Multilingual Currents in Literature, Translation, and Culture

At a time increasingly dominated by globalization, migration, and the clash between supranational and ultranational ideologies, the relationship between language and borders has become more complicated and, in many ways, more consequential than ever. This book shows how concepts of 'language' and 'multilingualism' look different when viewed from Belize, Lagos, or London, and asks how ideas about literature and literary form must be remade in a contemporary cultural marketplace that is both linguistically diverse and interconnected, even as it remains profoundly unequal. Bringing together scholars from the fields of literary studies, applied linguistics, and translation studies, the volume investigates how multilingual realities shape not only the practice of writing but also modes of literary and cultural production. Chapters explore examples of literary multilingualism and their relationship to the institutions of publishing, translation, and canon-formation. They consider how literature can be read in relation to other multilingual and translational forms of contemporary cultural circulation—such as music and film—and what new interpretative strategies such developments demand. In tracing the multilingual currents running across a globalized world, this book will appeal to the growing international readership at the intersections of comparative literature, world literature, postcolonial studies, literary theory and criticism, and translation studies.

Rachael Gilmour is Reader in Postcolonial and World Literatures in the Department of English at Queen Mary, University of London, UK.

Tamar Steinitz is Lecturer in the Department of English and Comparative Literature at Goldsmiths, University of London, UK.

Routledge Interdisciplinary Perspectives on Literature

For a full list of titles in this series, please visit www.routledge.com.

Multilingual Currents in Literature, Translation, and Culture

Edited by Rachael Gilmour
and Tamar Steinitz

NEW YORK AND LONDON

First published 2018
by Routledge
711 Third Avenue, New York, NY 10017

and by Routledge
2 Park Square, Milton Park, Abingdon, Oxon OX14 4RN

Routledge is an imprint of the Taylor & Francis Group, an informa business

© 2018 Taylor & Francis

The right of Rachael Gilmour and Tamar Steinitz to be identified as the authors of the editorial material, and of the authors for their individual chapters, has been asserted in accordance with sections 77 and 78 of the Copyright, Designs and Patents Act 1988.

Library of Congress Cataloging-in-Publication Data
CIP date has been applied for.

ISBN: 978-1-138-12053-2 (hbk)
ISBN: 978-1-315-65167-5 (ebk)

Typeset in Sabon
by codeMantra

Contents

List of Figures

1 Introduction

Multilingual Currents

Rachael Gilmour and Tamar Steinitz

The current state of globalization is daily questioning—through the expansion of capital, new financial circuits, technoglobalism, and massive migrations—national ideals and principles about the purity of language, the homogeneity of literature, and the distinctiveness of national cultures.

Walter Mignolo[1]

—*We only ever speak one language...*
(yes, but)
—*We never speak only one language...*
Jacques Derrida[2]

This book is concerned with the circuits of language in the contemporary world, and with their implications for our understanding of literature now. While making no claims for a new global linguistic order entirely ruptured from those which came before, it argues that existing literary paradigms ill equip us to understand the complex forces that shape language in the present as they impact upon the production and circulation of literature. In tracing these forces, it takes up questions which, in many ways, define the current moment: the impact of accelerated patterns of migration precipitated by war and conflict, economic pressures, and environmental degradation; the relationship between national and supranational political formations and ideologies; and the transformative effects of transnational flows of culture, capital, electronic media, and technology. As we argue here, literature is sensitive and responsive to these developments, registering new kinds of linguistically and symbolically complex contexts and cultures. These trends shape not only the practice of writing, but also its production and circulation in a cultural marketplace that is increasingly interconnected even as it remains profoundly unequal. And so, the chapters in this collection explore how ideas about literature, literary form, and organizing concepts such as language itself must be rethought in light of these accelerating processes, which operate at scales from the local to the global. The contributions here operate on the premise that monolingual paradigms are inadequate in a world dominated by globalization and migration. Furthermore, they seek alternatives to a homogenizing tendency in the still-emerging field of World Literature that emphasizes the rise of so-called global English and relies on Western, often Anglophone, systems of production and circulation, both of literary and cultural texts and of scholarly discourses about them. Conventional national categorizations no longer adequately reflect a literary world in flux, and traditional disciplinary divisions also come under pressure as literary studies seek new critical paradigms. This collection, therefore, approaches the field of contemporary multilingual literature and culture from a range of locations and disciplinary intersections, bringing to bear insights from translation studies and linguistics, and considering literature in relation to other forms of cultural production.

Although paradigms of monolingual, national literatures continue to dominate literary scholarship at an institutional level, it is nevertheless true that they have long been problematized. Postcolonial literary studies, even in their persistent concern with the former European colonial languages (primarily English), see those languages reterritorialized away from their conventional centres of gravity in Europe—as, in the well-known formulation by Ashcroft et al., in the shift from "English" to "englishes"—and historicize and materialize that reterritorialization, through global linguistic flows precipitated by European colonialism and continued by contemporary globalization.[3] Postcolonial literary scholars have also had to find ways to conceptualize the literary effects both of linguistic diversity, and of power differentials in and between languages largely conditioned by colonial history, and we take many of our cues here from them. In one influential early intervention, Samia Mehrez coins the term "radical bilingualism" to describe the traces of multiple languages contained within one ostensibly monolingual postcolonial text, and to underline the counter-hegemonic power of such bilingualism to make the colonial language "'foreign' to its own monolingual native speaker."[4] Much more recently, Rey Chow has argued for mediation between unequal languages, and the sense of language as alien and "prosthetic" which this produces, as a definitively postcolonial experience.[5]

This volume is informed by these ideas, in concert with that broader transnational turn in literary studies, strongly influenced by postcolonial scholarship, which concerns itself with the processes and effects of globalization.[6] It is, at the same time, driven by a scepticism towards synoptic, systemist models of World Literature, not least—although not only—for their assumptions about language and translatability. Christopher Larkosh, for example, reflects here on how differently contemporary configurations of World Literature might look if viewed from the perspective of Québec, reminding us not only of the dominant Anglocentrism of world-circulation models like that of David Damrosch, but also how contemporary world Francophonie, notably in the influential work of Pascale Casanova, pivots around Paris.[7] But just as we must question monolingual literary models, whether national or transnational, we also need to critique prevailing literary-critical paradigms of language diversity that have become, in their own way, hegemonic. And so, Larkosh's chapter challenges the academic dominance of English–Spanish in the US as the pre-eminent model for contemporary literary 'bilingualism'; what, he asks, would happen if the focus turned from the United States' southern border with Mexico, to its northern border with Canada? In such a decentring spirit, working from multiple locations and disciplinary specialisms, we go on to consider how questions of language, culture, and translation in contemporary literature look different when addressed from Lagos, Belize City, or Glasgow; in configurations of the contemporary 'global novel,' or avowedly local/national/regional models of publishing; or indeed, how we can read 'multilingualism' or 'translation' in literature in relation to other contemporary cultural forms such as film. In attending to diversity and difference, at the same time we assume connectivity between literary texts and their production in different contexts within the circuits of an uneven, but intricately connected, contemporary world-system.[8] We are also keenly aware that academia itself operates in a related system of production and circulation that is implicated in the processes and discourses of globalization, even as it attempts to define and interrogate them.

It is worth saying that the literary phenomena that we explore here are by no means new. We need only think of Beckett, to give one often-cited example, to recall that writers have long written and published in different languages, and self-translated. But these forces are undoubtedly proliferating and accelerating, rupturing conventional assumptions (conventional, not least, within literary studies) of languages as stable entities, rooted in a particular territory, and of literary texts as 'in' one language. On the one hand, and connected to dominant configurations of World Literature, there is an ever-increasing market-driven tendency towards translation and translatability, commensurability and legibility as conceived within the "US–Anglo–global" publishing industry, as texts travel further and faster than ever before, and appear simultaneously in multiple languages—"born translated," in Rebecca Walkowitz's terms.[9] In the field of Anglophone literature, we see the rise of what Tim Parks somewhat tendentiously describes as the "dull new global novel," written for an international English readership and for translation.[10] Denuded of distinctive acoustic effects or idioms, this is language that aspires to be any language: the language equivalent of the empty, placeless space–time of late-modernity, the airport departure lounge or the shopping mall. Indeed, in many ways, the forces of contemporary globalization tend to the flattening out or homogenizing of language and culture, as certain valuable kinds of linguistic and cultural resources (for example standard varieties of English, French, Arabic, or Chinese)

spread ever more widely. Pierre Bourdieu's ideas about language as symbolic capital, and its uneven distribution and circulation, remain as
important now as they ever were.[11] Yet at the same time, these forms
of language—used as media of wider communication, "in-addition-to"
rather than "instead-of" other codes—reveal to us a global scene becoming ever more, rather than less, linguistically complex in its local/global
dimensions and kaleidoscopic shifts (multilayered processes that tend,
in contemporary global cities like London, to what Stephen Vertovec
has defined as "super-diversity").[12] Thus in literary studies, taking a
cue from applied linguistics, we are faced with the challenge of developing new paradigms whereby we can "shift our gaze from stability to
mobility," and "take diversity [...] as normal."[13] In the context of accelerated patterns of migration, electronic media and global communication, and surrounded in everyday life by diverse symbolic resources of
all kinds, "the late-modern urban subject is distinctly and intensely polyglot."[14] As Rita Wilson suggests in this volume for Trieste and Milan,
for example, and Rachael Gilmour for Glasgow, the global and the local
clash and merge in the world city: polyphony is a model for the linguistic and literary realities of late-modern urban life. Here, too, in Polo
Moji's Paris, a hybrid "Afropean" subjectivity recalibrates Francophonie
transnationally and multilingually, locating it in a network of connections that links Africa, Europe, and the Americas, and language to other
forms of signification and cultural production. Contemporary writers,
as these chapters argue, are faced with the diverse aesthetic possibilities
of the "intensely polyglot," as well as the task of representing the social
dynamics and affective experience of moving between different forms
of language, while at the same time being governed by the essentially
monolingual demands of the publishing industry. Thus not only literary texts themselves, but their publishing and circulation, in relation to
linguistic diversity and the politics of language and translation, demand
new kinds of critical focus. Brian Lennon, in a recent intervention, has
called for "a radically, anarchically plurilingual literature"—which may
only be possible through electronic publication, with its potential to represent different lects, scripts, and modes, and its circumvention of the
conventions and demands of commercial print publishing—as the route
to "a renovated and radically plurilingual 'new American studies.'"[15]
Lennon's "anarchic plurilingualism," like Emily Apter's recent valoriza-
tion of "untranslatables," poses language difference against neoliberal
models of commensurability and equivalence.[16]

Approaches such as those of Lennon and Apter, which place critical,
politicized approaches to language diversity and translation at the centre
of contemporary literary study, are vitally important to this project.
They serve as useful models, too, in their principled interdisciplinary engagements with applied linguistics, in the case of Lennon, and
translation studies in the case of Apter. In the US academy, studies of

literary 'multilingualism' have, since the 1990s, challenged the assumed Anglophony of 'American literature' and what might be called its language-political correlate, 'English Only' language policies.[17] Nevertheless, we wish to move decisively beyond the dominance of US scholarship and institutional contexts, which place at the centre of this field discussions of US domestic language politics, US foreign policy, and disciplinary formations of world/comparative literature within the US academy—significant as these are as forces in the world. Our aim is to explore a set of interlinked questions from a diversity of local contexts and critical formations, in order to think about how different kinds of writing, different language contexts, and symbolic economies, different versions of translation, or of market forces, may be interpreted in relation to one another.

In doing so, our shared interests are, first of all, literary-critical: considering literary texts which are produced in contemporary multilingual contexts, by writers moving between multiple languages: from the conditions (political, social, economic, psychic) that govern writers' language choices, to the linguistic and formal innovations by which they register and explore linguistic diversity, and the reading strategies such writing demands. Second, we explore how language and linguistic exchange in the field of literature relates to the institutions of publishing and translation, the demands of literary markets (local, national, and transnational), and the formation and contestation of literary canons. Third, we place literature in relation to other forms of cultural production—such as music and film—that offer new, or different, ways to think about how forms of language travel and interact. Addressing ourselves to these questions helps us to map a variety of contemporary constellations of literature, language diversity, cultural forms, and translation practice; which is to say that we are concerned with the differences, as well as the homologies, between the contexts we explore: the politics of literary "multilingualism" and its marketing in Belize, and in Scotland; interlingual writing as "predicament," or as "motor of critique." In all of this, we treat literature not as a rarefied sphere separate from, but as both imbricated in and critically engaged with, the operations of language in the world. We require, and this book sets out to establish, critical formulations and disciplinary paradigms that foreground the relationship of literary praxis to language as situated social practice, embedded in social, material, and political realities.

So far, we have been using phrases like 'language diversity' and 'language repertoires' to denote the complex array of symbolic resources which constitute most people's experience of language in the world, the way in which they practice communication within it, and the ways in which literature explores and mediates those experiences and practices. But this, of course, is not how language is generally talked about, either in everyday life or in literature. Though long assaulted from within both critical theory and applied linguistics, it is hard to overemphasize either the ideological power or the durability of the idea of 'a language' or 'the language' as a bounded, stable, entextualized, somehow natural, and self-evident entity, which is the full inheritance and possession of its 'native' or 'mother tongue' speakers, distinct from other such 'languages' even as it is substitutable for them through translation. As Derrida tells us in *Monolingualism of the Other*, this notion of "the language," or "a language," is a fiction. Writing from the perspective of colonial Algeria about his relationship to French, Derrida at the same time makes it clear that what he reveals through colonialism holds for us all: "the language" is something both multiple and ineluctable, which nobody can fully possess.[18] Yet it is, equally, an idea with pervasive, and perhaps even escalating, real-world force. In Europe and the US, for example, we see renewed emphasis on the relationship between language and national belonging in the context of debates about asylum and immigration, borders and citizenship, and the prevention of "terror."[19] As Sinfree Makoni and Alastair Pennycook have argued, the idea of languages as "discrete entities in the world" developed through both the emergence of the modern European nation-state, and the work of colonial linguistics to develop languages as distinct, reifiable units of knowledge. Its force has been to shape

> how language policies have been constructed, how education has been pursued, how language tests have been developed and administered, and how people have come to identify with particular labels and at times even to die for them, as the violent nature of ethnic rivalry in Africa, South Asia and elsewhere amply demonstrates.[20]

The "monolingual paradigm" that posits a coherence of language and national identity is disrupted both by a long-term plurality of languages in a single geopolitical unit, and by more recent and ongoing processes of migration and globalization.[21] These factors call into question, too, notions of 'multilingualism'—for example, as encoded in state language policies in places like South Africa, or via supranational entities like the European Union—which continue to be conceived as relations between multiple 'languages' that are still imagined as bounded, singular entities.[22] For a number of reasons, it is not possible to pose a distinction between a bad, old monolingualism, and a good, new multilingualism; nor indeed, to assume that we all share the same understanding of 'multilingualism.' Multilingualism after all must imply not just the plurality of language forms, but also the range of relationships that are conceived between them: from a "hard multilingualism" that insists on linguistic difference and incommensurability, to a "soft multilingualism" that emphasizes "translatability and inter-linguistic transparence."[23] As Blommaert et al. have recently argued, forms of multilingualism which deviate from prescribed language norms—norms which include both state monolingualism and forms of multilingualism which are conceived as legitimate by the state or wider culture—can be "dangerous." This means, at one level, of course, posing a danger to conventional ideologies of language and the systems they shore up; but also dangerous in the sense of being "unwanted, disqualified or actively endangering" to the people who practice them.[24] And so, even as 'multilingualism' becomes increasingly an object of *literary* scholarship, we must be careful to recognize that it has no fixed valency: it may serve dominant visions of the nation-state, or cosmopolitanism, or the effects of global cultural exchange, or unsettle them profoundly.

All of the above goes to suggest that, in order to adequately understand the pull-and-push of these forces as they act in and on literature—normative visions of language on the one hand, and radical, improvisational, everyday forms of communication and meaning-making on the other—literary scholarship needs to pay attention to the insights of those other disciplines that concern themselves with language, principally applied linguistics and translation studies, and to do so with precision. This is vital as literary texts themselves reflect with increasing self-consciousness on the processes and experiences of language and translation as they are refracted by globalization, while their production and circulation are impacted by the same processes. Precedents for such interdisciplinary literary scholarship range from Elizabeth Klosty Beaujour's engagement with neurolinguistic theories of bilingualism, through Doris Sommer's exploration of bilingual practices such as code-switching, to Yasemin Yildiz's engagements with the "postmonolingual."[25] Recent years have also seen a translational turn in literary and cultural studies, extending the category of translation from a textual or linguistic practice to a conceptualization of global cultural exchange.[26] More than a metaphor or theme, translation becomes a structuring feature and analytical concept in contemporary literary works, as "translational literature" foregrounds and problematizes the act of translation.[27] In this volume, Fiona Doloughan argues that translation has become an integral part of the production and reception of the narratives of multilingual writers. As Doloughan's chapter, amongst others, goes to demonstrate, the study of literary texts has a particular value in thinking about language, from which applied linguists and translation scholars too may learn a great deal. Works of literature, in their linguistic self-reflexivity, are richly, if not uniquely, suited to the exploration of some of the questions at the heart of contemporary studies of language, translation, and globalization: the complex local/global dynamics of language, its power differentials, and the affective experience of its use. Reflection on this interdisciplinary flow between linguistics, translation studies, and literary studies—and developing the precision required for its execution—is at the heart of our project here.[28] Britta Schneider's sociolinguistic perspective on literary multilingualism in Belize is a case in point, exploring how language choices in literature can index a network of local, national, and transnational contexts, with connections to Latin America, West Africa, the UK, the US, and the Caribbean.

Chapters in this book explore the relationship between language and mobility from numerous angles, as transnational authors—migrants, exiles, and the bicultural first-generation descendants of migrants—register the realities and effects of border crossing both thematically and formally. Linguistic border crossing, like its geographic counterpart, presents opportunities and possibilities, but also involves dislocation and estrangement. Literary multilingualism has often been conceived of as the domain of "great, often polyglot, cosmopolitan figures of the world of letters" who act as "foreign exchange brokers" and even "legislators" of the "Republic of letters": of a version of *Weltliteratur* associated with European Enlightenment; yet the current moment demands a less rarefied view of multilingualism in literature, of its dynamics and discomforts.[29] Here, for example, Steven G. Kellman examines the spatial metaphors employed by translingual writers in their memoirs, from those who choose to make language itself their home, to others who are left disoriented by the linguistic switch and caught in the gap between languages, a gap that can resemble a no-man's land or a demilitarized zone. Carli Coetzee problematizes the transnationalism of the African diasporan novel: a growing genre that extends debates about the use of English by former colonial subjects to reflect new realities of migration from the global south. Against the success of NoViolet Bulawayo's *We Need New Names* in the Anglophone metropolitan markets, a success that is measured and confirmed in no small part by the literary prize industry and mainstream Anglo-American media, Coetzee offers the idea of a conspiratorial "local" reading that excludes an Anglophone reader through linguistically coded references to Zimbabwean history and literary tradition. Indeed, as this chapter for one suggests, the focus on movement—of writers and texts—in many debates around contemporary World Literature can obscure the everyday multilingualism that constitutes the lived experience of individuals and communities in many parts of the world, and which is not necessarily linked to mobility or privilege. Thus, Moradewun Adejunmobi here examines subtitling practices in Nollywood, the popular film industry in multilingual Nigeria, showing how polyglot films can circulate in different contexts—national, transnational African, and global—and offering a valuable alternative paradigm to the travelling texts of literature, which often require a monolingual address, usually in a European language, to access global markets.

As these examples show, this volume, in its search for paradigms for the theorization of World Literature, highlights a key tension between the decentring impulse of multilingualism in its various configurations and contexts, and the centralizing tendency of English as a global language. On the one hand, the perspectives offered here on "World Englishes"[30]—in local varieties from Scotland to Belize—show English becoming diversified by its contact with other forms of language, resisting the idea of a homogeneous lingua franca, and destabilizing the core of English as a monolingual and monolithic construct. On the other hand, as the examples of literature written and marketed "in English" demonstrate—we cannot fail to recognize the spread and power of English as the language of commerce, of new and proliferating digital media, and of increasingly consolidated publishing markets.[31]

The English language is not only the key to cultural capital, but *is itself* capital in a primary, material sense: English language teaching is, Alastair Pennycook reminds us, "big business" that involves native English speakers "[travelling] the world, able to market their monolingual skills above their bilingual counterparts."[32] English plays a similar role in higher education, where it has cemented its status as the international language of academic exchange, asserting the Anglo-American hegemony of academic institutions and academic publishing. The dominance of English in academia is related to processes of circulation, marketization, and homogenization that, in many ways, echo the wider circuits of literary and cultural production. Bill Readings observed, two decades ago, a link between economic globalization and the rise of the university as a "transnational bureaucratic corporation,"[33] and more recently, Stefan Collini has noted a shift in the "communities of reference" of the university, from the national to the international.[34] Paul Jay sees the opening up of American and other Western academic institutions to "minority and postcolonial students" and the movement of some of these students into the professoriate as playing a key role in challenging Eurocentric critical and theoretical practices and transforming a "largely nationalist enterprise" of literary studies into "an increasingly transnational enterprise."[35] While this description is undoubtedly true, the academic migration to centres of scholarship and research (which are often dependent on multinational corporations for funding) results in a so-called brain drain in the countries of origin. And as Western universities open up to international students, the global university reaches out to new markets in a bid to recruit students or to open subsidiaries: both are lucrative revenue streams in which students become both consumers and commodities.

Thus, another tension emerges when we come to examine our own position in relation to the subject of our inquiries: contemporary scholarship engages critically with political and social processes of globalization on the one hand, and on the other—academia participates in various ways in the global marketplace and sustains global inequality. Indeed, this volume enacts and reflects the very processes and transformations it examines. Most of the contributing authors are multilingual; some are translingual and transnational; and yet, this collection cannot escape the predominance of English as the language of academic exchange. Moreover, we are the product of systems of knowledge and critical traditions forged in the West, depending on and sustaining an academic publishing industry that perpetuates an unequal distribution of knowledge. The transnational turn in the humanities and social sciences is not only attuned to, but also a product of, these tensions. As Jay observes, this turn is not simply a response to globalization—itself a process he traces back to the sixteenth century—but proceeds from decades-long processes of social and political movements that filtered into the academy through theoretical and critical practices "dominated by a sustained and critical attention to difference."[36]

This volume insists on the ongoing importance of such "sustained and critical attention to difference" as it traces the multilingual currents running through a globalized world. The present moment is marked by seismic shifts in the world order: the battle lines in political and military conflicts, for example in the Middle East, are not drawn along national borders; the current wave of migration, largely propelled by such crises, puts the post-war project of the European Union under extreme stress; this, in turn, may prove as foreshadowing mass migrations to come, as a result of economic instability and climate change. Literature, by and large, is not written on the move (Virginia Woolf's assertion that money and a room of one's own are necessary for the production of fiction[37] still resonates in these new contexts), and so the cultural field is in flux, as must be any attempt to theorize it. In this dynamic global and disciplinary context, our contribution to the debates surrounding World Literature engages in an emerging comparativism that troubles the alignment of language and nation, broadens the horizons beyond the dominant Anglo-American context, and delights in the tensions, contradictions, and possibilities presented by the intersections and mutual transformations of literature, language, and politics in the contemporary world.

Notes

1 Walter D. Mignolo, *Local Histories/Global Designs: Coloniality, Subaltern Knowledges, and Border Thinking* (Princeton, NJ: Princeton University Press, 2000), 229.
2 Jacques Derrida, *Monolingualism of the Other; Or, the Prosthesis of Origin*, trans. by Patrick Mensah (Stanford, CA: Stanford University Press, 1998), 10.
3 Bill Ashcroft, Gareth Griffiths and Helen Tiffin, *The Empire Writes Back: Theory and Practice in Post-Colonial Literature*, 2nd Edition (London: Routledge, 2002).
4 Samia Mehrez, "Translation and the Postcolonial Experience: The Francophone North African Text," in *Rethinking Translation: Discourse, Subjectivity, Ideology*, ed. Lawrence Venuti (London: Routledge, 1992), pp. 120–38 (130).
5 Rey Chow, *Not Like a Native Speaker: On Languaging as a Postcolonial Experience* (Columbia, NY: Columbia University Press, 2014).

6 Important studies in this field include Azade Seyhan, *Writing Outside the Nation* (Princeton, NJ: Princeton University Press, 2001), Paul Jay, *Global Matters: The Transnational Turn in Literary Studies* (Ithaca, NY: Cornell University Press, 2010), Emily Apter, *The Translation Zone: A New Comparative Literature* (Princeton, NJ: Princeton University Press, 2006) and *Against World Literature: On The Politics of Untranslatability* (London: Verso, 2013), and Yasemin Yildiz's *Beyond the Mother Tongue: The Postmonolingual Condition* (New York: Fordham University Press, 2012).

7 David Damrosch, *What Is World Literature?* (Princeton, NJ: Princeton University Press, 2003); Pascale Casanova, *The World Republic of Letters*, trans. by Malcolm B. DeBevoise (Cambridge, MA: Harvard University Press, 2004).

8 See Warwick Research Collective, *Combined and Uneven Development: Towards a New Theory of World-Literature* (Liverpool: Liverpool University Press, 2015).

9 Brian Lennon, *In Babel's Shadow: Multilingual Literatures, Monolingual States* (Minneapolis and London: University of Minnesota Press, 2010), 3; Rebecca Walkowitz, *Born Translated: The Contemporary Novel in an Age of World Literature* (New York: Columbia University Press, 2015), 1.

10 Tim Parks, "The Dull New Global Novel," *New York Review of Books*, 9 February 2010, www.nybooks.com/daily/2010/02/09/the-dull-new-global-novel/.

11 Pierre Bourdieu, *Language and Symbolic Power* (Cambridge: Polity, 1991).

12 Steven Vertovec, "Super-Diversity and Its Implications," *Ethnic and Racial Studies* 30 no. 6 (2007): 1024–1054. See also Susanne Wessendorf, *Commonplace Diversity: Social Relations in a Super-Diverse Context* (Basingstoke: Palgrave, 2014); Susanne Wessendorf, "'All the people speak bad English': Coping with Language Differences in a Super-Diverse Context," *IRiS Working Paper Series* No. 9, 2015, www.birmingham. ac.uk/Documents/college-social-sciences/social-policy/iris/2015/working-paper-series/IRiS-WP-9-2015.pdf.

13 Monica Heller, *Paths to Post-Nationalism: A Critical Ethnography of Language and Identity* (Oxford: Oxford University Press, 2011), 5, 7. See also Sinfree Makoni and Alastair Pennycook, "Disinventing and Reconstituting Languages," in *Disinventing and Reconstituting Languages*, eds. Sinfree Makoni and Alastair Pennycook (Clevedon: Multilingual Matters, 2007); Jan Blommaert, *The Sociolinguistics of Globalization* (Cambridge: Cambridge University Press, 2010).

14 Jan Blommaert, Sirpa Leppänen, and Massimiliano Spotti, "Endangering Multilingualism," in *Dangerous Multilingualism: Northern Perspectives on Order, Purity and Normality*, eds. Jan Blommaert, Sirpa Leppänen, Päivi Pahta, and Tiina Räisänen (Basingstoke: Palgrave, 2012), 9.

15 Lennon, *In Babel's Shadow*, 165.

16 See Lennon, *In Babel's Shadow*, footnote 3, 180–81.

17 See for example Michael North, *The Dialect of Modernism: Race, Language, and Twentieth-Century Literature* (Oxford University Press, 1994); Werner Sollors, ed. *Multilingual America: Transnationalism, Ethnicity, and the Languages of American Literature* (New York: New York University Press, 1998); Marc Shell and Werner Sollors, eds. *The Multilingual Anthology of American Literature: A Reader of Original Texts with English Translations* (New York: New York University Press, 2000); Martha J. Cutter, *Lost and Found in Translation: Contemporary Ethnic American Writing and the Politics of Language Diversity* (Chapel Hill: University of North Carolina

Press, 2005); Hana Wirth-Nesher, *Call It English: The Languages of Jewish American Literature* (Princeton, NJ: Princeton University Press, 2006), Joshua L. Miller, *Accented America: The Cultural Politics of Multilingual Modernism* (Oxford: Oxford University Press, 2011); Lennon, *In Babel's Shadow.*

18 Derrida, *Monolingualism of the Other*, 28–9.

19 Blommaert, *The Sociolinguistics of Globalization.*

20 Sinfree Makoni and Alastair Pennycook, "Disinventing and Reconstituting Languages," in *Disinventing and Reconstituting Languages*, eds. Sinfree Makoni and Alaistair Pennycook (Clevedon: Multilingual Matters, 2007), 2–3.

21 Yildiz, *Beyond the Mother Tongue*, 2.

22 See for example Sinfree Makoni, "From Misinvention to Disinvention of Language: Multilingualism and the South African Constitution," in *Black Linguistics: Language, Society and Politics in Africa and the Americas*, eds. Sinfree Makoni, Geneva Smitherman, Arnetha F. Ball, Arthur K. Spears (London and New York: Routledge, 2003), 132–52; Máiréad Nic Craith, *Europe and the Politics of Language: Citizens, Migrants and Outsiders* (Basingstoke: Palgrave, 2006). Another important example is Monica Heller's critique of Canadian bilingualism and the nation state in *Paths to Post-Nationalism: A Critical Ethnography of Language and Identity* (2011).

23 Yaseen Noorani, "Hard and Soft Multilingualism," *Critical Multilingualism Studies* 1 no. 2 (2013): 9.

24 Blommaert et al., "Endangering Multilingualism," 1.

25 Elizabeth Klosty Beaujour, *Alien Tongues: Bilingual Russian Writers of the "First" Emigration* (Ithaca, NY: Cornell University Press, 1989); Doris Sommer, *Bilingual Aesthetics: A New Sentimental Education* (Durham, NC: Duke University Press, 2004); Yildiz, *Beyond the Mother Tongue.*

26 For a discussion of translation as a "travelling concept" that moves across disciplinary divides, see Doris Bachmann-Medick, "Translation—A Concept and Model for the Study of Culture," in *Concepts for the Study of Culture*, eds. Doris Bachmann-Medick, Wolfgang Hallet and Ansgar Nünning (Berlin & Boston: De Gruyter, 2012), pp. 23–43; Doris Bachmann-Medick, ed. *The Translational Turn*: Special Issue of *Translation Studies* 2 no. 1 (2009).

27 Waïl S. Hassan, "Agency and Translational Literature: Ahdaf Soueif's 'The Map of Love,'" *PMLA* 121 no. 3 (2006): 754.

28 Analyses of literary explorations of language diversity and translation within applied linguistics and translation studies include: Mark Sebba, "Writing Switching in British Creole," in *Multilingual Literacies: Reading and Writing Different Worlds*, eds. Marilyn Martin-Jones and Kathryn Jones (Amsterdam and Philadelphia, PA: John Benjamins, 2000), 171–87; Rainier Grutman and Dirk Delabastita, eds. *Fictionalising Translation and Multilingualism*: Special issue of *Linguistica Antverpiensia New Series*, 4 (2005); Blommaert, *The Sociolinguistics of Globalization*, 64–77.

29 Casanova, *The World Republic of Letters*, 21.

30 Alastair Pennycook, "English as a Language Always in Translation," *European Journal of English Studies* 12 no. 1 (2008): 38.

31 Walkowitz, *Born Translated*, 21.

32 Pennycook, "English as a Language Always in Translation," 35.

33 Bill Readings, *The University in Ruins* (Cambridge, MA: Harvard University Press, 1996), 3.

34 Stefan Collini, *What Are Universities For?* (London: Penguin, 2012), 16.

35 Jay, *Global Matters*, 23.
36 Jay, *Global Matters*, 17.
37 Virginia Woolf, *A Room of One's Own* (London: Harcourt Brace & Company, 1989 [1922]), 4.

Bibliography

Apter, Emily. *Against World Literature: On The Politics of Untranslatability.* London: Verso, 2013.
———. *The Translation Zone: A New Comparative Literature.* Princeton, NJ: Princeton University Press, 2006.
Ashcroft, Bill, Gareth Griffiths, and Helen Tiffin. *The Empire Writes Back: Theory and Practice in Post-Colonial Literature*, 2nd Edition. London: Routledge, 2002.
Bachmann-Medick, Doris, ed. *The Translational Turn*: Special Issue of *Translation Studies* 2 no. 1(2009): 2–16.
———. "Translation—A Concept and Model for the Study of Culture.'" In *Concepts for the Study of Culture*, eds. Doris Bachmann-Medick, Wolfgang Hallet and Ansgar Nünning, 23–43. Berlin: De Gruyter, 2012.
Beaujour, Elizabeth Klosty. *Alien Tongues: Bilingual Russian Writers of the "First" Emigration.* Ithaca, NY: Cornell University Press, 1989.
Blommaert, Jan. *The Sociolinguistics of Globalization.* Cambridge: Cambridge University Press, 2010.
Blommaert, Jan, Sirpa Leppänen, and Massimiliano Spotti. "Endangering Multilingualism." In *Dangerous Multilingualism: Northern Perspectives on Order, Purity and Normality*, eds. Jan Blommaert, Sirpa Leppänen, Päivi Pahta and Tiina Räisänen, 1–21. Basingstoke: Palgrave, 2012.
Bourdieu, Pierre. *Language and Symbolic Power.* Translated by John B. Thompson. Cambridge: Polity, 1991.
Casanova, Pascale. *The World Republic of Letters.* Translated by Malcolm B. DeBevoise. Cambridge, MA: Harvard University Press, 2004.
Chow, Rey. *Not Like A Native Speaker: On Languaging as a Postcolonial Experience.* Columbia, NY: Columbia University Press, 2014.
Collini, Stefan. *What Are Universities For?* London: Penguin, 2012.
Cutter, Martha J. *Lost and Found in Translation: Contemporary Ethnic American Writing and the Politics of Language Diversity.* Chapel Hill: University of North Carolina Press, 2005.
Damrosch, David. *What Is World Literature?* Princeton, NJ: Princeton University Press, 2003.
Derrida, Jacques. *Monolingualism of the Other; Or, the Prosthesis of Origin.* Translated by Patrick Mensah. Stanford, CA: Stanford University Press, 1998.
Grutman, Rainier and Dirk Delabastita, eds. *Fictionalising Translation and Multilingualism*: Special issue of *Linguistica Antverpiensia New Series* 4 (2005). Antwerpen: Hogeschool Antwerpen, HIVT.
Hassan, Waïl S. "Agency and Translational Literature: Ahdaf Soueif's 'The Map of Love'." *PMLA* 121 no. 3 (2006): 753–68.
Heller, Monica. *Paths to Post-Nationalism: A Critical Ethnography of Language and Identity.* Oxford: Oxford University Press, 2011.

Jay, Paul. *Global Matters: The Transnational Turn in Literary Studies*. Ithaca, IL: Cornell University Press, 2010.

Lennon, Brian. *In Babel's Shadow: Multilingual Literatures, Monolingual States*. Minneapolis: University of Minnesota Press, 2010.

Makoni, Sinfree, and Alastair Pennycook. "Disinventing and Reconstituting Languages." In *Disinventing and Reconstituting Languages*, eds. Sinfree Makoni and Alastair Pennycook, 1–41. Clevedon: Multilingual Matters, 2007.

Mehrez, Samia. "Translation and the Postcolonial Experience: The Francophone North African Text." In *Rethinking Translation: Discourse, Subjectivity, Ideology*, ed. Lawrence Venuti, 120–38. London: Routledge, 1992.

Mignolo, Walter D. *Local Histories/Global Designs: Coloniality, Subaltern Knowledges, and Border Thinking*. Princeton, NJ: Princeton University Press, 2000.

Miller, Joshua L. *Accented America: The Cultural Politics of Multilingual Modernism*. Oxford: Oxford University Press, 2011.

Noorani, Yaseen. "Hard and Soft Multilingualism." *Critical Multilingualism Studies* 1 no. 2 (2013): 7–28.

North, Michael. *The Dialect of Modernism: Race, Language, and Twentieth-Century Literature*. Oxford: Oxford University Press, 1994.

Parks, Tim. "The Dull New Global Novel." *New York Review of Books*, 9 February 2010. www.nybooks.com/daily/2010/02/09/the-dull-new-global-novel/.

Pennycook, Alastair. "English as a Language Always in Translation." *European Journal of English Studies* 12 no. 1 (2008): 22–47.

Readings, Bill. *The University in Ruins*. Cambridge, MA: Harvard University Press, 1996.

Sebba, Mark. "Writing Switching in British Creole." In *Multilingual Literacies: Reading and Writing Different Worlds*, eds. Marilyn Martin-Jones and Kathryn Jones, 171–87. Amsterdam: John Benjamins, 2000.

Seyhan, Azade. *Writing Outside the Nation*. Princeton, NJ: Princeton University Press, 2001.

Shell, Marc, and Werner Sollors, eds. *The Multilingual Anthology of American Literature: A Reader of Original Texts with English Translations*. New York: New York University Press, 2000.

Sollors, Werner, ed. *Multilingual America: Transnationalism, Ethnicity, and the Languages of American Literature*. New York: New York University Press, 1998.

Sommer, Doris. *Bilingual Aesthetics: A New Sentimental Education*. Durham, NC: Duke University Press, 2004.

Vertovec, Steven. "Super-Diversity and Its Implications." *Ethnic and Racial Studies* 30 no. 6 (2007): 1024–54.

Walkowitz, Rebecca. *Born Translated: The Contemporary Novel in an Age of World Literature*. New York: Columbia University Press, 2015.

Warwick Research Collective. *Combined and Uneven Development: Towards a New Theory of World-Literature*. Liverpool: Liverpool University Press, 2015.

Wessendorf, Susanne. *Commonplace Diversity: Social Relations in a Super-Diverse Context*. Basingstoke: Palgrave, 2014.

———. "'All the People Speak Bad English': Coping with Language Differences in a Super-Diverse Context." *IRiS Working Paper Series* 9 (2015). www. birmingham.ac.uk/Documents/college-social-sciences/social-policy/ iris/2015/working-paper-series/IRiS-WP-9-2015.pdf.

Wirth-Nesher, Hana. *Call It English: The Languages of Jewish American Literature*. Princeton, NJ: Princeton University Press, 2006.

Woolf, Virginia. *A Room of One's Own*. 1922. London: Harcourt Brace & Company, 1989.

Yildiz, Yasemin. *Beyond the Mother Tongue: The Postmonolingual Condition*. New York: Fordham University Press, 2012.

2 Writer Speaks with Forked Tongue

Interlingual Predicaments

Steven G. Kellman

The literary achievements of Samuel Beckett, Joseph Conrad, and Vladimir Nabokov inspire such awe that the history of translingual literature (by writers who write in more than one language or in a language other than their primary one) often seems like a narrative of artistic triumph over linguistic handicap.[1] For some writers, switching languages appears seamless, painless, and complete. Petrarch managed to write enduring poetry in both Latin and Italian, Mirza Ghalib in both Urdu and Persian, and Uri Zvi Greenberg in both Yiddish and Hebrew. Rafael Sabatini wrote more than 30 novels in English, his sixth language (after Italian, Portuguese, French, German, and Spanish). Ha Jin arrived in the United States from China with barely a rudimentary knowledge of English, yet it took him only 11 years to win both the National Book Award and the PEN/Faulkner Award for his first novel, *Waiting* (1999). Many of the most celebrated contemporary novelists, poets, and playwrights—including Rabih Alameddine, Julia Alvarez, Louis Begley, Zehra Cerak, Edwidge Danticat, Junot Díaz, Assia Djebar, Gao Xingjian, Mohsin Hamid, Aleksandar Hemon, Milan Kundera, Amin Maalouf, Alain Mabanckou, Andreï Makine, Charles Simic, and Eli Wiesel, amongst others—write in an adopted tongue.

And translingual memoirs are a thriving—and reflexive—genre.[2] Because they tend to foreground and problematize the author's transition from one language to another, they are of particular interest to a study of interlingual predicaments. The implicit concluding sentence of translingual memoirs is often: "And so I arrived at the point at which I was able to write these pages, impeccably, in this rich adopted language that you are reading." Mary Antin's popular autobiography *The Promised Land* (1912) celebrates her ability "to think in English without an accent" but elides the arduous process of acquiring English, "this beautiful language in which I think," and in fact omits any mention of her first language, Yiddish.[3] For Edward W. Bok, who arrived in New York from the Netherlands without any English, learning the local language required little effort. Writing in English in the third person, he recalls that

> the national linguistic gift inherent in the Dutch race came to the boy's rescue, and as the roots of the Anglo-Saxon lie in the Frisian

tongue, and thus in the language of his native country, Edward soon found that with a change of vowel here and there the English language was not so difficult of conquest.[4]

Nevertheless, for many others, tongue-switching is agony, an excruciating ordeal that is never completely mastered. Indeed, the translingual project is sometimes a failure or even a pathology. Inability or refusal to accept the language of exile may not have caused the suicides of Klaus Mann, Ernst Toller, and Stefan Zweig—writers who, driven into exile by Nazism, could not count on a wide readership when continuing to write in their native German—any more than it drove Paul Celan, Romain Gary, Arthur Koestler, Jerzy Kosinski—each of whom wrote well in an adopted language—to kill themselves. But linguistic disorientation does contribute to despondency. In her own travails going from Russian to French to English, Natasha Lvovich recalls "an emotional dysbalance, a psychic discomfort, similar to nostalgia, a 'language sickness.'"[5] Elsa Triolet, writing in French rather than her native Russian, bemoans the bilingual malaise that has afflicted her: "On dirait une maladie: je suis atteinte de bilinguisme" [One could call it a disease: I am afflicted with bilingualism].[6] Amongst translingual Russian émigrés in general, Elizabeth Klosty Beaujour diagnoses a tendency to "experience the pangs of infidelity and guilt, as well as a sense of self-mutilation."[7] Few writers demonstrate as severe and dramatic a case of *taedium lingua* as Louis Wolfson, who was institutionalized with schizophrenia. His 1970 book *Le Schizo et les langues* documents how Wolfson's revulsion towards his maternal language, English, the language of his terrifying mother, propelled him towards several other languages—including French, Hebrew, Russian, and German—that he did not entirely inhabit. At the very least, linguistic displacement creates a fracture in personal identity that is impossible to restore. At best, a coherent new self is created.

The Phases of Transition Between Languages

The ordeal resembles rites of passage as analysed by British anthropologist Victor Turner. Studying the Ndembu of Zambia, Turner found three phases defining their initiation rituals: "separation, margin (or *limen*), and aggregation."[8] After a neophyte is isolated from the community, a period of disorientation and ambiguity ensues. During this marginal interim, initiates experience self-abasement, a conviction that they are worthless and unclean. In a successful *rite de passage*, such feelings eventually dissolve, and the outcast—during what Turner calls "aggregation"—is reintegrated into the community. Employing some of the same terminology in what she terms "a psychoanalytic reading" of second-language learning, Colette A. Granger diagnoses the plight of the "liminal self, living unsteadily in two languages and therefore living fully in neither."

Using a familiar spatial metaphor, she finds the second-language learner "positioned on the blurred border-line between first and second languages, unable either to turn back and regain the old self or to move forward, unencumbered, into a new one."[9]

For much of her memoir, Eva Hoffman is just such a liminal self. Relocated at 13 from Cracow to Vancouver, Hoffman is, for many years, what she calls "lost in translation." Her native Polish, now useless, slips away, and her command of English is embryonic and clumsy. However, Hoffman's *Lost in Translation*, written 30 years later in dexterous and sophisticated English, testifies to the successful conclusion of the liminal phase. Nevertheless, a writer as accomplished as Hoffman must be regarded as an anomaly. Millions of people have attempted to start their lives anew in a different culture with a different language, and very few have become as articulate as Hoffman. Of the hundreds of thousands of human beings who began new lives after surviving the devastation of the Third Reich, few managed to be as expressive in an adopted language as Aharon Appelfeld, Louis Begley, Paul Celan, and Elie Wiesel. Translingual literature is the creation of extraordinary nomads who succeed in passing through all three of Turner's phases. There are, according to the United Nations Refugee Agency, more than 19.5 million refugees in the world today.[10] Aggregation is a phase of translingualism never attained by most.

Except in linguistic atlases, language is not defined by latitude and longitude. Language is a process, a performance, a system of communication—not a place. Yet spatial metaphors are frequently invoked to explain the translingual situation or even culture in general. In *The Location of Culture*, Homi K. Bhabha repeatedly employs spatial tropes when he invokes "'in-between' spaces," "the site of cultural difference," and "that Third Space of enunciations which I have made the precondition for the articulation of cultural difference."[11] Much analysis of second-language acquisition accepts this notion of "third space" or "third place," so that, as Claire J. Kramsch puts it, "the major task of language learners is to define for themselves what this 'third place' that they have engaged in seeking will look like, whether they are conscious of it or not."[12] The equation of locution with location becomes even more explicit in a formulation by Daisy Cocco de Filippis, a native of the Dominican Republic who came to the United States when she was 13: "El lenguaje ha sido el espacio habitado por aquellos a quienes se le ha negado un lugar" [Language has been the space inhabited by those who have been denied a place].[13] Assia Djebar writes in a French that, though enriched with resonances of Arabic and Berber from her native Algeria, she calls "Mon seul véritable territoire" [My only true territory].[14] After all of her dislocations, from Russia to Italy to the United States, Lvovich makes a similar claim about the memoir that she wrote in English, *The Multilingual Self*: "This book is my home."[15] And when Eva Hoffman

concludes her memoir by stating: "I am here now," she, too, is positioning herself within both the English language and the book that she has
written in it—as if languages and books possessed cartographical coordinates and every speaker could be located through a linguistic GPS.[16]
A writer who travels between languages is what George Steiner, who
moves amongst English, French, and German, calls "extraterritorial."[17]
Thus can Anton Shammās, a Palestinian, worry that he has strayed into
hostile territory by writing in Hebrew, committing "a sort of cultural
trespassing and I might one day be punished for it."[18]

Language as Home

Of course, languages and texts do not occupy physical space, except
symbolically, but that symbolism is a commonplace in discussions of
translingual experience. And, since there is no place like home, many
translinguals refer to their language of choice as home. Though he was
born in Lithuania, Czesław Miłosz spent most of his life in the United
States but insisted on writing in Polish, declaring, at a poetry reading at
the 1998 MLA Convention: "Language is the only homeland."[19] Despite
extensive immersion in both Japanese and Chinese, Gary Snyder writes
exclusively in English, about which his poem "It" declares: "my language
is home."[20] Asked whether he still had a homeland, Albert Camus,
torn between his restive native Algeria and the imperial metropolis,
Paris, replied: "Oui, j'ai une patrie, la langue française" [Yes, I have a
homeland, the French language].[21] He was echoing what Louis Martin
Chauffier wrote a decade earlier in defiance of the German occupation of
France: "ma Patrie, c'est la langue française" [My homeland is the French
language]. Chauffier added that the French language is "une patrie sans
frontière" [a homeland without borders].[22] Similarly, for Céline Dion,
the French Canadian singer who tours widely and records in both French
and English: "Le français c'est ma maison" [French is my home].[23] When
asked what she considers home, Julia Kissina, who writes in Russian,
Ukrainian, and German, replied: "Heimat ist für mich meine Sprache—
ganz egal welche: Russisch, Ukrainisch oder Deutsch" [Homeland
is for me my language—no matter whether Russian, Ukrainian, or
German].[24] Noting that many fellow Chicanos are dispersed throughout
the Midwest and the Northeast, Gloria Anzaldúa, too, insists that what
you speak is where you are: "For some of us, language is a homeland
closer than the Southwest."[25]

During the age of nation-states that confounds language and
nationality, that considers facility in Polish requisite for Polish identity,
in Norwegian for Norwegian identity, those who abandon one language
but are not yet secure in another can feel as if they have vacated one
apartment but not yet moved all of their belongings into another.
Many translinguals suffer from a permanent sense of homelessness.

J.M. Coetzee, who grew up speaking Afrikaans and English, mastered the latter well enough to have earned the Nobel Prize for Literature by writing in it. Nevertheless, he told an audience in India that the language he writes in, English, is not his home:

> As a child in South Africa, I was sent to an English medium school because my parents thought it was a way to the future. I then studied in English at the university level. Yet I can't say that I can feel at home in English. I feel I am writing in someone else's language.[26]

Edward Said, who grew up speaking both English and Arabic, confesses: "I *have never known* which was *my first language*, and have felt fully at home in neither, although I dream in both. Every time I speak an English sentence, I find myself echoing it in Arabic, and vice versa."[27]

According to Gustavo Pérez Firmat, Ricky Ricardo, the TV persona of Cuban émigré Desi Arnaz, embodies the pathos of translingual muddle. On the long-running *I Love Lucy* show, while Ricky's Spanish, corrupted by anglicisms and enfeebled by a diminishing vocabulary, deteriorated, his heavily accented English never improved. "He is homeless in two languages," concludes Pérez Firmat.[28] Ricky, and the actor who played him, are examples of the "nilingüe," which Pérez Firmat defines as "someone who doesn't speak either: 'ni español ni inglés.'"[29] The metaphor of homelessness posits language as a matter of realty, if not reality. And if, as Martin Heidegger contended, language is the House of Being ("Die Sprache is das Haus des Seins. In ihrer Behausung wohnt der Mensch" [Language is the House of Being. In its habitation resides man]),[30] those who are not housed securely in a specific language suffer from an ontological deficiency.

Or else they revel in a deconstructionist decentring. Jacques Derrida spatializes language when, in *Monolinguisme de l'autre: ou la prothèse de l'origine*, he recounts how he, a Jew growing up in Muslim Algeria, resided "au bord du français, uniquement, ni en lui, ni hors de lui, sur la ligne introuvable de sa côte"—in a liminal position neither inside nor outside the French language but at its very edge.[31] He poses the paradox of being monolingual in a language that was not his own, to the extent that "depuis toujours, à demeure, je me demande si on peut aimer, jouir, prier, crever de douleur ou crever tout court dans une autre langue ou sans rien en dire à personne, sans parler même"—he has always wondered whether it is possible to love, enjoy, pray, die of pain, or die at all in another language or without saying anything to anyone, without even speaking.[32] Banished to the margins of a destabilized French, Derrida is able to employ it with reflexive sophistication.

It is the language of the metropolis that governed the colonized Algiers of his childhood, that he did not leave until he went off to Paris to attend the École normale supérieure at age 19. Although Derrida was not an observant Jew and did not particularly embrace his ethnic heritage, he was directly affected by the Crémieux Decree of October, 1870, which bestowed French citizenship on Maghreb Jews, as well as by the revocation of that citizenship by the Vichy régime in October, 1940 (his altered legal status resulted in expulsion from his *lycée*), and, again, by its restoration following the Second World War. The vagaries of national identity complicated Derrida's relationship to the nation whose language he spoke as his primary one. He could thus pronounce the typically Derridean paradox that: "Oui, je n'ai qu'une langue, or ce n'est pas la mienne" [Yes, I have only one language, but it is not mine].[33] Though he was fluent enough in English to teach in it at the University of California at Irvine, Derrida contends that he is condemned to "ce solipsisme intarissable" [this inexhaustible solipsism] of monolingualism and that it is a universal as well as personal condition.[34] "On ne parle jamais qu'une seule langue" [One never speaks anything but one language], he insists but, recognizing that all language is hybrid and interpersonal, immediately follows that with the declaration that: "On ne parle jamais une seule langue" [One never speaks only one language].[35] Situating himself both inside and outside French, Derrida presents his ambivalent thoughts about language by conceiving of language as a place, "un milieu absolu" [an absolute milieu].[36] It is an imaginary place whose peripheries he inhabits.

Betwixt and Between

Langue of course manifests itself as *parole*, as performance, a succession of symbols in time. Conceiving of language not temporally but spatially reifies it, reduces it to a static entity that can be located with coordinates of latitude and longitude. Literature offers the same conceptual temptation. Its representation on a printed page leads many readers to regard it as a commodity, to confuse the leaves of Whitman's published book with *Leaves of Grass*. As Stanley Fish, endorsing Gotthold Ephraim Lessing's assignment of poetry to the category of temporal, not spatial, art, insists, a poem is not a well-wrought urn but rather "the developing responses of the reader in relation to the words as they succeed one another in time."[37] Johann Wolfgang von Goethe's conception of *Weltliteratur* insidiously invites us to think of literature as congruent with the world, hence, like language, occupying positions on a map. So, too, do discussions of Eurocentrism and Afrocentrism place literature, assign it positions in space. Thinking of languages and literatures as spaces implies territoriality, conflating Dutch, Japanese, and Persian with the geopolitical constructs in which they are spoken.

If languages occupy space and the space they occupy is a mental homeland, the preposition *between* (*entre, zwischen, mellan, inter, между, בין*) becomes indispensable to any discussion of translingualism. "Betwixt and Between" is the way Turner characterizes initiates in the liminal phase, and Marie Arana uses the same phrase to describe her own divided loyalties to the United States and Peru, English and Spanish.[38] "I live on bridges," she reports, using a familiar spatial metaphor. "I've earned my place on them, stand comfortably when I'm on one, content with betwixt and between."[39] Describing Samuel Beckett's relationship to English and French, Brian T. Fitch contends: "Beckett is the Man-between and each of his books is a Work-between."[40] Djebar diagnoses her bilingual dilemma as a condition she calls "entre-deux-langues" [between-two-languages].[41] Translinguals tend to conceive of themselves as being situated between—or among—languages. A Canadian living in Paris, Nancy Huston imagines herself suspended at an exact midpoint between the two languages in which she writes, French and English. She describes: "Cette sensation de flottement entre l'anglais et le français, sans véritable ancrage dans l'un ou l'autre— de sorte que, au bout de dix années à l'étranger, loin d'être devenue 'parfaitement bilingue,' je me sens doublement mi-lingue" [This feeling of floating between English and French, without real anchoring in one or the other—so that, after ten years abroad, far from becoming "fully bilingual," I feel doubly mid-lingual].[42] Ariel Dorfman projects a similar consciousness of being located between two languages, in his case Spanish and English. Geography is destiny for Dorfman, who has written about half of his books in English and the other half in Spanish and calls himself "a bigamist of language."[43] The very title of his memoir *Heading South, Looking North* imagines the author poised somewhere above Central America equidistant from the two poles of his existence, Chile and the United States. However, his vantage point is *utopian* in the root sense—it is a *no place* that is impossible to inhabit since each language keeps jockeying for primacy; at various times, Dorfman even determines to speak one language to the total exclusion of the other.

Thus, because translingual writers often feel closer to one language than another, when they locate themselves *between* languages, the figure described is not necessarily an equilateral triangle—or, in the case of trilinguals such as Vladimir Nabokov, George Steiner, and Edwidge Danticat, a square. Pérez Firmat titles his study of Cuban-American culture *Life on the Hyphen*, but his position between English and Spanish is a precarious perch. "Hyphens hurt," he admits.[44] In the topological geometry of language, he, like many other Latinos in the United States, does not calibrate himself exactly "mi-lingue," but tilts more towards North America than Latin America, towards English than Spanish. Brought from his native Havana to Miami as a child, Pérez Firmat identifies himself as a cohort of the "1.5" American immigrant generation, one that, though more assimilated than his parents, still suffers from "a spiritual bilocation, the sense of being in two places at once, or of living in one residing in another."[45] Spatiality is again invoked to evoke the feeling of dis*place*ment.

Kathleen Saint-Onge, too, employs the metaphor of hyphen, but her language memoir *Bilingual Being: My Life as a Hyphen* asserts not that she is situated on a hyphen but that her life *is* a hyphen. And, in contrast to Pérez Firmat, for whom hyphens hurt, in Saint-Onge's case hyphens heal. A Canadian who associates the trauma of childhood sexual abuse with her native French, she uses a spatial metaphor to express the relief she felt after drifting from French to English, a language that, she explains, "created an alternative social space where I made a new life for myself, one so different from that inscribed by my hereditary French setting."[46] However, if switching languages can be liberating, remaining suspended in the space between languages can be exceedingly uncomfortable. Even writers who make a successful transition into another language often feel the residual pain of separation.

Julia Alvarez grew up in the Dominican Republic, but after several decades in Vermont, she explains: "I lost the capacity to really express myself in my native tongue. It remains a childhood language, but one that still exerts a gravitational pull."[47] In a poem whose title, "Leaving English," reinforces the spatial metaphor, as if language were a point of embarkation, Alvarez emphasizes the disparate distances between her and her two languages: "Even if Spanish made me who I was, it's English now that tells me who I am."[48] Hannah Arendt also adopted English as her medium of written expression, but, in contrast to Alvarez, she continued to feel a gap between it and her that she did not feel with her native German. She observed, in German: "Ich schreibe in Englisch, aber ich habe die Distanz nie verloren," [I write in English, but I have never lost a sense of distance from it].[49] Distance is debilitating, but it can also nourish. In Jean Buridan's famous philosophical paradox, a donkey standing equidistant between two bales of hay starves to death because it is unable to choose. And someone poised on the precise midpoint of Pérez Firmat's hyphen would be rendered what he calls "nilingüe." It is the tongue-tied condition in which Celaya, the "bilingual" protagonist of Sandra Cisneros's *Caramelo*, finds herself. "I don't have the words for what I want," she laments. "Not in English. Not in Spanish."[50]

No Man's Land

When the rhetoric about translingualism combines the connotations of peril and place, it often ends up invoking the image of no man's land, the term applied in the First World War to the area between the trenches of opposing armies that was not safe for anyone. Thus, faulting Robert Browning's translation of Aeschylus's *Agamemnon* for being "interlingua," "a centaur-idiom" that imposes the vocabulary, syntax, and phonology of ancient Greek on his own Victorian English, George Steiner (the trilingual critic who pointedly titled a 1972 volume of essays on language and literature *Extraterritorial*) pronounced it "a no-man's-land in psychological and linguistic space"—hence a text treacherous for both Hellenophones and Anglophones because it occupies a space outside either language.[51] In a similar vein, Ilan Stavans, describing how his identity was split between Spanish-speaking and English-speaking selves, recalls: "Every so often I would have a *tête-à-tête* with my *doppelgänger*, which resulted in a moment of intense confusion and despair, making me feel as the personification of a no-man's-land."[52] The metaphor takes even more dramatic form in the polyglot pun that Lise Gauvin employs to describe the dangerous zone that Francophone writers of Quebec, trying to assert themselves within the French literary world as well as against the Anglophone Canadian majority, inhabit. She contends that their struggle "peut conduire à l'aphasie, au silence littéraire ou au no man's langue" [can lead to aphasia, to literary silence, or to no man's language].[53]

The phrase "no man's langue" was probably coined by Ghérasim Luca, a Romanian Surrealist who wrote in French but advanced a programme of alienation from all languages, native and adopted. An online literary magazine based in Berlin called *No Man's Land* (www.no-mans-land. org) serves to make contemporary German-language poetry and fiction accessible to readers of English. As the website explains, "Ours is a virtual no man's land between languages and cultures—one which, like the former no man's land of the Berlin Wall, is now open for exploration."[54] But it was not until after childhood's end that the linguistic space favoured by Hugo Hamilton became habitable and safe. Hamilton wrote his memoir, *The Speckled People*, in English, but he recalls his Dublin childhood as a "language war" in which his mother spoke German and his nationalist father, who insisted on speaking Irish, prohibited the use of English at home, trying to enforce the rule with his fists.[55]

A demilitarized zone is *terra nemo* that, while remaining contested territory, has been declared off-limits to combat. Across the 38th Parallel, hostile armies of North and South Korea face off against each other, and the UN Buffer Zone in Cyprus separates Greek and Turkish adversaries. From Quebec to Catalonia to Cape Town and beyond, confrontations between languages have generated fighting words. Anton Shammās likens his own situation as a Palestinian writing in Hebrew to a kind of demilitarized zone, a battlefield from which a truce has forced antagonists to withdraw, at least temporarily. Shammās titles his 1979 volume of poetry שטח הפקר [*No Man's Land*] and concludes it with a poem called, with obvious homage to Wallace Stevens, "י״ג דרכים להסתכל בזה" ["Thirteen Ways of Looking at This"]. In the final lines of that poem, he declares:

אני לא יודע
שפה מעבר מזה
ושפה מעבר מזה
ואני הוזה בשטח ההפקר

[How could I know, if you don't mind –
one language ahead,
another behind.
And here I am,
imagining things in my no man's land.][56]

But of course in his poetry Shammās stands in treacherous space, daydreaming—perhaps hallucinating—in Hebrew, one of his two adversarial languages.

The Texas–Mexico border has become a dangerously militarized zone, but for Gloria Anzaldúa it is a symbolic space of linguistic freedom. In *Borderlands/La Frontera*, a book whose bilingual title in itself heralds hybridity, she catalogues the eight languages that she inhabits to one degree or another—"1. Standard English/ 2. Working-class and slang English/ 3. Standard Spanish/ 4. Standard Mexican Spanish/ 5. North Mexican Spanish dialect/ 6. Chicano Spanish (Texas, New Mexico, Arizona, and California have regional variations)/ 7. Tex-Mex/ 8. *Pachuco* (called *caló*)."[57] This heteroglossia is a product of her residence in the borderlands of south Texas, a contested space between the United States and Mexico in which her people, Chicanos, were conquered and oppressed. But Anzaldúa also uses "borderlands" figuratively, to apply to a state of mind. "La frontera" is the liminal condition, betwixt and between, that causes acute anxiety and cognitive dissonance in other translinguals. However, for Anzaldúa, who declares: "I am my language," the motley nature of that language is the source of strength, not, as with Wolfson, of malaise.[58] Translingualism becomes transcendence, not transgression.

Walter D. Mignolo uses Anzaldúa as a reference *point*, to use a spatial metaphor, in his own spatializing polemic on behalf of hybridity. Studying the tensions between imperial cultures and languages and indigenous ones that he locates in "the border or line that divides and unites modernity/coloniality," Mignolo calls for what he terms "border thinking"—"an epistemology, an ethic and politics that emerge from the experiences of people taking their destiny in their own hands and not waiting for saviors."[59] It is, he explains, "tantamount to engaging decoloniality; that is, in thinking and doing decolonially."[60] In a revolutionary project that must also transcend the territoriality of scholarly disciplines, what he also calls "border gnosis" includes "languaging," which he defines as "thinking and writing between languages."[61] Instead of the endangered no-man's-land that others describe as the space between languages, Mignolo conceives of it as a privileged vantage point from which to launch a successful foray against hegemonic thinking. "I have to be at war, constantly," he declares, "against competitive ideologies, as well as with decolonial ideologies that do not intend to compete but to delink."[62] For Mignolo, as for Hamilton and Stavans, the space between languages is a locus for hostility, though he is confident of worthy purpose and ultimate victory.

Hybrid Pollution and Invigoration

Tatyana Tolstaya was considerably more ambivalent in writing about the Russian-French translingual Andreï Makine. In fact, her two reviews of the same novel, Makine's *Le Testament français*, are a striking illustration of the relation between language and thought. Writing in English, in *The New York Review of Books*, Tolstaya praised Makine's novel for its ability to express quintessentially Russian attitudes in evocative adopted French.[63] However, writing in Russian and defending the honour of her own native language, Tatyana Tolstaya denounced Makine, who abandoned their shared L1 to write in French, as "a philological mongrel, a cultural hybrid, a linguistic chimera, a literary basilisk, who, if you believe the old books, was a combination of a rooster and snake, something that flies and crawls at the same time."[64] Tolstaya's pungent attack on Makine's translingualism draws on a long tradition of disparaging as traitors those who move between languages. When national identity is embodied in language, forsaking or abusing it becomes as reprehensible as burning the flag. After all, according to the hoary Italian adage "*Traduttore, traditore*," to translate is to betray.

Linguistic patriotism is the motive behind the various authoritative institutions, including the Académie française, the Latvian State Language Centre, and the Institute of the Czech Language, that attempt to enforce verbal conformity, and governments from Malaysia to Poland to Quebec that impose fines on those who pollute the official language, especially by adulterating it with words from another tongue. It is the source of establishment disdain for Franglais, Spanglish, Deutschrussisch, Chinglish, and other macaronic tongues. Proper use of the national language is associated with notions not only of loyalty but also of what Deborah Cameron calls "verbal hygiene";[65] a spurious belief in 'linguistic purity' leads many to regard those who mix tongues as unclean. They are polluting the 'spaces' that languages occupy. Tolstaya's image of "something that flies and crawls at the same time" suggests that translingualism is unnatural and loathsome.

In racial terms, mixing languages is tantamount to miscegenation, and xenophobic projects of ethnic cleansing have often been accompanied by demonization of those who sully the national tongue (according to Judges 12, the Gideonites identified Ephraimites by their inability to pronounce *shibboleth* and then killed them; and in 1937, during the "Parsley Massacre," Dominican authorities slaughtered approximately 20,000 people, reputedly when their inability to trill the 'r' in *perejil* exposed them as Haitians). Moreover, if many languages encourage us to regard L1 as the 'mother tongue' (*maternam locutionem,*

Muttersprache, langue maternelle, madrelingua, idioma materno, 語, *modersmål, anyanyelvük,* שפת אם, *Язык матери,* מאמע-לאשן, اللغة الأم), abandoning it for another constitutes a kind of psychic matricide.

Yet hybridization of crops—heterosis—yields more robust corn and rice than the conventional kind, lending genetic support to Anzaldúa's defence of heteroglossia and to the code-switching practised by her and other Chicano writers. Anzaldúa's work is congruent with the contemporary postcolonial multicultural moment, in which alterity is valorized and *métissage* and *Mischling* become virtues, not vices. Notions of cultural and linguistic purity such as Tolstaya's are condemned as what Albert Memmi calls "heterophobia," fear of difference.[66] Thus does translingual (French, Creole, English) Françoise Lionnet, employing a spatial metaphor and emphasizing language as a crucial element in global mixing, extol "all those who must survive (and write) in the interval between different cultures and languages."[67] Likewise, in addition to race, religion, and culture, language is crucial to the syncretism that Antillean writers Jean Bernabé, Patrick Chamoiseau, and Raphaël Confiant call for in their 1989 manifesto for "creolization," *Éloge de la Créolité.* "La Créolité," they proclaim, "est une annihilation de la fausse universalité, du monolinguisme et de la pureté" [Creolization is an annihilation of false universality, monolingualism, and purity].[68]

Such exaltation of heterogeneity recalls the mysticism of José Vasconcelos, who in 1925 heralded what he called "la raza cósmica," the glorious cosmic race of the future that will be a synthesis of all the disparate elements—racial, cultural, and linguistic—found in Latin America. Looking forward to a supreme *mestizaje,* he prophesied that out of the human mix will emerge "la raza definitiva, la raza síntesis o raza integral, hecha con el genio y con la sangre de todos los pueblos y, por lo mismo, más capaz de verdadera fraternidad y de visión realmente universal" [the definitive race, the synthetical race, the integral race, made up of the genius and the blood of all peoples and, for that reason, more capable of true brotherhood and of a truly universal vision].[69] Even more grandiose was Walt Whitman's conception of English as the supreme syncretic language:

> View'd freely, the English language is the accretion and growth of every dialect, race, and range of time, and is both the free and compacted composite of all. From this point of view, it stands for Language in the largest sense, and is really the greatest of studies. It involves so much; is indeed a sort of universal absorber, combiner, and conqueror.[70]

Whitman's conception of English as "universal absorber, combiner, and conqueror" anticipates Léopold Sédar Senghor's glorification of French as the universal language of civilized humanity. A translingual, from

Serer to French, Senghor hailed the Francophone movement for spreading an egalitarian humanism: "La francophonie, c'est l'humanisme intégral qui se tisse autour de la terre, cette symbiose des énergies dormantes de toutes les races, de toutes les consciences et qui se réveillent à leur chaleur complémentaire" [Francophonie is that integral humanism that is woven into the earth: that symbiosis of dormant energies of all races, all forms of consciousness awakening to their complementary ardour].[71] The exalted claims by Whitman and Senghor echo the historical ambitions of imperial languages such as Latin, Farsi, and Han Chinese that presumed to subsume scattered vernaculars within a single language that embodied the highest values of the human race. Though postcolonial discourse, by contrast, rejects the hegemony of any particular language, it, too, yearns to transcend local languages that are partial and divisive.

Panlingual Aspirations

The translingual project is ultimately and implicitly panlingual. The urge to accumulate languages culminates in a *reductio ad infinitum*, the dream of transcending all languages to arrive at a space of universal Truth. It would shatter the "monolingual paradigm" that, according to Yasemin Yildiz, developed in the eighteenth century with the rise of the monolingual nation state.[72] Though most people speak more than one language, hegemonic nation-states could define and police their borders by insisting on the congruence of one nation and one language. By contrast, the panlingual space of universal Truth is currently symbolized by the 17 acres in the Turtle Bay neighbourhood of Manhattan that are occupied by the United Nations. The property of no nation, the UN Headquarters, where six languages are deemed official and another 469 languages are recognized as equally valid for articulating the Universal Declaration of Human Rights, is legally extraterritorial. It is simultaneously no-man's-land and everyman's (and every person's) land. The UN is a site of global pathology, for focusing the conflicts of the world and, occasionally, resolving them. However, as an embodiment of humanity's highest aspirations for peace and justice, but also as a place that is no place, it is translingual utopia.

Notes

1 See Steven G. Kellman, *The Translingual Imagination* (Lincoln: University of Nebraska Press, 2000).
2 Kellman, *Translingual Imagination*; Mary Besemeres, "Language and Emotional Experience: The Voice of Translingual Memoir," in *Bilingual Minds: Emotional Experience, Expression, and Representation*, ed. Aneta Pavlenko (New York: Multilingual Matters), 34–58.
3 Mary Antin, *The Promised Land* (New York: Penguin, 1997), 282, 164.
4 Edward V. Bok, *The Americanization of Edward Bok: The Autobiography of a Dutch Boy Fifty Years After* (New York: Charles Scribner's Sons, 1920), 4.

5 Natasha Lvovich, *The Multilingual Self: An Inquiry into Language Learning* (Mahwah, NJ: Lawrence Erlbaum, 1997), 71.

6 Elsa Triolet, *La Mise en mots* (Geneva: Albert Skira, 1969), 54.

7 Elizabeth Klosty Beaujour, *Alien Tongues: Bilingual Russian Writers of the "First" Emigration* (Ithaca, NY: Cornell University Press, 1989), 42.

8 Victor Turner, *In the Forest of Symbols* (Ithaca, NY: Cornell University Press, 1967), 94.

9 Colette A. Granger, *Silence in Second Language Learning: A Psychoanalytic Reading* (Tonawanda, NY: Multilingual Matters, 2004), 62.

10 United Nations High Commissioner for Refugees, "Facts and Figures about Refugees," www.unhcr.org.uk/about-us/key-facts-and-figures.html.

11 Homi K. Bhabha, *The Location of Culture* (New York: Routledge Classics, 1994), 2, 46, 56.

12 Claire J. Kramsch, *Context and Culture in Language Teaching* (New York: Oxford University Press, 1993), 257.

13 Daisy Cocco De Filippis, *Desde la diáspora: selección bilingüe de ensayos* (New York: Ediciones Alcance, 2003), 149.

14 Assia Djebar, *Ces Voix qui m'assiègent ... en marge de ma francophonie* (Montreal: Les Presses de l'Université de Montréal, 1999), 44.

15 Lvovich, *The Multilingual Self*, xv.

16 Hoffman, *Lost in Translation*, 280.

17 George Steiner, *Extraterritorial: Papers on Literature and the Language Revolution* (New York: Atheneum, 1971), 3 ff.

18 Hannan Hever, "Hebrew in an Israeli Arab Hand: Six Miniatures on Anton Shammās's *Arabesques*," *Cultural Critique* 7 (1987): 72.

19 Luz María Umpierre, "Unscrambling Allende's '*Dos palabras*': The Self, the Immigrant/Writer, and Social Justice," *MELUS* 27 (2002): 135.

20 Gary Snyder, *Regarding Wave* (New York: New Directions, 1970), 42.

21 Albert Camus, *Carnets II Janvier 1942–Mars 1951* (Paris: Gallimard, 1964), 337.

22 Louis Martin Chauffier, "Ma patrie, la langue française," in *Domaine Français: Messages 1943*, ed. Jean Lescure (Geneva: Editions des Trois Collines, 1943), 62.

23 Céline Dion, "Français ou anglais?" Celine Dion Website, www.celinedion.com/fr/francais-ou-anglais/2012.

24 Anastasia Poscharsky-Ziegler, "Heimat ist für mich meine Sprache," *Der Neue Tag*, 30 March 2006, www.oberpfalznetz.de/onetz/860891-131-heimat_ist_fuer_mich_meine_sprache,1,0.html.

25 Gloria Anzaldúa, *Borderlands/La Frontera: The New Mestiza* (San Francisco: Aunt Lute, 1987), 55.

26 Wasfia Jalali, "Can't Feel At Home in English: Coetzee." *Outlookindia.com*, 24 January 2011, http://news.outlookindia.com/items.aspx?artid=7095892011.

27 Edward Said, *Reflections on Exile: And Other Essays* (Cambridge, MA: Harvard University Press, 2001), 557.

28 Gustavo Pérez Firmat, *Life on the Hyphen: The Cuban-American Way*, revised edition (Austin: University of Texas Press, 2012), 43.

29 Pérez Firmat, *Life on the Hyphen*, 43.

30 Martin Heidegger, *Über den Humanismus* (Frankfurt am Main: Vittorio Klostermann, 2000), 5.

31 Jacques Derrida, *Monolinguisme de l'autre: ou la prothèse de l'origine* (Paris: Galilée, 1996), 14.

32 Ibid., 14.

33 Ibid., 15.

34 Ibid., 14.

35 Ibid., 21.

36 Ibid., 13.

37 Stanley Fish, "Literature in the Reader: Affective Stylistics," *New Literary History* 2.1 (1970): 126–7.

38 Turner, *In the Forest of Symbols*, 97.

39 Marie Arana, *American Chica: Two Worlds, One Childhood* (New York: Dial, 2005), 301.

40 Brian T. Fitch, *Beckett and Babel: An Investigation into the Status of the Bilingual Work* (Toronto, ON: University of Toronto Press, 1988), 156.

41 Djebar, *Ces Voix qui m'assiègent*, 33.

42 Nancy Huston and Leila Sebbar, *Lettres parisiennes: Histoires d'exil* (Paris: Bernard Barrault, 1986), 77.

43 Ariel Dorfman, *Heading South, Looking North: A Bilingual Journey* (New York: Farrar, Straus & Giroux, 1998), 270.

44 Pérez Firmat, *Life on the Hyphen*, ix.

45 Ibid.

46 Kathleen Saint-Onge, *Bilingual Being: My Life as a Hyphen* (Montreal, QC: McGill-Queen's University Press, 2013), 325.

47 Robert Birnbaum, Interview with Julia Alvarez, *Identity Theory*, 22 May 2006, www.identitytheory.com/julia-alvarez/.

48 Julia Alvarez, "Leaving English," in *The Woman I Kept to Myself* (Chapel Hill, NC: Algonquin, 2011), 111.

49 Günter Gaus, *Zur Person: Porträts in Frage und Antwort* (Munich: Deutscher Taschenbuch Verlag, 1987), 24.

50 Sandra Cisneros, *Caramelo, or, Puro Cuento* (New York: Knopf, 2003), 60.

51 Steiner, *After Babel*, 332.

52 Ilan Stavans, *Art and Anger: Essays on Politics and the Imagination* (Albuquerque: University of New Mexico Press, 1996), ix.

53 Lise Gauvin, *L'écrivain francophone à la croisée des langues: entretiens* (Paris: Karthala, 1997), 9.

54 *No Man's Land: New German Literature in English Translation*. Berlin. www.no-mans-land.org/.

55 Hugo Hamilton, *The Speckled People* (London: Harper Perennial, 2003), 278.

56 Anton Shammās, שטח הפקר. [Shetakh Hefker] (Tel Aviv: Hakibbutz Hameuchad, 1979), 46. Author's translation from Anton Shammās, "Three Poems," *Banipal: Magazine of Modern Arab Literature* 3 (1998), www.banipal.co.uk/selections/17/165/anton-shammas/.

57 Anzaldúa, *Borderlands/La Frontera*, 55.

58 Ibid.

59 Walter D Mignolo, *Local Histories/Global Designs: Coloniality, Subaltern Knowledges, and Border Thinking*, rev. edition (Princeton, NJ: Princeton University Press, 2012), xvi, xxii.

60 Mignolo, *Local Histories/Global Designs*, xvi.

61 Mignolo, *Local Histories/Global Designs*, 309, 226.

62 Mignolo, *Local Histories/Global Designs*, xvii.

63 Tatiana Tolstaya, "Love Story: Dreams of My Russian Summers," *New York Review of Books*, November 20, 1997: 4–5.

64 Quoted in Adrian Wanner, *Out of Russia: Fictions of a New Translingual Diaspora* (Evanston, IL: Northwestern University Press, 2011), 27.

65 Deborah Cameron, *Verbal Hygiene* (London: Routledge, 1995).

66 Albert Memmi, *Le Racisme: description, définition, traitement* (Paris: Gallimard, 1982), 115.

67 Françoise Lionnet, *Autobiographical Voices: Gender, Race and Self-Portraiture* (Ithaca, NY: Cornell University Press, 1989), 1.

68 Jean Bernabé, Patrick Chamoiseau, and Raphaël Confiant, *Éloge de la Créolité* (Paris: Gallimard, 1989), 28.

69 José Vasconcelos, *The Cosmic Race/La raza cósmica. A Bilingual Edition*, trans. Didier T. Jaén (Baltimore: Johns Hopkins University Press, 1997), 60.

70 Walt Whitman, "Slang in America," in *Prose Works 1892, Volume 2 Collect and Other Prose*, ed. Floyd Stovall (New York: New York University Press, 1964), 572.

71 Léopold Sédar Senghor, "Le français langue de culture," *Liberté I: Négritude et humanism* (Paris: Editions du Seuil, 1964), 363.

72 Yasemin Yildiz, *Beyond the Mother Tongue: The Postmonolingual Condition* (New York: Fordham University Press, 2011), 2 ff.

Bibliography

Alvarez, Julia. "Leaving English." In *The Woman I Kept to Myself*. Chapel Hill, NC: Algonquin, 2011.

Antin, Mary. *The Promised Land*. 1912. Edited by Werner Sollors. New York: Penguin, 1997.

Anzaldúa, Gloria. *Borderlands/La Frontera: The New Mestiza*. San Francisco, CA: Aunt Lute, 1987.

Arana, Marie. *American Chica: Two Worlds, One Childhood*. New York: Dial, 2005.

Bernabé, Jean, Patrick Chamoiseau, and Raphaël Confiant. *Éloge de la Créolité*. Paris: Gallimard, 1989.

Besemeres, Mary. "Language and Emotional Experience: The Voice of Translingual Memoir." In *Bilingual Minds: Emotional Experience, Expression, And Representation*, edited by Aneta Pavlenko, 34–58. New York: Multilingual Matters, 2006.

Bhabha, Homi K. *The Location of Culture*. New York: Routledge Classics, 2004.

Birnbaum, Robert. Interview with Julia Alvarez. *Identity Theory*, 22 May 2006. www.identitytheory.com/julia-alvarez/.

Bok, Edward W. *The Americanization of Edward Bok: The Autobiography of a Dutch Boy Fifty Years After*. New York: Charles Scribner's Sons, 1920.

Cameron, Deborah. *Verbal Hygiene*. London: Routledge, 1995.

Camus, Albert. *Carnets II Janvier 1942–Mars 1951*. Paris: Gallimard, 1964.

Chauffier, Louis Martin. "Ma patrie, la langue française." In *Domaine Français: Messages 1943*, edited by Jean Lescure, 61–8. Geneva: Editions des Trois Collines, 1943.

Cisneros, Sandra. *Caramelo, or, Puro Cuento*. New York: Knopf, 2003.

Cocco-DeFilippis, Daisy. *Desde la diáspora: selección bilingüe de ensayos*. New York: Ediciones Alcance, 2003.

Derrida, Jacques. *Monolinguisme de l'autre: ou la prothèse de l'origine*. Paris: Galilée, 1996.

Dion, Céline. "Français ou anglais?" Céline Dion Website. www.celinedion.com/fr/francais-ou-anglais/.

Djebar, Assia. *Ces Voix qui m'assiègent... en marge de ma francophonie*. Montreal: Les Presses de l'Université de Montréal, 1999.

Dorfman, Ariel. *Heading South, Looking North: A Bilingual Journey*. New York: Farrar, Straus & Giroux, 1998.

Fish, Stanley. "Literature in the Reader: Affective Stylistics." *New Literary History* 2 no. 1 (1970): 123–62.

Fitch, Brian T. *Beckett and Babel: An Investigation into the Status of the Bilingual Work.* Toronto, ON: University of Toronto Press, 1988.

Gaus, Günter. *Zur Person: Porträts in Frage und Antwort.* Munich: Deutscher Taschenbuch Verlag, 1987.

Gauvin, Lise. *L'écrivain francophone à la croisée des langues: entretiens.* Paris: Karthala, 1997.

Hamilton, Hugo. *The Speckled People.* London: Harper Perennial, 2003.

Heidegger, Martin. *Über den Humanismus.* 1947. Frankfurt am Main: Vittorio Klostermann, 2000.

Hever, Hannan. "Hebrew in an Israeli Arab Hand: Six Miniatures on Anton Shammās's *Arabesques.*" *Cultural Critique* 7 (1987): 47–76.

Hoffman, Eva. *Lost in Translation: A Life in a New Language.* New York: E.P. Dutton, 1989.

Huston, Nancy, and Leila Sebbar. *Lettres parisiennes: Histoires d'exil.* Paris: Bernard Barrault, 1986.

Jalali, Wasfia. "Can't Feel At Home in English: Coetzee." *Outlookindia.com,* 24 January 2011. http://news.outlookindia.com/items.aspx?artid=709589.

Kellman, Steven G. *The Translingual Imagination.* Lincoln: University of Nebraska Press, 2000.

———. "Translingual Memoirs of the New American Immigration." *Scritture migranti: rivista di scambi interculturali* 3 (2009): 1–14.

Kramsch, Claire J. *Context and Culture in Language Teaching.* New York: Oxford University Press, 1993.

Lionnet, Françoise. *Autobiographical Voices: Gender, Race and Self-Portraiture.* Ithaca, NY: Cornell University Press, 1989.

Lvovich, Natasha. *The Multilingual Self: An Inquiry into Language Learning.* Mahwah, NJ: Lawrence Erlbaum, 1997.

Memmi, Albert. *Le Racisme: description, définition, traitement.* Paris: Gallimard, 1982.

Mignolo, Walter D. *Local Histories/Global Designs: Coloniality, Subaltern Knowledges, and Border Thinking,* rev. edition Princeton, NJ: Princeton University Press, 2012.

No Man's Land: New German Literature in English Translation. www.no-mans-land.org/.

Pérez Firmat, Gustavo. *Life on the Hyphen: The Cuban-American Way,* rev. edition. Austin: University of Texas Press, 2012.

Poscharsky-Ziegler, Anastasia. "Heimat ist für mich meine Sprache." *Der Neue Tag,* 30 March 2006. www.oberpfalznetz.de/onetz/860891-131-heimat_ist_fuer_mich_meine_sprache,1,0.html.

Said, Edward. *Reflections on Exile: And Other Essays.* Cambridge, MA: Harvard University Press, 2001.

Saint-Onge, Kathleen. *Bilingual Being: My Life as a Hyphen.* Montreal, QC: McGill-Queen's University Press, 2013.

Senghor, Léopold Sédar. "Le français langue de culture." *Liberté I: Négritude et humanisme,* 358–63. Paris: Editions du Seuil, 1964.

Shammās, Anton. הפקר שטח [Shetakh Hefker]. Tel Aviv: Hakibbutz Hameuchad, 1979.

———. "Three Poems." *Banipal: Magazine of Modern Arab Literature* 3 (1998). www.banipal.co.uk/selections/17/165/anton-shammas/.

Snyder, Gary. *Regarding Wave*. New York: New Directions, 1970.

Stavans, Ilan. *Art and Anger: Essays on Politics and the Imagination.* Albuquerque: University of New Mexico Press, 1996.

Steiner, George. *Extraterritorial: Papers on Literature and the Language Revolution.* New York: Atheneum, 1971.

———. *After Babel: Aspects of Language and Translation.* Oxford: Oxford University Press, 1998.

Tolstaya, Tatiana. "Love Story: Dreams of My Russian Summers." *New York Review of Books*, November 20, 1997: 4–5.

Triolet, Elsa. *La Mise en mots*. Geneva: Albert Skira, 1969.

Turner, Victor. *In the Forest of Symbols*. Ithaca, NY: Cornell University Press, 1967.

Umpierre, Luz María. "Unscrambling Allende's '*Dos palabras*': The Self, the Immigrant/Writer, and Social Justice." *MELUS* 27 (2002): 129–36.

United Nations High Commissioner for Refugees. "Facts and Figures about Refugees." www.unhcr.org.uk/about-us/key-facts-and-figures.html.

United Nations Office of the High Commissioner of Human Rights. "Universal Declaration of Human Rights." www.ohchr.org/EN/UDHR/Pages/Introduction.aspx.

Vasconcelos, José. *The Cosmic Race/La raza cósmica. A Bilingual Edition.* Translated by Didier T. Jaén. Baltimore: Johns Hopkins University Press, 1997.

Wanner, Adrian. *Out of Russia: Fictions of a New Translingual Diaspora.* Evanston, IL: Northwestern University Press, 2011.

Whitman, Walt. "Slang in America." In *Prose Works 1892, Volume 2 Collect and Other Prose*, edited by Floyd Stovall. New York: New York University Press, 1964.

Wolfson, Louis. *Le schizo et les langues*. Paris: Gallimard, 1970.

Yildiz, Yasemin. *Beyond the Mother Tongue: The Postmonolingual Condition.* New York: Fordham University Press, 2011.

3   The Worlds of Québec

On Post-Bilingualism, Multidirectionality, and Other Critical Detours

Christopher Larkosh

Et Héloïse, elle ne va plus à la messe. Elle n'a plus de temps, écrit-elle. Elle ne va plus communier le dimanche, il fait trop froid, dit-elle. Elle dit qu'il y a un téléphone à l'auberge. Et l'électricité. Ah! Ce n'est pas comme ici. La vie à l'étranger est bien appréciable, bien sûr, Emmanuel, mais malgré tout on est bien ici, le soir, avec notre lampe à l'huile. Ton père ne veut pas l'électricité, et il a raison. Moi aussi je suis contre le progrès. Et toi, Emmanuel, qu'est-ce que tu en penses, hein?

[As for Héloïse, she no longer goes to Mass. She writes that she no longer has time. She doesn't take Holy Communion on Sunday, as she says it's too cold outside. She says that she has a telephone at the hostel. And electricity. Oh, it's not like here. Life out there is something to appreciate, of course, Emmanuel, but in spite of everything we're fine here, in the evening, with our oil lamp. Your father doesn't want electricity, and he's right. I am also against progress. And you, Emmanuel, what do you think, hmm?]

—Marie-Claire Blais, Une saison dans la vie d'Emmanuel[1]

Québec Literature: World Literature?

Why is it that rereading a quote from a familiar work by an iconic twentieth-century author from Québec—in this case, one from a 1965 novel by Marie-Claire Blais—so often fills me with an ambivalent mélange of rare aesthetic pleasure, along with a lingering, almost gnawing, cultural melancholy? Despite the widespread recognition of this work by now as a classic in Québec, and its long-standing, near-universal availability at any bookstore or library there, going back to reread this work still imparts the sensation of entering once again into a vast open secret, available to anyone who cares to enter, and yet one that so few close to it, beyond the specialists and other committed readers, have made much effort to get to know. To be blunt, so many of those we encounter on a daily basis, whether in Québec or elsewhere, are simply not as interested in the question of literature as many of us might like to believe. As we see above, many are even unapologetically sceptical as to what a novel or poem might be able to offer in the way of reshaping one's view of the world. Even so, literature's critical potential still ends up at times remaking the world we come to live in, often thoroughly, and irreversibly, whether we consider ourselves readers or not.

And yet, I continue to return to this world of books from Québec I have read, and will continue to read, again and again, ones that I never seem to be completely finished with. This is the true mark of a literary classic for me: not necessarily its level of international academic or critical recognition or the number of translations it has engendered, but the enduring nature of the literary world that it creates, one unlike any other. Yet how to explain to others unfamiliar with such a work how it served as an entryway into the unique world of its own narrative and that of other related works, illuminating along the way so many aspects of Québec's history and political culture, precisely at that pivotal historical moment when the dark world of often crushing monotony, rural poverty, social injustice, and religious control it described was at the point of irreversible transformation?

To be honest, there are times that I wish I could write of this work as I would of any recognized classic of world literature; elliptically, even blithely, assured of other readers' familiarity with its well-worn narrative and cast of characters.* There would be no need to reintroduce

---

* Such a familiarity with said narrative and cast of characters would clearly extend to the political and cultural events already unfolding at this time: that is, la Révolution Tranquille that gave French-speaking people of Québec greater influence in economic and political life; the 1967 Montréal World's Fair, Expo '67; le Front de Libération du Québec (FLQ)'s 1970 kidnapping and murder of Labour Minister Pierre Laporte, as well as Prime Minister Pierre Trudeau's subsequent declaration of a state of emergency, also known as the October Crisis; the 1969 Official Language Act, which made Canada an officially bilingual country; and the 1977 Loi N° 101, which in turn made French Québec's sole official language. And yet, already I find I am reconstructing the very kind of introduction to the uninitiated that I had wished I could avoid in the first place.

So with these basic history lessons now set aside, the more important question for me here remains: is there any work of Québec literature that would be considered indisputably an example of 'World Literature' as it is currently being reconsolidated and promoted? Some Anglophone-centred specialists in this enterprise of World Literature (most notably, Damrosch 2003) who make it their business to select, critique, organize and anthologize these seminal works as part of a renewed push to arrive at a world literary canon, apparently don't seem to think so; or if they do (Casanova 2004), apparently not enough to highlight more than perhaps one or two literary works from Québec in their admittedly wide-reaching overview of world literature from a markedly Parisian perspective: they either focus on ones that make use of a spoken dialect of *joual*, most notably as in the works of playwright and novelist Michel Tremblay, or make generalizations that reduce the importance of the entire Québec literary tradition to nationalistic or separatist concerns that, while no doubt serving an important purpose of individuation in the 60s and 70s, are hardly representative of the broad range of literature produced in Québec since then (Casanova 232, 283–4). Perhaps more troubling is the repeated cataloguing of Québec literature under the rubric of so-called 'small literatures,' most often alongside another prime example of a historically suppressed literary and linguistic

Grand-Mère Antoinette, the matriarch in charge of keeping this traditional family intact in the face of constant misery, shame and deprivation; or Héloïse, the granddaughter expelled from the convent, whose work as a prostitute now provides an unspoken but nonetheless much welcome source of income for the family; or her brother Jean le Maigre, sickly, infested with fleas since birth, yet possessed of a literary passion that no amount of familial neglect and disapproval can diminish. As the Father remarks to Grand-Mère Antoinette at the outset, "On n'a pas besoin de livres dans cette maison" ['we don't need books in this house'] (16), and ultimately it is still into this resolutely non-literary world that so many people continue to be born. For this reason, it is Jean le Maigre's poetic struggle with this unresponsive society, in league with his brother, bedmate, and companion le Septième, which remains at the heart of this novel's hardly concealed undercurrent of sarcasm and social critique.

So if the novel actually devotes most of its attention to the memoirs of Jean le Maigre that are to be left behind as his *œuvre posthume*, along with the intermittent travails of his sister Héloïse, first at the convent and later at the "Auberge de la Rose Publique," what then of the title character Emmanuel, the newborn baby in this family whose arrival provides his grandmother with an attentive, if still unresponsive, listener? As the novel's final pages suggest, he may well meet the same fate as Jean le Maigre—that of sexual abuse, premature death from scarlet fever, and subsequent, if belated, beatification at the hands of the religious authorities—or he and others like him just might emerge over the next few generations into the new and different world that awaits them: one that we shall begin by calling here, however tentatively, modernity.

Moving Towards Post-Bilingualism in Québec and North America

Ultimately, so much of what Blais identifies not only as a culture in transition, but as one perhaps in the midst of its most profound societal transformation, can now be identified at a nexus of a full-fledged cultural model, one that has not only established French as its sole official language at the national (i.e. provincial) level, but one that continues to renegotiate its relationship with the bilingual confederation of which it remains a part. So how would one characterize this multilayered literary,

tradition of another bilingual semi-autonomous region, that of Catalonia, but without any concrete examples that might show how precisely these two literary traditions might dialogue with one another (Casanova 104, 195). But then again, why should I or anyone else feel troubled by that? One might just continue to delight in the relative non-recognition of this lesser-known literary canon, aware that, in alternative reformulations of world literature, it is as central and indispensable as any other.

linguistic, and cultural landscape? Is it still largely monolingual or bilingual in practice? Or does it represent an even more complex model of multilingualism that might be characterized differently? One term one might want to consider for the purposes of this discussion, then, is yet another: *post-bilingual*, that is, one in which the inherent hierarchies of official bilingualism and/or belonging ('bilangue-ing'?) as they are traditionally understood have already been laid bare in their incapacity to manage a number of re-emergent linguistic relationships, especially, at least for the purposes of this study, with indigenous communities, immigrant groups, or a necessary set of ever-developing cultural relationships with other cultures around the globe.

The opportunity to revisit Québec culture and its developing understanding of its own globalized late-modernity, both through its own literature and culture and as part of a continually developing set of intercultural and interlinguistic relationships, arrives at a moment when the questions I wish to raise on the globalizing terms of this modernity are unavoidably projected against a background of conflicting cultural politics.[†] The perhaps unavoidable series of recent official statements against multiculturalism on either side of the conventional Western left/right political divide, both from politicians and from cultural critics, challenge me to reinterpret texts and materials at hand in the context of what they might have to contribute to an ongoing transnational discussion taking place in the here-and-now: namely, on the sustained viability of multicultural models of subjectivity, of which multilingualism is an inseparable part, at least in my view. In this context, what is at stake for literary scholars, committed not only to the study, but also to a lifelong practice, of multilingual multiculturalism, to develop projects outside of their areas of assigned disciplinary and linguistic expertise: that is, not only to cross new borders of language and culture, but just as important, to challenge the well-worn lines of disciplinary specialization and institutional affiliation? To what extent are we willing to interrogate the ways that our own academic, cultural, and linguistic personae might be subject to the same kind of critical multilingual interrogations, both through the languages we speak and choose to learn, the texts we read, the materials we research, and cultural contact to which we expose ourselves and others, whether nominally Western or non-Western, major or minor, through our continuing professional engagement in the humanities and social sciences?

† Here I wish to thank once again the Ministry of International Relations of the Government of Québec and Québec Government Office in Boston for providing me with the Québec Studies Program travel and research grant in June 2010 that allowed me to reconnect with Québec and its diverse landscape of languages and cultures for the purposes of this work.

In this particular case, this approach to transnational studies and border crossing involves reading Québec literary and cultural production not only from its conventionally constructed 'inside' (its major cities and other established cultural centres, universities, and other points of academic specialization, along with sites of political and economic power both national and federal), but also from across its borders and outlying spaces, both internal and external. Reading culture across the current, continually crisscrossing its possible points of reference, not only prefigures a number of ways that the complexities of the cultural, linguistic, and political space known as Québec can be reinterpreted, but also how such cultural examination, as it continues to circulate outward, may also begin to alter and transform other spaces outside of its borders.

With this question in mind, I also ask: which are the circulating cultural models that might be suspended, at least temporarily interrupted, before we begin? Some spring to mind more readily than others: we could no doubt begin with the resurgent calls to repudiate multiculturalism that are presently claiming the attention of many on both sides of the Atlantic, ones I might simply dismiss out of hand if it were not for the fact that many of our academic responses to them have often been far too timid to make much of a difference. Consider, for example, a recent academic address entitled "English Is Not Enough," which contents itself with advancing such presumably controversial proposals as second-language study and bilingualism.[2] Such goals, however admirable they might appear at first glance, would still probably be considered by many of us who study multilingualism a case of preaching to the choir at best, and setting the bar too low at worst.

What is perhaps most puzzling is that this and other programmatic manifestos for language study in the US all too often overlook the long-standing debates on this subject that have taken place a few hours away across the nearest border in Québec, thus confirming a trend of rendering Québec studies invisible that is still all too common in the vast majority of US French departments to this day, to say nothing of France and those global areas still largely subject to its understandings of linguistic normativity and cultural superiority and prestige. In this light, would it be admissible to propose that, given the current crisis, perhaps it is not merely monolingualism, whether English, French, or Spanish, but also the most common combinations of these, that is, conventional North American bilingualisms, that are also simply "not enough"? While some might make mention of the growing importance of West or South Asian languages (even if all too often for clearly 'strategic'/military reasons), no one would deny that the overwhelming emphasis remains on Spanish and French. With this in mind, one might begin instead by asking: how is the act of continually turning in the direction of a single pair or reduced set of Western European languages—most often in those metropolitan accents or dialects perceived as having the greatest cultural prestige[‡]—also a form of linguistic limitation bordering on the monolingual? In spite of the all-inclusive ways that it might be argued that the term 'bilingualism' has been employed to subsume all other forms of multilingual expression, I would still contend that the term remains insufficient to serve as a shorthand for a truly globalized multilingualism, especially if we are to extend the discussion beyond those models of bilingualism that merely institutionalize the predominance of a self-proclaimed lingua franca (English, French, etc.) from which any number of functional and officialized bilingualisms are seen to radiate.[3]

Meanwhile, 'south of the border' (i.e. in the present-day US), conversations on bilingualism and borders have also all too often been used as a shorthand for a single form of bilingualism or a single border, namely, Spanish–English bilingualism and the US–Mexico border, with academic responses all too simplistic in their aims, often through proposals to enshrine this single form of bilingualism as official for the entire country, in which "Spanish must identify and occupy the most enabling structural situation from which to articulate its agenda as a second national language."[4] This kind of self-interested political manoeuvre on the part of academics who act almost exclusively on behalf of a single language (usually their own) only underscores how the politics of bilingualism is not always an opening to knowledge, but can also act to shut down or disable the development of a more diverse multilingual landscape, and can even act to the detriment of other languages, especially those minority languages that in many cases are truly endangered.

While most scholars of multilingualism are no doubt familiar with the important contributions of Latino authors, border theorists, and performance artists such as Gloria Anzaldúa and Guillermo Gómez-Peña to this discussion, not to mention numerous others dedicated to the study of Latin American cultures who have theorized border crossing and cultural hybridity,[5] my aim here is not to debate, much less displace these particular politicized strategies of living in/between different languages and cultures in North America, but rather to continue to create space for alternative and

---

[‡] Even in the few programs where Québécois literary texts have been included in the French curriculum, language units that provide exposure to the differences in vocabulary, syntax, pronunciation, and code-switching in North American French remain decidedly rare. This is certainly not due to a lack of materials: there are numerous guides and dictionaries of French as spoken in Québec (Bélanger 1997/2004; Bergeron 1980/1997; Corbeil 2010). Such selective exposure to local variants of the French language, one which often continues to privilege the written over the spoken idiom, may do as much, if not more, to undercut claims of multiculturalism than the monolingual projects of world literature that are based overwhelmingly if not exclusively on translated texts and are so often proposed by present-day English departments in the US and elsewhere with little or no concern for what one might call the multilingual imperative of multicultural life.

quite often pre-existing cultural models still circulating here, especially those in which no single interlinguistic construct is privileged institutionally merely on the basis of sheer numerical, or worse yet, political strategic concerns. What I would like to return to by way of Québec are a series of approaches to multilingualism and transculture[§] that need no specific bordered political entity in order to legitimize themselves, but that simply recognize the wide range of multilingual discourses that are already circulating against the current. What I wish to explore here is the fundamentally multidirectional nature of languages and cultures in global transit.

Post-Bilingual Blues: Détour-ing from Québec Through Its Literature

That said, I would like to continue this discussion of post-bilingual linguistic transit in North America by returning to another novel that has left its mark on my understanding of Québec culture for some time, the 1984 road novel by Jacques Poulin with the English-language title of *Volkswagen Blues,* as well as a series of what one could consider contrapuntal literary works: perhaps we could even see them as textual or critical *détours* that serve to supplement, if not interrupt, or even overturn, many of the initial work's thematic premises or limitations.[6]

From the very beginning, by way of the novel's title, one that can be said, precisely in its combination of two internationally recognizable terms, to need no translation, the text moves continually between French-language narration and English-language dialogues to explore a particularly North American way of being in/between languages, in the way that French–English border crossers continually blur the boundary between Francophone Québec and the rest of North America, along with less immediately visible linguistic and cultural transients. The novel tells the story of a writer known by the pseudonym of Jack Waterman, who sets out on a transcontinental road trip from Gaspé in eastern Québec all the way to San Francisco in search of his brother Théo, who disappeared many years before. On the way, he passes through other North American cities and across vast expanses of landscape, crossing the US–Canadian border between Detroit and Windsor; but what this novel seems to question more than anything else through this continual movement is the permanence of such cultural and linguistic distinctions predicated upon geographic

[§]   It would be difficult to evoke this concept of transculture and transculturation in this particular context of Québec without some mention of the influential cultural journal *Vice Versa* (1983–1996), founded by a group led by Italian migrants to Montréal, most notably the brothers Gianni and Fulvio Caccia, a project that promoted a truly multilingual, multicultural model of Québec culture, open to both a wide range of cultural positions and languages (most often left untranslated), and even a measure of Québec nationalist counterargument (Moser 2010: 48–50).

divisions. Here we still have the chance of imagining borders—whether political, cultural, or linguistic—as unstable, shifting, even permeable, a possibility that, ironically enough, this and many other borders have surrendered to the exigencies of an increasingly 'securitized' present.

There are nonetheless certain textual elements that serve to complicate a bilingual or any other binary conceptualization of the novel: first, the vehicle that is introduced in the title, the 1971 Volkswagen bus that provides for the novel's mobility. The narrative and dialogue also underscore that it is more than a scenic element but actually a character in and of itself, with its own personality, life story, and language. Long before this particular voyage, this Volkswagen was imported from Germany, and before that it had apparently travelled all over Europe with its previous owner, who even left an inscription on the dashboard: "Die Sprache ist das Haus des Seins."[7] These words are also left untranslated in the text, but many of us would recognize them immediately as those of the German philosopher Martin Heidegger:

> Die Sprache ist das Haus des Seins. In ihrer Behausung wohnt der Mensch. Die Denkenden und Dichtenden sind die Wächter dieser Behausung. Ihr Wachen ist das Vollbringen der Offenbarkeit des Seins, insofern sie diese durch ihr Sagen zur Sprache bringen und in der Sprache aufbewahren.

> [Language is the House of Being. Human beings live in the dwelling of language. Thinkers and poets are the guardians of this dwelling. Their guardianship is the achievement of being able to reveal Being, insofar as they bring it to language through their speech and preserve it in language.][8]

If we are still predisposed to accept that language is indeed at the core of our being, that we learn languages to come closer to an understanding of our human experience, what should we make of the reappearance of these words in their original language here, in this space where language cannot possibly be one, where it must continually reaffirm itself as multiple in order to tell the story that unfolds before it? What kind of linguistic dwelling is this? Certainly not the kind with a fixed address and concrete foundation, but perhaps one that is continually on the move, though in order to experience it we may have to break out of Heidegger's metaphorical house as he has constructed it. For my part, at this point in time at least, I don't want language to be a house. I want to get into its driver's seat and take language for a ride across boundaries. This is the point of a linguistic model that remains singular while no longer dual and continually on the way towards the increasingly multiple. In the spirit of Poulin's novel, I too want language to be continually on the move, no longer the house of being, but perhaps more the Volkswagen bus of being.

After all, if it is truly the thinkers and poets who are the guardians of this inhabitation, then what does this imply about the lives in language of those who live far from the formalized, urban, national, or academic worlds of poetry and philosophy? In order to complete this understanding, might it be necessary to revise our understanding of thinking to accommodate alternative models of 'dwelling' in language, as watched over by thinking and poetics, especially those transitory, seasonal, and makeshift structures that place fewer claims to perennial stability, much less permanence, especially on landscapes where the Western house as dwelling is a relative newcomer?

For this very reason, it is important in this context to point out how Jack's travel companion, La Grande Sauterelle, not only transits and mediates the space between French and English with Jack, but also that between the Innu First Nation (referred to in the novel by its French name Montagnais, though one used much less today than only a few years ago) and 'white' culture, a cultural divide with which the primary boundaries between European languages and attendant North American colonial settler cultures (whether English, French or Spanish) seem insignificant in comparison. This is not to say that the casting of an indigenous, female sidekick should not provoke a measure of cultural discomfort and thereby open this work up to a certain measure of cultural critique, especially at this late hour. Even so, since the publication of Poulin's novel, authors from Québec's 11 recognized indigenous cultures have already been receiving increased international attention, both in their own native languages and in French,[¶] even as the challenge that

---

[¶]   It would be impossible for me to overlook the important work of Italian-born scholar Maurizio Gatti in researching, compiling and popularizing so many of the French-language First Nation authors and poets writing in Québec today (Gatti 2006, 2009). It is equally important to recount here the difficulties that Gatti originally had when explaining his research project to a Québec cultural representative in Paris:

> Elle a eu une réaction inattendue. Visiblement vexée et offusquée, comme si j'avais mis le doigt sur une vieille blessure encore ouverte, elle a dit fermement que [la littérature amérindienne au Québec] n'était pas une littérature mais uniquement une série de documents ethnologiques à visée informative, rien de plus; qu'elle ne comprenait pas pourquoi les Européens étaient toujours si attirés par les Indiens, et que l'étude de la littérature québécoise, 'une vraie littérature,' me permettrait de faire une recherche plus stimulante.

> [She had an unexpected reaction. Visibly perturbed and offended, as if I had stuck my finger in an old, open wound, she said firmly that Amerindian literature was not a literature but only a series of ethnological documents of an informative nature, nothing more, and that she didn't understand why Europeans were still so attracted by Indians, and that the study of Québec literature, 'a true literature,' would permit me to carry out more stimulating research.]

(Gatti 2009: 15)

Then again, one would do well to recognize that the tendency to dismiss out of hand both the 'true' literary dimensions and autonomous configurations of Native cultures still persists throughout North America, not only in Québec.

the name la Grande Sauterelle suggests, of literally jumping back and forth between these cultures, remains as daunting as ever.

It is for this reason that I juxtapose, not only as a point of contrast but perhaps as an overt counterexample, the recent bilingual French-Cree poem "Mahiganou" by the Cree poet Romeo Saganash. A portrait of the existential conflicts of a Métisse woman as she talks to the mythical she-wolf Mahiganou reflected in the frozen, mirror-like surface of Lake Mishigamish, the poem rearticulates this sentiment of transiting spaces in different languages, even while holding out the possibility of an eventual transvalorization of this in-between subject for both cultures:

> "Nimaii apatou innou, apatou wèm-shtigoushiou-ji":
> non, tu n'es pas la moitié de l'un et la moitié de l'autre
> tu es l'un et l'autre
> Une Blanche avec une âme crie
> Une Crie avec une âme blanche
> C'est toi qui décides quoi en faire
> Je suis l'héritière des beautés et des malheurs de deux mondes
> Je vois
> Nôtre grande île de la Tortue
> Est devenue un immense lit d'échange, d'amour, de métissage.
> Les échos de tambours viennent me flatter doucement
> Mes larmes surgissent de nouveau
> Je me lève la tête
> Mahiganou n'est pas là
> Dans la glace, elle y est toujours…
> Que je suis belle, Mahiganou
> Que je suis métisse.

> ["Nimaji apatou innou, apatou wèm-shitgoushiou-ji"; No, you are not half of one and half of the other / you are one and the other / White with a Cree soul / Cree with a White soul / It's you who decides what to make of it / I am the inheritor of the beauties and misfortunes of two worlds / I see / our great Turtle Island / has become an immense bed of exchange, of love, of métissage. / The echoes of drums come to caress me softly / My tears well up again / I lift my head / Mahiganou is no longer there / On the ice, she is still there… / For I am beautiful, Mahiganou / For I am métisse.][9]

It may no doubt be tempting for many of us based in urban environments to entertain the notion that most if not all cultures in Québec and beyond can find a place as part of a continually repeated model of multilingualism or translation culture that places the urban experience at its undisputed centre.[10] Yet what First Nation cultures often emphasize is precisely the opposite: that is, that there is something to be said for the cultural specificities separated by vast geographical expanses from the self-styled global or translational city, in indigenous languages that often not only resist translation, but are in many cases geographically non-transferable to an urban metropolis.[**] Another important question resurfaces on this frozen lake: to what extent do indigenous models of multilingualism and translational culture not only allow for, but actually reaffirm, the need for such separate and untranslatable cultural spaces, especially in relation to endangered peoples and their cultural patrimony?

A final example of the kind of nascent post-bilingual multidirectionality that I wish to trace out here is represented by the novel's destination: the city of San Francisco on the edge of the Pacific Ocean, where so many cultures run into and mix with one another, not as the exception, but as the rule: Asian, Latin American, African-American, and European, along with any number of political, social, and sexual subcultures, all combined with a distinct Native significance: the city boasts one of the highest percentages of Native people of any major US city, and Alcatraz, the island occupied by separatists of the American Indian Movement in the early 1970s, remains right offshore, a beacon of Native peoples' recent struggles for political and cultural autonomy across North America.

For the moment, however, I wish to focus on the three-way intersection through which this Volkswagen bus must unavoidably pass as the search continues: that of Broadway, Grant, and Columbus, at the shifting and always uncertain border between the traditionally Italian–American and bohemian neighbourhood of North Beach and the ever-expanding Chinatown, the largest outside Asia, where we find the City Lights Bookstore and its owner Lawrence Ferlinghetti, who enters the novel as another character who helps point Jack and La Grande Sauterelle in the direction of the elusive man they are looking for. But then again, one could say that Ferlinghetti and the rest of the Beat poets have been present in this novel from the very beginning: at one point as Jack investigates his brother's whereabouts, for example, he finds out that Théo had a copy of Jack Kerouac's *On the Road* among his possessions. Even if no explicit mention of Kerouac and his work were made in the text, it would still be difficult to imagine this or any other subsequent crossing of this continent without acknowledging the mark that this Franco-American writer

---

[**] This is not to say, however, that they are not translatable: one example is the groundbreaking 1995 bilingual collection of poetry by Innu poet Rita Mestokosho, *Eshi uapataman Nukum/Comme je perçois la vie, Grand-Mère*, recently translated into Swedish with a preface by J.M.G. Le Clézio. If Québec literature is to be increasingly recognized as an unavoidable part of world literature, as Le Clézio did in his 2008 Nobel Prize acceptance speech, highlighting Mestokosho's importance alongside that of two other canonical Québec literary figures, Émile Nelligan and Réjean Ducharme, it has already become all the more evident that Québec literature's circuitous route towards global recognition will pass not just through metropolitan centres such as Montréal or Québec (or New York, London, Paris, and Stockholm, for that matter), but also through small towns like Mingan and the vast territorial expanses connected to the Innu language, as well as other spaces of indigenous language and culture.

has left on this and other Québec writing (Nicole Brossard's 1987 lesbian feminist postmodern road novel *Le Désert mauve*, with its character Kathy Kerouac, providing another prime example[††]), to say nothing of the rest of late twentieth-century North American literary and intellectual culture. Ultimately, this work is just as much a search for Kerouac and his gang of Beats as anyone else: whether it is Jack the transcontinental drifter, or 'Ti-Jean,' the bilingual son of a French-Canadian immigrant family from Lowell, Massachusetts, Kerouac as cultural icon continues to draw Québec culture back across its southern border, to explore that often ignored part of itself that has long been located outside of itself, and in so doing may even draw the occasional French-Canadian descendant on the other side of the border[‡‡] back into a renewed conversation about what Québec continues to share with its nineteenth-century cross-border New England diaspora after all these years.

But what of the end of the novel, one might ask? In the end, Théo is indeed found in San Francisco, although, as is the case with so many lost relatives, the actual reunion is often a pale reflection of the process of travel and introspection that led to it. Théo is by now in the grip of what his doctors have called "creeping paralysis," a progressive breakdown of the body.[11] He is in a wheelchair, has joined the ranks of the homeless, cannot recognize his own brother and no longer speaks French. Some critics have posited this final scene as a cautionary tale about Québec culture, suggesting that in its contact with the outside world it may just lose its way, but I would venture another reading, that living on the edge

---

[††]   And here, with Nicole Brossard at the wheel, we take yet another *détour critique*: aside from the international recognition that *Le Désert mauve* has received over the years in the French original, its English translation by Susanne de Lothbinière-Harwood— herself a key cultural theorist of bilingualism in her own right (as evinced in her 1991 work *Re-belle et infidèle*)—is also a literary achievement that has not only solidified the novel's cult status and stature in Canadian literature as a whole, but perhaps also present and future Anglophone configurations of world literature as well. For example, consider its selection in the recent online blog project on works of world literature undertaken by Ann Morgan called "A Year of Reading the World" (www. ayearofreadingtheworld.com) and a subsequent book (2015). In each, Morgan takes Lothbinière-Harwood's translation of Brossard's novel as the single work that would be read to represent Canada in this year-long reading project; she goes so far as to say that it was "one of the most innovative things I've ever read." Such an assessment, even when relying exclusively on a translation for an Anglophone understanding of what it means to "read the world," still calls attention both to its compelling depictions of living between languages and/or in translation and to a geographical mobility across a North American landscape stretching far beyond Québec's borders. Perhaps most importantly, this point of view also speaks powerfully, both in the original or in translation, to yet another more recent configuration of world literature, without recurring to any of the tropes or defining characteristics (e.g. overt nationalism, use of dialect) that Casanova identifies as Québec literature's most important contributions to a world literary system (232, 283–4).

[‡‡]   *Oui, comme moi-meme* (Larkosh 2006, 2007, 2009, 2010).

always involves a measure of risk, and Théo is just one of two brothers; Jack continues to move on, boarding a plane back to Québec, while la Grande Sauterelle does not return to Québec at all, choosing instead to stay with the Volkswagen bus in California as part of her own as yet unfinished voyage of self-discovery. As both Poulin's novel and the necessary contrapuntal *détours* that the act of critical rereading calls forth here would suggest, the possible directions are endless, with this particular part of the literary trip only the beginning.§§

§§ At least, that's what it was for me, that is, if you will allow me a single (if extended) personal anecdote to explain. You see, as I began this research project, I was faced with two main options: simply to go to Montréal, rent an apartment for a few weeks and immerse myself in the libraries, archives, bookstores, and cultural life of the multilingual metropolis; or to hit the road, transiting the smaller towns and vast expanses of road, looking out at the visual representations of rural and regional cultures, as well as stopping at those Mi'kmaq, Innu, Cree, Algonquin and Abenaki reserves whose perspectives would turn out to be instrumental in devising any possible cultural and critical *détours* from what I considered comfortable and familiar. I ended up heading off alone, in my own Volkswagen (not a classic camper van, but a more modest 2004 Jetta), on what would eventually be a three-week, 4000-mile road trip from my home in Providence, Rhode Island, crossing into Québec from New Brunswick at the Mi'kmaq community of Listuguj, continuing on to Gaspé; crossing the St. Lawrence by ferry at Matane to Baie-Comeau and on to Sept-Îles and the Mingan archipelago and Innu communities at Uashat and Mingan; through the forests, communities and lakes of the Saguenay–Lac-St.-Jean region, both Chicoutimi and the Innu town of Mashteuiash; into the wilderness to Cree towns at Oujé-Bougamou, Nemaska and finally Waskaganish on the shores of James Bay; through the Algonquin town at Pikogan, back down through Ottawa/Gatineau and Montréal for research in libraries and archives, and then up the St. Lawrence River Valley through the Abenaki town of Odanak to end up in Québec City to see Robert Lepage's sound and light show created in honour of its 400th anniversary: *Le Moulin à Images* (2008).

Soon after I arrived in Nemaska, the capital of the Cree Nation located halfway up the seemingly endless and sparsely travelled gravel highway called La Route du Nord, I stopped into the *dépanneur* for provisions. Apparently the occasional outsider is met with a certain curiosity in these parts, and it was thus that I met Michael, a resident of this Cree reserve who, it turns out, had once lived in Hamburg in the 1970s. When he found out that I too had lived in West Germany a few years later, he began to speak German with me, and as he showed me around the town, I was confronted with the fact that this place was not at all somehow out of the picture as some urban cultural critics or proponents of urban-centred perspectives might imply, but quite the opposite: it was in fact an equally viable point from which to survey and transit global cultures, one in which the same elements of multilingualism and translation that both of us had experienced on another continent and in another language and culture remained very much in play, still providing the common terms of our present communication between our divergent points of departure. Ultimately, how does Michael's preference for German when speaking with me on Cree nation land in Québec transform what languages are functioning as either Western or not, or necessarily hegemonic or subaltern? In any case, how far we seem to be from Heidegger here! Even as we speak to each other about life on a First Nation reserve in a European language, it is in neither of Canada's two official languages; this too is what we can identify as yet another momentary instance of an emergent post-bilingualism.

Into a Globalized Present: Asian Cultures, Transcultural Destinations

And thus this complex web of linguistic reference points continues to expand; with this in mind, I would like to revisit here, if briefly, a set of more recent examples, beginning with Robert Lepage's 1997 film *Nō*, examined both as a model of cultural critique and a means of imagining alternative forms of transculture between contemporary Québec and other, often distant cultural traditions in a global context.[12] Central to this discussion is Lepage's ongoing artistic engagement with East Asian cultures and dramatic traditions, with which Québec culture traditionally has maintained relatively few extended exchanges, or even discussions about what a possible contact between these two divergent cultures might look like.

Lepage nonetheless appears prepared for such an extended conversation: the first of his dramatic works to consider this relationship was his 1985 *Dragons' Trilogy*, which, as the title suggests, is a three-part piece which follows a set of Québécois and Asian characters, first in Québec City's Chinatown in the 1920s, through Toronto in the Second World War, and then finally to Vancouver at the end of the century. In the same way, although *Nō* is of normal feature length, it is only a fragment of a more extended seven-hour theatrical piece from 1994, *The Seven Streams of the River Ota*.[13] As for the film *Nō*, the obvious play on words in its succinct title continually alternates between an explicit reference to Japanese Nō drama and the political atmosphere of opposition (whether through affirmation or negation) that characterized Québec in the late 1960s and 1970s, both in the new political identity as embodied in the Révolution Tranquille and the FLQ October Crisis, and the resulting polarized political atmosphere, one that culminated in the 1980 'No' vote against Québec independence.

The plot revolves around two stories: that of Sophie, an actress performing a French farce by Feydeau at the Osaka World's Fair, Expo '70, with not surprisingly disastrous results, while her boyfriend back in Montréal becomes involved in the FLQ bombings that led Prime Minister Pierre Trudeau to declare a state of emergency. These thematic elements are thus set against the backdrop of an equally ambivalent global cultural environment that combines World's Fairs (as much the Montréal Expo in '67 as the one featured in the film), and the still unresolved conflicts of a post-war, nuclear age, as epitomized by the character Hanako, the simultaneous interpreter of the piece from French to Japanese. She is a *hibakusha*, a survivor blinded by the light of the atomic blast at Hiroshima. In this far-reaching juxtaposition of historical events and cultural objects (albeit in a much more critical way than one might find at a World's Fair, with its emphasis on translated official discourses for mass consumption and clearly delineated national pavilions), Lepage's film raises a number of questions about such improbable transcultural encounters in the present age of global communication and exchange.

Most important of these for the purposes of this discussion might be not only how we interpret or translate a single language or culture, but also a continually expanding set of cultural connections and ever unfolding historical events, in this case, through the Japanese dramatic tradition of Nō. After all, to what extent can Québec truly say 'Nō/ no'—whether to the English language, the rest of Canada, cultural and linguistic metropolises such as the US, France, or the Commonwealth, or any number of other forms of Western cultural hegemony—even if Québec is in many ways yet another form of that cultural hegemony for many, especially for Native peoples and more recent non-Western arrivals?

For that matter, how is it truly possible for this West to say 'yes' to Japanese culture? That is to say, how might it stage a complex and meaningful encounter with a centuries-old dramatic tradition characterized by what can only be considered a minimalistic approach to emotion or humour in comparison to those forms of cultural critique produced in French? By this I mean not only that oft-revisited "Empire of Signs" that the French cultural critic Roland Barthes identified in the Japan of precisely this same year, even if it does retain a measure of its semiotic complexity and its irreconcilable difference, never a completely 'know'-able object of knowledge, and not only in relation to Québec, but to all cultures, Western or otherwise.[14] Ultimately, how is the political and cultural promise of 'no drama' still not only an undeniable form of drama in and of itself, but one potentially equally as powerful as other circulating modes of affirmation or opposition, if not more so?

Moreover, what are the unspoken forms of *farce* (and not only the French theatrical caricatures such as those of Feydeau depicted in Lepage's film) that continue to circulate in Francophone cultural discourse, and how might such experimental and linguistically hybrid approaches to literature, theatre, and film represent a potent alternative, both now and in the future? With so many writers intent on hastening "l'acte de decès de la francophonie" in favour of a "littérature-monde en français," it might appear that either the French language still remains central to their vision, or that even this centre cannot hold.[15] As Dany Laferrière, the Haitian writer now inextricably linked to Québec literature in spite of his own continual cross-border migrations, evokes in the title of one of his latest books—*Je suis un écrivain japonais*—he has every right to claim for himself what Poulin, Lepage and many other Québec authors can take for granted: in Laferrière's own words, "la liberté de circuler":

Peut-on gagner sa vie avec des rêves? Le seul métier que le permet, m'a t-on dit, c'est celui d'écrivain. C'est pour moi, ça! Une longue préparation consistant a me débarrasser de tous les clichés crasseux qui m'encombraient la tête. L'écrivain libre au retour de la nuit profonde les bras charges de fruits rares á offrir au monde. Quel monde? Dans quelle langue? Je n'étais plus un rêveur, mais un immigré, un exilé, un Noir, un Caribéen, un Québécois parfois (on me garde toujours dans la section des écrivains immigrés dans les anthologies publiées au Québec). Quelqu'un peut-il me dire ce qu'est un écrivain immigré? Peut-être une façon de vous garder dans une réserve.

[Can one earn one's keep with dreams? The only job that allows this, they have told me, is that of a writer. That's the thing for me! A long preparation consisting of getting rid of all the crass clichés that filled my head. The free writer returning from the dark of night, his arms filled with rare fruits to offer the world. What world? In which language? I was no longer a dreamer, but an immigrant, an exile, a Black man, a Caribbean, a Québécois at times (they still put me in the immigrant writer section in anthologies published in Québec). Can someone tell me what an immigrant writer is? Maybe a way of keeping you on a reservation.][16]

All the same, Laferrière hardly needs permission in claiming this freedom for himself, exercising it whether or not anyone else grants it to him, which is in itself a form of freedom, especially considering how farcical the lingering claims of equal access to it may prove to be.

Concurrently, other authors continue to complete the picture, connecting Québec to an ever-wider set of global points of reference. While Ying Chen's 1993 epistolary novel *Les letters chinoises* continues to stand out as an emblematic literary sign of Québec's increasingly frequent look towards the Far East, mapping out what would become the recurrent thematic contours of Québec's literary exploration of Asia—separation, an encounter between languages and cultures of origin and those of global migration, and the ongoing flows and interruptions of this encounter—it is clearly not to be the last.[17] Consider, for example, the Québec cartoonist Guy Delisle, whose popular graphic novels that describe a wide range of cultural encounters on his visits to lesser-known locales in Asia—not only of central points such as the Special Economic Zones of mainland China that will continue to shape our cultural and economic reality in the coming century, but also those still entrenched totalitarian spaces most resistant to this process of global transformation, such as North Korea under Kim Jong-il, or Burma under military dictatorship.[18] Such moves continue to extend the boundaries of Québec literature not only beyond its well-worn lines of cultural interaction,[¶¶] but also in relation with other forms of visual culture. Another is Kim Thúy's recent semi-autobiographical memoir entitled *Ru* (2009), which recounts the story of a girl and her family as they flee their home in Vietnam to make a new life for themselves, first as boat people interned in a Malaysian refugee camp, then as immigrants in the town of Granby in the Eastern Townships/Cantons de l'Est.[19] As in Lepage's film, a two-letter bilingual title once again allows for an exchange of meanings between languages: as Thúy explains in the novel's epigraph, in French the word means a small stream, whether of river water or of tears; in Vietnamese, it means a cradle or the act of cradling. Both of these images find a place in this narrative of loss and refuge; the narrative first charts its way out of Vietnam towards Canada, learning both French and English in the process, albeit in a way that the author herself is quick to recognize as always incomplete by its very nature—"je ne maîtrisais que ce qui m'avait été spécifiquement enseigné, transmis, offert... j'accumulais des connaissances au hasard" [I mastered only what had been specifically taught, transmitted or offered to me... I accumulated knowledge by chance].[20] The work thus also charts a return, not only for its author, who eventually takes a job as an interpreter in Hanoi, thereby relearning her native language, but also for its reader, who may well have to sacrifice some of his or her own cherished preconceptions about "le rêve américain,"[21] not only as that faraway ideal set against the Communist regime that forced her departure so many years before, but also in light of the lingering vestiges of Western languages and cultures left there by French colonialism and US Cold War imperialism. In the end, the exchange of language that *Ru* maps out is multidirectional; after all, the rest of us in North America have also been assigned our own 'Vietnamese lessons' by now: ones which we must either continue to study to this day, for better or for worse, as part of our own language and culture by the sheer force of historical necessity, or else ignore at our own peril.

By Way of Conclusion: A Final Détour

Ultimately, rereading Québec in this way—not only its entire literary tradition as a now indisputable representative chapter of world literature, but those canonical texts against the backdrop of its other media,

---

[¶¶] Such official points of cultural interaction can be imagined most clearly as Québec continues to expand its diplomatic presence throughout the world by the establishment of Québec Government Offices: not only in the US and Western Europe, but also in Latin America (Mexico City, Santiago, São Paulo) and across Asia (Damascus, Mumbai, Hong Kong, Taipei, Shanghai, Beijing, Seoul, and Tokyo). As this new mapping indicates, the continually expanding exercise of political and cultural autonomy through diplomatic soft power is by now an inseparable part of Québec's developing foreign policy.

languages, popular traditions, and landscapes through direct lived experiences, that is, simultaneously from within, across, and outside of its conventionally recognized political and linguistic borders and academic institutions—may even have an unintended effect. After all, what may well be most at stake here are the ways that cultural and institutional politics of multilingual practices are approached both in this particular corner of the North American continent and across the globe, where any number of linguistic and cultural vehicles remain 'on the road' and in circulation, and in which any one intellectual paradigm, however all-encompassing it may appear, can only scratch the surface of its own implications and future possibilities, both for and beyond itself. With no clear distinctions between presumably distinct and competing models, each of them alternating and multidirectional, connective and critical, while incorporating both traditional and innovative elements from indigenous cultures, a distinctly North American set of French-language traditions begins to emerge, as well as continually emerging post-bilingual contacts with both other Western and distinctly non-Western elements. This diverse set of cross-cultural connections holds out at least some promise to keep a now recognizably multilingual Québec more fully connected to an ever-expanding global information society.

And believe it or not, this is still surprisingly close to where I find myself, both in Québec and the rest of North America today. As I have stated here, my aim in drawing forth these particular and often contrapuntal examples is not to displace any particular cultural or linguistic model of bi- or multilingualism presently in use by others, but simply to affirm that there are those who may already approach these questions of language and culture in a perhaps radically different way on a daily basis, not only on both, but on all sides of present cultural and linguistic borders, and whose readings and interpretations are inextricably connected to a praxis of continual cultural and linguistic multidirectionality that need not inscribe itself within any single institutional, governmental, academic, or disciplinary programme, or any established metropolitan hierarchy of global literary, linguistic, or cultural reference in order to realize, defend, or justify itself. At times this praxis demonstrates its power to destabilize narratives of origin, fixed identity and institutional affiliation, providing thereby a measure of cultural autonomy from both the roles we are assigned and even those we continue to assign ourselves. And as each of us steps outside and crosses the line of those previous engagements, we might even find a measure of future there.

Notes

1 Marie-Claire Blais, *Une saison dans la vie d'Emmanuel* (1965; repr. Montréal, QC: Boréal, 1991), 133. My translation.
2 Catherine Porter, "English is Not Enough," *PMLA* 125 no. 3 (2010): 546–55.

3 Jean Laponce, *Loi de Babel et autres régularités des rapports entre language et politique* (Québec City, QC: Presses de l'Université Laval, 2006).

4 Carlos Alonso, "Spanish: The Foreign National Language," *Profession* (2007): 228.

5 Gloria Anzaldúa, *Borderlands/La frontera* (San Francisco, CA: Aunt Lute Books, 1988); Guillermo Gómez-Peña, *Border Brujo.* (San Diego, CA: Cinewest 1989), VHS; Néstor García Canclini, *Hybrid Cultures: Strategies for Entering and Leaving Modernity* (Minneapolis: University of Minnesota Press, 1995); Walter Mignolo, *Local Histories/Global Designs: Essays on the Coloniality of Power, Subaltern Knowledges and Border Thinking* (Princeton, NJ: Princeton University Press, 2000).

6 Jacques Poulin, *Volkswagen Blues* (Montréal, QC: LEMEAC Éditeur, 1988).

7 Ibid.

8 Martin Heidegger, *Holzwege* [1946] (Frankfurt am Main: Klostermann, 1947/2003), 310. My translation.

9 Romeo Saganash, "Mahiganou," in *Être écrivain amérindien au Québec,* ed. Maurizio Gatti (Montréal, QC: Hurtubise, 2006), 127. My translation.

10 See Sherry Simon, "Crossing Town: Montreal in Translation," *Profession* (2002): 15–24; *Translating Montreal: Episode in the Life of a Divided City* (Montreal, QC: McGill-Queen's University Press, 2006); *Cities in Translation: Intersections of Language and Memory* (London: Routledge, 2012).

11 Poulin, *Volkswagen Blues,* 315.

12 Robert Lepage, *Nô,* In Extremis Images (1998), VHS.

13 Saša Aleksandar Dundjerović, *The Theatricality of Robert Lepage* (Montreal, QC: McGill-Queen's University Press, 2007), 75–96, 123–51.

14 Roland Barthes, *L'Empire des signes* (1970; repr. Paris: Points, 2005).

15 Lise Gauvin, ed., *Les littératures de langue française à l'heure de la mondialisation* (Montréal, QC: Hurtubise, 2010), 169, 173.

16 Ibid., 95. My translation.

17 Ying Chen, *Les lettres chinoises* (Montréal, QC: Leméac Éditeur, 1993).

18 Guy Delisle, *Pyongyang: A Journey in North Korea,* trans. Helge Dascher (Montreal, QC: Drawn & Quarterly, 2004); *Shenzhen. A Travelogue from China,* trans. Helge Dascher (Montreal, QC: Drawn & Querterly, 2006); *Burma Chronicles,* trans. Helge Dascher (Montreal, QC: Drawn & Quarterly, 2008).

19 Kim Thúy, *Ru* (Montréal, QC: Éditions Libre Expression, 2009).

20 Ibid., 82. My translation.

21 Ibid., 84.

Bibliography

Alonso, Carlos. "Spanish: The Foreign National Language." *Profession* (2007): 218–28.

Anzaldúa, Gloria. *Borderlands/La frontera.* San Francisco, CA: Aunt Lute Books, 1988.

Barthes, Roland. *L'Empire des signes.* 1970. Reprint, Paris: Points, 2005.

Belanger, Mario. *Petit guide du parler québécois.* 2ème édition. Outremont, QC: Éditions internationales Alain Stanké, 2004.

Bergeron, Léandre. *Dictionaire de la langue québécoise.* 1980. Reprint, Montréal, QC: Éditions Typo, 1997.

Blais, Marie-Claire. *Une saison dans la vie d'Emmanuel.* 1965. Reprint, Montréal, QC: Boréal, 1991.

Brossard, Nicole. *Le Désert mauve.* Montréal, QC: Éditions de l'Hexagone, 1987.

———. *Mauve Desert.* Translated by Susanne de Lothbiniere-Harwood. Toronto, ON: Coach House Books, 1990.

Caccia, Fulvio, ed. *La transculture et Vice-Versa.* Montréal, QC: Triptyque, 2010.

Casanova, Pascale. *The World Republic of Letters.* Translated by Malcolm B. Debevoise. Cambridge, MA: Harvard University Press, 2004.

Chen, Ying. *Les lettres chinoises.* Montréal, QC: Leméac Éditeur, 1993.

Corbeil, Pierre. *Le québécois pour mieux voyager.* 5ème édition. Montréal, QC: Ulysse, 2010.

Damrosch, David. *What is World Literature?* Princeton, NJ: Princeton University Press, 2003.

Delisle, Guy. *Pyongyang: A Journey in North Korea.* 2003. Translated by Helge Dascher. Montreal, QC: Drawn & Quarterly, 2004.

———. *Shenzhen. A Travelogue from China.* 2003. Translated by Helge Dascher. Montreal, QC: Drawn & Quarterly, 2006.

———. *Burma Chronicles.* Translated by Helge Dascher. Montreal, QC: Drawn & Quarterly, 2008.

Dundjerović, Aleksandar Saša. *The Theatricality of Robert Lepage.* Montreal, QC: McGill-Queen's University Press, 2007.

García Canclini, Néstor. *Hybrid Cultures: Strategies for Entering and Leaving Modernity.* Minneapolis: University of Minnesota Press, 1995.

Gatti, Maurizio. *Être écrivain amérindien au Québec: indianité et creation littéraire.* Montréal, QC: Hurtubise, 2006.

———, ed. *Littérature amérindienne du Québec. Écrits de language française.* Nouvelle édition revue et augmentée. Montréal, QC: Bibliothèque québecoise, 2009.

Gauvin, Lise, ed. *Les littératures de langue française à l'heure de la mondialisation.* Montréal, QC: Hurtubise, 2010.

Gómez-Peña, Guillermo. *Border Brujo.* San Diego, CA: Cinewest, 1989. VHS.

Heidegger, Martin. *Holzwege.* 1946. Frankfurt am Main: Klostermann, 2003.

Kerouac, Jack. *On the Road.* 1957. London: Penguin Classics, 2002.

Laferriere, Dany. "Est-il possible d'aller n'importe où, Lise?" In *Les littératures de langue française à l'heure de la mondialisation*, edited by Lise Gauvin, 93–7. Montréal, QC: Hurtubise, 2010.

Laponce, Jean. *Loi de Babel et autres régularités des rapports entre language et politique.* Québec City: QC: Presses de l'Université Laval, 2006.

Larkosh, Christopher. "Je me souviens… *aussi*: Microethnicity and the Fragility of Memory in French-Canadian New England." *TOPIA* 16 (2006): 111–27.

———. "Allophone Presences: In the Here-And-Now of the Humanities." In *Producing Presences: Branching Out from Gumbrecht's Work*, edited by Victor Mendes and João Cezar de Castro Rocha. 22941. Dartmouth: Adamastor Book Series, University of Massachusetts Dartmouth, 2007.

———. "QuébEx: Post-Nations, Translations and Other Forms of Multiple Identity." *Contemporary French and Francophone Studies/Sites* 13 no. 1 (2009): 55–65.

————. "Alternative Passages: Cultural Autonomy and Border Crossing in Contemporary North America." In *Remapping the World, Culture and Border-Crossing,* edited by Steven Tötösy de Zepetnek and I-Chun Wang, 70–83. Kaohsiung: NSYSU Press, 2010.

Le Clézio, Jean-Marie Gustave. "Dans le forêt des paradoxes/In the Forest of Paradoxes." 7 December 2008. www.nobelprize.org/nobel_prizes/literature/laureates/2008/clezio-lecture.html.

Lepage, Robert. *Nô.* In Extremis Images, 1998. VHS.

————. *Dragons' Trilogy.* First performed 6 June 1987, Hangar 9, Vieux-Port de Montréal, Festival de théâtre des Amériques.

Lothbinière Harwood, Susanne de. *Re-belle et infidèle: la traduction comme pratique de réécriture au féminin/The Body Bilingual: Translation as a Re-writing in the Feminine.* Montréal, QC and Toronto, ON: Les éditions de remue-ménage and Women's Press, 1991.

Mestokosho, Rita. *Eshi uapataman Nukum/Comme je perçois la vie, Grand-Mère.* 1995. Edition bilingue, préface de Jean-Marie Le Clézio. Sweden: Editions Beijbom Books, 2010.

Mignolo, Walter. *Local Histories/Global Designs: Essays on the Coloniality of Power, Subaltern Knowledges and Border Thinking.* Princeton, NJ: Princeton University Press, 2000.

Morgan, Ann. *Reading the World: Confessions of a Literary Explorer.* London: Harvill Secker, 2015.

————. A Year of Reading the World. https://ayearofreadingtheworld.com.

Moser, Walter. "Transculturation: Métamorphoses d'un concept migrateur." In *La transculture et Vice-Versa,* edited by Fulvio Caccia, 33–59. Montréal, QC: Triptyque, 2010.

Nepveu, Pierre. "Qu'est-ce que la transculture?" *Paragraphes,* 4ème trimestre (1989): 16–31.

Porter, Catherine. "English is Not Enough." *PMLA* 125 no. 3 (May 2010): 546–55.

Poulin, Jacques. *Volkswagen Blues.* Montréal, QC: LEMEAC Éditeur, 1988.

Quijano, Aníbal. "Coloniality of Power, Ethnocentrism, and Latin America." *Nepantla* 1 no. 3 (2000): 533–80.

Saganash, Romeo. "Mahiganou." In *Être écrivain amérindien au Québec: indianité et creation littéraire,* edited by Maurizio Gatti, 124–7. Montréal, QC: Hurtubise, 2006.

Simon, Sherry. "Crossing Town: Montreal in Translation." *Profession* (2002): 15–24.

————. *Translating Montreal: Episode in the Life of a Divided City.* Montreal, QC: McGill-Queen's University Press, 2006.

————. *Cities in Translation: Intersections of Language and Memory.* London: Routledge, 2012.

Thúy, Kim. *Ru.* Montréal, QC: Éditions Libre Expression, 2009.

4 Narrating the Polyphonic City

Translation and Identity in Translingual/Transcultural Writing

Rita Wilson

The exponential increase in international migratory flows in the late twentieth century has given rise to a new polyphonic linguistic and literary reality in which identity and otherness are constructed in relation to a "sense of place" that merges global influences with localized place meanings.[1] The fluctuation and intermingling of identities, languages, and cultures through their complex permeations has had its repercussions on literary narratives, prompting a new engagement with the interrelated issues of linguistic and cultural diversity and the spatial construction of identity. This has led, in turn, to an awareness of the need for a new geocritical reading[2] of discourses of identity that takes into account the key role played by translation in plurilingual places where diverse cultures meet.

A remarkable case of a rapidly developing transcultural space is contemporary Italy, a country that, because of its geographical location, has received large numbers of immigrants in comparison to other western European countries and is still attracting new migrants. The major transformations that have occurred in Italian society as a result of the ever-increasing flow of inward migration over the last three decades[3] has been reflected in literary production by a new generation of translingual/transcultural writers.[4] This chapter focuses on the construction of cultural identity as it appears in narratives written in Italian by writers who are variously described as 'migrant,' 'Italophone' and, more recently, 'translingual.'[5] As Armando Gnisci notes, translingual writers have already undertaken "il salto triplo" (the triple jump), going beyond multi- and interculturalism and providing a new model of reciprocal education that can be defined as 'transcultural.'[6] Adopting the spatial rhetoric of 'in-betweenness' as a discursive strategy—that 'third space' that Homi Bhabha has described as "a contradictory and ambivalent space of enunciation"[7]—their polyvocal works test the boundaries of form as they explore the limits of expression and thus the boundaries of the self. By carrying with them a variety of native languages, these authors add to the various languages spoken already in Italy: that is, standard Italian, regional dialects, and global languages such as English. In this chapter, I aim to show that their narratives give prominence to the relationship between the transnational and the translational,[8] thus highlighting the centrality of both language and place in a global world as well as signalling how patterns of mobility affect cultural orientations, sensibilities, and, consequentially, creative (literary) expressions.[9]

Migration, Translation, Identity

Migration is directly and inevitably a process of cross-cultural translation, a passage between different languages, cultures, and worlds. This is especially evident in the migrant landscapes of the contemporary metropolis where cultures are always vectors of movement and translation as much as they are modes of being in place.[10] Central to understanding the specificities of transcultural identity formation—predicated on a process by means of which one or both of the cultures in touch may be modified and lead to new creations that emerge from that encounter—is the concept of space as dialogic. In order to develop a complex discussion of the relations between urban space and migration literature, it is useful to begin with Giuliana Benvenuti's expansion of the notion of "contact zones."[11] In Benvenuti's formulation, contact zones are locations where cultural exchanges are enacted and which "consentono di riarticolare la segregazione e di costruire nuove identità ibride e nuovi spazi trasgressivi" (allow for a re-articulation of segregation and the construction of new hybrid identities and new transgressive spaces).[12] Benvenuti focuses in particular on how fiction can inflect perceptions of the 'real,' and therefore on the impact that imagined spaces can have on the construction of the urban space that we encounter in our daily experiences: literary discourse is

> una delle forme discorsive che interagiscono con la percezione e la produzione dello spazio e lo modificano: questo l'assunto centrale della geocritica, un metodo di studio dei luoghi che propone una prospettiva multifocale, ovvero l'analisi di piu sguardi su e rappresentazioni di, un luogo, ed esige un'attenzione polisensoriale, che non indulga alla centralità del visivo, ma tenga presente il corpo in tutte le sue possibilità percettive.[13]

> [one of the discursive forms that interact with the perception and production of space and consequently modify it: this is the central assumption in geocriticism, which is a methodology for studying locations that proposes a multifocal perspective, that is, an analysis of the multiple gazes directed at a specific place and its representations, demanding a polysensorial attention that does not only privilege the visual, but rather takes into consideration all of the body's perceptual capabilities.]

The fictional context theorized by Benvenuti allows for interpretations of the ever-changing relations of the subject with the space s/he inhabits. This, in turn, leads us to think about translation in relationship with the exosomatic phenomenological dimension of our human existence.[14] In this context, translation can be examined as a 'sensory activity' born of our relationship with the world around us, which is formed through sound, touch, taste, and smell as much as sight.

Over time, "the contact zone has become more jagged" and the experience of increased global migration suggests that translation occurs not simply between one culture and another but between fragments.[15] Not least because migrants are by definition fragmented beings, who, to use Salman Rushdie's words, have experienced a "triple disruption": loss of place, entering into an "alien language," and being "surrounded by beings whose social behaviour and codes are very unlike, and sometimes even offensive to, [their] own."[16] Rushdie's formulation, together with the analogous articulation by Gnisci of the "triple jump," enables us to draw the parallels between migration and translation with confidence. This nexus is particularly applicable to translingual narratives that seek to highlight the ways that translation has been or can be used to (re)negotiate identity, by focusing on how cultural heterogeneity is produced in the dialectic between the local and the global, and through the spatial displacement of people.[17]

Public discourse about immigration in Italy continues to focus largely on new arrivals and the security and cultural threats that they allegedly pose.[18] Both in political campaigning and in the media, the discussion is generally centred around notions of criminalization and racialization reinforced by an exclusionary discourse in which migrants are categorized as 'outsiders' though the use of terms such as *extracomunitari* (non-EU citizens) and *clandestini* (illegal immigrants).[19] The focus on recent migrants and the construction of their otherness within Italian society serves to perpetuate the myth of a clear split between a unified national culture and identity ('us'), and the foreigners ('them'), while ignoring the fact that many of the country's immigrants are long-term residents, some of whom have made Italy their home for over 30 years. A primary theme to emerge from such one-sided portrayals is the issue of labelling: in particular, there is a lack of consensus with regard to the use of terms such as 'Italian-born' and 'second generation' to refer to any person who has at least one foreign-born parent. The terms are methodologically imprecise because they do not distinguish between those who have Italian citizenship (and are usually referred to as 'native' Italians) and those who do not; nor whether they have grown up within the Italian school system and/or are native speakers of Italian. Italian citizenship law privileges *ius sanguinis* over *ius soli*, making naturalization based on residence a drawn-out and complex process, particularly for non-EU citizens. Moreover, the assumption of biological otherness, implicit in the *ius sanguinis* framework, effectively impedes certain forms and expressions of cultural insiderness. Despite Italy's history and present reality of localized, fragmented, and hybrid identities, Italianness is still widely constructed as something culturally and socially homogeneous.[20]

Literary fiction, however, follows a different pattern of representation. Since the 1990s, with the rise of so-called migration literature, questions of ethnicity and citizenship have gained major visibility in the Italian literary context.[21] In particular, literary narratives have become instrumental in shaping contemporary notions of 'national' identity according to which the adjective 'national' is a concept that should never be taken for granted, but should be constantly renegotiated. The last two decades have seen the emergence of a large group of foreign-born writers who have introduced new subject positions that are responsible for what is arguably the most significant reinvention of Italian literary and cultural geography in recent years.[22] They represent Italianness as a plural concept, which involves the voices of its new inhabitants in literary products that appropriate the 'national' language and turn it into "a new system of signification" that describes the transformation of Italian society as it incorporates people with diverse cultural heritages, who are uprooted and 'thrown together' in diverse ways.[23]

The 'first wave' of migrant writing in the 1990s was largely confined to the space of testimonial writing.[24] The shift from testimony and autobiography to more imaginative forms that address the formation of new hybrid subjectivities in recent literary production—experimenting with both the dispersion of different stories and their translation into new forms—reflects the change which has occurred in Italian society. The new generation of translingual/transcultural writers includes those born in Italy either to a non-Italian parent or parents (Gabriella Kuruvilla, Cristina Ali Farah, Gabriella Ghermandi, Igiaba Scego) or who have been living in the country for several decades (Amara Lakhous, Tahar Lamri, Laila Wadia). This group stresses the interconnectedness of mobility, (urban) space and language choice in the construction of their complex identities. Although they opt for genres as diverse as crime fiction (Lakhous) and family sagas (Ghermandi, Scego), what they have in common, in addition to personal biographies inscribed with mobility and multiple cultures, is the deployment of polylingual practices to portray a "genuine polyphony of fully valid voices."[25] In their polyphonic writing, they give agency to the multiple voices that constitute contemporary Italian society—including those marginal voices that had previously been excluded—thus challenging normalized positionings within discursive spaces.

If polyphony demands relationship and difference, then textual polyphonic production provides alternative voices in relation to dominant discourses through dialogical agency.[26] Such texts contribute to what sociologist Melita Richter refers to as the emergence of "translated identities," a process that "is even more visible to those passing through different geographical and cultural contexts."[27] Richter notes that as a "diversified space with a plurality of identities around us becomes more and more the normal context of our existence," there is an increased need for "some sort of *mobile citizenship*, separate from nationality."[28] From the perspective of the everyday and the urban places of the city, this suggests a world in constant movement, a mobility constantly bringing previously disparate and distant ideas, representations and experiences into local frames of reference. For some, this process has been identified as a destructive force, threatening to disrupt cultural homogeneity and unique 'identities of place,' and is seen as inevitably leading to strange, illegible, and unfamiliar environments in which once-familiar places can no longer be recognized. For others, like anthropologist Massimo Canevacci, this epitomizes the "polyphonic city," that is, a city which communicates though a multitude of autonomous voices that are related, intersect and overlap, or contrast with one another, analogous to the "textured" singing of a polyphonic choir.[29]

Polyphonic Cityscapes

Acclaimed writers like Lakhous, Lamri, and Scego, amongst others, challenge the grand narrative of multiculturalism and reveal the limited permeability of Italian society through representations of multi-ethnic and polyphonic urban scenarios. While stories by the so-called first generation of migrant writers were organized around the "trajectories"[30] of marginal characters, creating an alternative topography of the city by linking places that might be called peripheral (social centres, railway stations, prisons, sidewalks), in more recent novels the focus has narrowed even further to an extremely localized space, such as a neighbourhood or a condominium: the city within a city, a 'laboratory' to reproduce on a small scale what Henri Lefebvre called the "corps polyrythmique" of the metropolis.[31] The two texts selected for discussion in this chapter, *Amiche per la pelle* (Best friends, 2007) by Laila Wadia[32] and *Milano, fin qui tutto bene* (Milan, so far so good, 2012) by Gabriella Kuruvilla[33] are representative of a "politics of microspection" which recognizes that the local is constantly open to the global and that the degree of complexity in globalized societies remains constant across scales.[34] Both authors employ a multifocal and multisensory hermeneutics in which both language and spatiality function as symbolic conduits between the plotting of identity constructions and Italian realities.

To date, the ways in which knowledge in and of the city is shaped by linguistic and aural aspects has been largely neglected in favour of the visual.[35] In contrast, translingual/transcultural narratives bring to the fore how the interplay of languages within urban spaces contributes to an individual's experience of the city. The different configurations of

linguistic forces put into play translational responses, creating a heightened awareness of the plurality of meaning systems, of the testing of the
limits of expression, where dissonance is understood as a productive
force. In the opening chapter of *Amiche per la pelle*, the translational
forces that drive a city like Trieste are revealed through the representation of urban spaces in which languages (and their associated cultures)
have attached themselves symbolically to sites and landmarks, influencing the creation of architectural form:

> Il centro storico di Trieste incorpora tre tipologie di case. L'elegante
> Borgo Teresiano, voluto dall'imperatrice Maria Teresa d'Austria,
> sfoggia imponenti palazzi color pastello, grondanti di bassorilievi e
> statue allegoriche. [...] Poi c'è la Città Vecchia con le sue vie strette
> in un abbraccio popolano, le sue palazzine degradate [...] Ora, gra-
> zie all'aiuto della Comunità Europea, questa zona è stata sottoposta
> a un restyling [...] per fare più chic. [...] Da poco questo quartiere,
> ribattezzato Zona Urban, ospita solo atelier e boutique, alberghi
> di charme e attici alla portata esclusivamente di professionisti dal
> gusto eclettico.
>   Sebbene si trovi a ridosso di queste due aree, via Ungaretti appar-
> tiene a una terza fascia del centro storico, quella di cui parrebbe che
> sia il sole che il Comune si siano dimenticati.[36]

> [The historical centre of Trieste incorporates three types of houses.
> The elegant Borgo Teresiano, commissioned by Empress Maria
> Theresa of Austria, boasts impressive pastel-coloured palaces,
> dripping with allegorical bas-reliefs and statues. [...] Then there
> is the Old Town with its narrow streets in a plebeian embrace,
> its deteriorating buildings [...] Now, with aid from the European
> Community, this area has undergone gentrification [...] to make it
> more chic. [...] Recently this neighbourhood, dubbed Zona Urban,
> only accommodates artists' workshops and boutiques, charming
> hotels, and penthouses that can be afforded solely by professionals
> with eclectic tastes.
>   Despite bordering on these two areas, via Ungaretti belongs to
> a third band of the historic centre, one that both the sun and the
> Municipality seem to have forgotten.]

Here urban space is represented as a compound of succeeding layers of
building or 'writing,' where previous strata of cultural coding underlie
the present surface and each waits to be uncovered and 'read.' Throughout the narrative, Wadia marks out Trieste's topography as a series of
shifting historical boundaries and changing neighbourhoods, one that
recognizes that national spaces are not completely self-contained and
that traditions, people, and languages are both mobile and inherently
heterogeneous.[37] The specificity of Trieste as a setting for this story is

significant. Because of its complicated history and its geographical position, Trieste has an unusually high number of widely spoken languages and dialects. Indeed, Sherry Simon considers Trieste to be exemplary of the "translational city," that is, a city in which languages connect as they move across space.[38] The polylingual setting is directly addressed in the novel through the presence of a varied cast of characters that brings into relief the complexity of linguistic identification and highlights the city as "a vantage point for the study of conceptions of Italian national identity and nationalizing practices."[39]

The plot of *Amiche per la pelle* is shaped around a condominium located in the imaginary Via Ungaretti that is home to four migrant families and a single local man, Signor Rosso. Mr Rosso is a misanthrope who avoids any contact with anyone in or outside the building: the relationship between him and the four families is difficult and the cohabitation arduous. Wadia deploys the metalanguage of liminality to reflect how institutional actions (law, urbanizing policy) and social practices (work and leisure places) designate the limits of an individual's mobility within the city and within society.[40] She also emphasizes how the "potency and potentiality" of liminality nurtures the play of ideas, words, symbols, and metaphors.[41] For instance, locating Via Ungaretti in "the third band of the historic centre" creates a spatial metaphor that represents the condition of its inhabitants, who live both inside and outside Italian society and evokes Homi Bhabha's conceptualization of a 'third space' as "a form of liminal or in-between space," where the "cutting edge of translation and negotiation occurs."[42] In addition, naming the imaginary street after the famous poet, Giuseppe Ungaretti, who was born and raised in Egypt during the years of Italian settlement in East Africa, alerts the reader to the link with Italy's repressed colonial past. This connection is made explicit at the end of the story when the unexpected appearance of Mr Rosso's grandson from Addis Ababa reveals a complex backstory of métissage and divided loyalties. Wadia plays with received notions of 'national' and 'cultural' in transnational contact zones, and in so doing helps reveal the artifice, the contextually specific nature of all identity labels and the ways in which all labels can be reread, rewritten, and/or be perceived as prejudice.

The multiform forces that create the polyphonic, translational city—a space of heightened language awareness, of intensified intercultural exchanges—are brought together particularly, though not exclusively, in the figures of the novel's four female protagonists. The four immigrant women are from very diverse cultural backgrounds and ethnicities: the narrator, Shanti, comes from India, Lule from Albania, Marinka from Bosnia, and Meigui, better known as Bocciolo di Rosa (Rosebud) from China. Implicitly autobiographical (the perspective of the narrator parallels the transcultural perspective of the author), *Amiche per la pelle* is the cross-fertilization of the four women's voices in a polyphonic narrative that enacts and embodies plurality and space as well as (or instead of) timelessness and unity.[43] The layered meanings of the cityscape (introduced in the first chapter) function in parallel with the characters' intersecting and contrasting viewpoints. In other words, the novel offers a new angle of approach to the multilingual city, by deploying a form of literary polyphony that accentuates the movement, complexity, and texture of urban language interactions. This particular form of polyphony is developed even more by Kuruvilla, who connects the interactions, convergence, indifference, or interference amongst the different languages and dialects spoken by the characters in *Milano, fin qui tutto bene* to the particular spaces they occupy in the city. In both cases, the voices and viewpoints of the characters (a plurality of consciousnesses, with equal rights and each with its own world) combine but are not merged in the unity of the event.[44] Rather, it is a cohabitation of voices in which no one holds homophonic sway.

Localizing Language(s)

As Simon observes, the ways in which languages converge within public space to create a common place of conversation and debate provide insight into the translational dynamics that contribute to the redefinition of civic space.[45] The new language acquired by migrants shapes the passage into the new society: for the individual, who is obliged to learn a new way of communicating, translating between different linguistic and cultural codes becomes a way of life. Such daily acts of (self-)translation typify a process of acculturation though which new conversations can be initiated. In this context, it is important to reflect on how the image transmitted by a novel like *Amiche per la pelle* differs from mainstream discourses that often characterize migrant women, especially those from the global south, as passive. The four female characters, each in her own way, prove active and persistent, creating alliances with each other, overcoming cultural differences in search of mutual solidarity.[46] Wadia's overarching thesis is that the solidarity amongst immigrant women is a catalyst for achieving small, but significant, things, and that, as Cronin has observed, "language (and by extension cultural difference) should not be seen as a 'barrier' or an 'obstacle' but as an opportunity":[47]

> La cosa che mi colpisce di più di questo piccolo e perfetto mondo multiculturale che siamo riusciti a creare in via Ungaretti 25 è l'idioma in cui ci confidiamo le cose. Provenienti dai quattro angoli del mondo, ci troviamo in questo stretto lembo di terra [...] a comprenderci in una lingua adottiva. È uno sforzo che abbiamo fatto noi, non per semplice necessità, ma per la voglia di diventare amiche, di poter andare oltre un semplice 'Buongiorno, come stai?' scambiato per le scale.[48]

[The thing that strikes me most about this small and perfect multicultural world that we have created at no. 25 via Ungaretti is the language in which we confide things. Coming from the four corners of the world, we now live in this narrow strip of land [...], making ourselves understood in an adoptive language. We've made this effort not just out of necessity, but because we wanted to become friends, to be able to go beyond a simple 'Good morning, how are you?' exchanged on the stairs.]

For Wadia, as for Walter Mignolo, "bilanguaging" opens new perspectives onto a way of life between languages: a mode of critique and an avenue towards aesthetic and political processes of transformation.[49] Wadia's female characters are resolved to integrate into the host society and, believing that mastering the language will enable them to better comprehend the culture, they decide to pay for Italian lessons despite their husbands' disapproval. As Shanti explains,

> due persone che vogliono abbattere il muro linguistico tra di loro, sono due esseri ansiosi di costruire un mondo migliore. E noi, armate di mattoni—libri di grammatica e di esercizi, vocabolari e audiocassette—e con tanto di cemento di buona volontà, stiamo tirando su con non poco sacrificio l'impalcatura del nostro futuro.[50]

> [two people who want to overcome a linguistic wall are two beings eager to create a better society. And our group, armed with bricks—grammar books and exercises, dictionaries and audiocassettes—and the cement of good will, is laying the foundation of our future, despite considerable sacrifices.]

The Italian lessons are given by Laura, a retired schoolteacher and regional activist, who divides her time between the "Comitato per la salvaguardia dei fiori del Carso" (Committee for the preservation of the flowers of the Carso) and the "Comitato per il bilinguilismo a Trieste" (Committee for bilingualism in Trieste).[51] Laura's fictional committees are an ironic allusion to the dominant negative discourse on migrants in Italy, particularly prevalent in the early 2000s with the blossoming of 'comitati di quartiere' (neighbourhood committees): grassroots residents' associations set up to 'safeguard' quality of life and security in their neighbourhoods and discursively constructed around issues of community and identity.[52] At the heart of this discourse is, of course, the question of national unity and the treacherous myth of monoculturalism, as is the notion that language is at play in everything; questions of national belonging, racial exclusion, and cultural production are all equally tied up with issues of language. Laura's advocacy, though, is presented with good-natured irony partly because it reflects the uneasy, multilayered coexistence of the old and the new in Italian landscapes, which seems to foster a sort of hyper-environmental self-awareness in its inhabitants that is inextricably bound up with (localized) language practices. More interesting is Wadia's portrayal of Laura as a "language activist," that is, someone who displays "a languaging response to the phenomena that present themselves in the world" and, by engaging "with the world-in-action," attempts "to develop different, more relational ways of inter-acting with the people and phenomena that one encounters in everyday life."[53] Arguably, then, Laura embodies the positive ideals that drive the four friends towards each other, personifying the means—learning the language as an essential moment of emancipation and thereby integration—through which to build their future in their adopted land.

The response of the women students is complicated: language lessons serve as a space to bond across cultural and linguistic difference but they also recognize their learning as a symbolic and practical gesture of "translational assimilation."[54] Michael Cronin asserts that there are two basic strategies adopted by immigrants in response to their new linguistic situation: "translational assimilation, where they seek to translate themselves into the dominant language of the community, and [...] translational accommodation, where translation is used as a means of maintaining their languages of origin."[55] The right to exercise autonomous forms of translation (the immigrant woman is in control of the translation situation) as opposed to heteronymous forms (others control the translation exchange) is seen as a crucial element in the emancipation of immigrants. In *Amiche per la pelle*, the goal of learning a shared vernacular is not conformity but community. In other words, this is a notion of language learning as world-building: language acquisition becomes a mode of bridging and integrating difference. Writing 'across' languages, Wadia is deeply aware that language "provides privileged access to the community" and "becomes a metonymic representation of the culture as a whole."[56] The shared language lessons could thus be seen as an example of the kind of intervention that is able to fashion a sense of togetherness out of the "throwntogetherness," fostering positive ways of living with difference and presenting an opportunity for new formative experiences.[57]

During these lessons, the unique intersections of the women's languages in transplanted accents—as evidenced, for instance, by Bocciolo di Rosa's inability to pronounce 'r's and Marinka's distinctive enunciation of 'qu' as 'kv'—creates a complex polyphonic rhythm reminiscent of Canovacci's formulation of urban communication as a 'singing choir.' The emphasis on pronunciation also draws attention to the audible surface of the city: the sensory landscape in which polyglot soundscapes form an integral part of everyday living experiences. Drawing on Arjun Appadurai's concept of 'scapes,' which he uses to theorize the ways that flows of people, money, technology, media, and ideologies move through the world, I would like to suggest that soundscapes cast new light on the linguistic aspects of globalization. Auditory impressions of languages, as are heard daily in urban spaces, can complement visually perceivable textual multilingual communication. Soundscapes paint an intricate picture of multilingual communication in urban "non-places" (bus stops, restaurants, airports).[58] Linguistic actors within the soundscape display a wide variety of multilingual practices, ranging from 'pragmatic borrowings' such as the use of single 'transnational' expressions (e.g. greetings) to those for whom languages not only coexist but form a new linguistic representation and identification, as Jørgensen puts it, a polylanguaging.[59] In short, urban soundscapes attest that contemporary multilingual identity is no longer characterized by languages which coexist as consciously registered separate languages, each having separate functions in different communication spaces, but rather by forms of translanguaging, in which language users employ whatever linguistic features are at their disposal to achieve their communicative aims as effectively as possible.[60]

Together with sounds, the circulation of material cultural objects contributes to the possibility of perceiving the global city in a multisensory way as a mobile, 'polyrhythmic body' of transcultural space. Transnational objects appear, and are interrogated, as spatial extensions of the self, which connect translocated users, and are fundamental to a rethinking of the 'sense of place' which Massey locates in the "conjunction" of trajectories that form both a material and a socio-political crossroad.[61] The interior of the building at number 25 via Ungaretti exemplifies this "particular constellation of social relations meeting and weaving together at a particular locus."[62] A closer look at Wadia's detailed portrayal of the domestic interiors of the four migrant families reveals an idiosyncratic configuration of objects and furnishings which, in each case, reflect important elements of their migration stories. The first floor is occupied by a large Chinese family, the Fongs. Their home is the most "eccentrica e esotica"[63] (eccentric and exotic), with red lacquered wardrobes and rice paper lamps. On the second floor, we find the supposedly well-to-do Albanian couple, Lule and Besim Dardani, whose blue and green neon lighting creates a "Star Trek" effect,[64] while the third floor is inhabited by two families whose apartments are illuminated by unadorned 100w bulbs: the Bosnian refugees Slobodan and Marinka Zigović and their twin children, and the Indians Shanti and Ashok Kumar and their young daughter Kamla. The description of the lighting in these interiors alludes to the reframing of self-familiarizing cultural practices of migrant life, with the Fongs and the Dardanis representing two ends of the spectrum of migrant home-building: for the former, material objects function as cultural-memory portmanteaux, while for the latter, the selection of furnishings implies they have chosen to cut ties with their (national) past in favour of new affiliations which exist outside national time and space. In line with the quasi-autobiographical

nature of the narrative and the author's own transcultural subjectivity, it is the décor of the Kumars' living room that exemplifies the
"micro-globalisation of the world city's everyday life and the globalisation of the biographies that are participating in it."[65] Colourful cushions
and silk screens of miniatures from the Mughal court are placed alongside gifts from the other residents: a brass plate from Durazzo, a Chinese
vase, a framed handwritten copy of Umberto Saba's poem "Trieste."[66]
Cultural material objects form part of the communicative activity of
these transnational families, functioning as meaning-bearing elements
(accentuated here by the addition of a linguistic dimension through the
inclusion of the framed poem) and giving a vivid sense of a global space
of cultural connection and dissolution, where local authenticities meet
and merge in transient urban and suburban settings.

Widening the Focus: From Building-Community to Urban Neighbourhoods

Wadia's depiction of a transcultural building-community concentrates attention on "the inner tensions of the already multilayered local culture."[67]
A similar process is undertaken by Gabriella Kuruvilla in *Milano, fin qui
tutto bene*. Kuruvilla shares the method of microhistory employed by
Wadia, but widens the scope: from exploring the sociability patterns of
a single building-community to focus on the processes of identity and
otherness construction in relation to city neighbourhoods—a context
in which physical proximity can create a sense of "public familiarity,"
where people see each other as belonging to a local community, intended
as a particular kind of social relation, warm, and intimate.[68] However,
the feeling of 'being at home' that we may get when we are close to
home and start to see recognizable faces does not necessarily mean that
we share any particular relation with these people that justifies the use
of the term 'local community,' intended as a spatialized sense of 'us,' a
cultural and symbolic local sense of belonging.[69] Situations in which established residents are surprised by the rapid and deep transformations
in their neighbourhood brought about by the arrival of newcomers can
lead to defensive reactions rhetorically grounded in the existence of a
community, more or less imagined, and the construction of socio-spatial
boundaries which shape neighbourhood belonging and mark the exclusion or partial inclusion of those considered outsiders.

The stories in *Milano, fin qui tutto bene* emerge from a decision by Kuruvilla and photographer Silvia Azzari to explore the ghettoized districts
affected by new by-laws limiting night-time opening hours for shops,
introduced by the local administration as a measure to preserve public
safety after a series of inter-ethnic riots erupted following the murder of
a young Egyptian man in February 2010. Kuruvilla's aim was to gather
first-hand accounts of everyday life in these constantly transforming

neighbourhoods. The result is a multifocal narrative structured around the distinctive topography of cultures found in four districts in Milan: Via Padova, Viale Monza, Via Sarpi, and Piazzale Corvetto, each of which offers a glimpse of the complex pattern of socio-cultural interactions in these superdiverse communities. Every street, piazza, restaurant, community centre, is seen from a different perspective and is transformed depending on the point of view of the observer. The protagonists of the stories are constantly moving within an urban fabric, which is also on the move and in which there is no stability but rather a precarious economic and affective identity. For Kuruvilla's characters, social life begins with the assumption that one is going to engage with people speaking different languages on an everyday basis and that linguistic interactions need to be constantly negotiated. Thus, in effect, they perform multiple acts of translation: translating their 'other' identity, moving across languages, spaces, and traditions.

The multifocalization adopted by Kuruvilla implies not only negotiation between individual representations of one and the same space, but also of their intersections. It is in these intersections that conflicting and concurring zones can be identified.[70] In the case of *Milano, fin qui tutto bene* this is reflected in the dismantling of the binary opposition of centre-periphery in favour of a "multiply stratified whole where the relations between centre and periphery are a *series* of oppositions."[71] To take just one example: geographically, Via Padova is a road that connects the centre with the distant suburbs. Since the 1980s, the many new arrivals (Filipinos, Chinese, Egyptians, Peruvians, Senegalese, Romanians, Moroccans, and Indians) have transformed its identity with "their music, their spices and their colours."[72] It has become a place where everyone feels welcome: "tutti si salutano, e si parlano: è tutto un gran vociare, in tutte le lingue" (people greet each other and everyone talks to each other: there's a great deal of clamour, in all languages),[73] and now it seems to be more central in many ways than other streets located in the geographic centre of Milan.[74] Thus, in Kuruvilla's narrative the centre is, to use Westphal's formulation, "the crystallization of a moment that *was*," and is coupled to a periphery that is always plural.[75] Such an approach corresponds to a central idea of polysystem theory: that is, that constituent elements of a system are constantly viewed in relation to other elements and derive their value from their position in a network.[76] By adopting a relational approach, analogous to Edouard Glissant's attempt to think identity via the "poetics of relation," Kuruvilla seeks a way to maintain both cultural difference and localized identity without falling into the exclusionary tendencies of ethnic and national identity.[77]

In addition to weaving together the stories of a series of endogenous, exogenous, and allogeneous characters,[78] Kuruvilla proposes a new sensory geography of the city, in which the voices of new arrivals, their customs, the smells of their cuisines and even the variety of the ringtones of their mobile phones mingle with local sounds and smells, thereby constructing a new reality, a representation of a contemporary city with a fast-paced syncopated rhythm.[79] Kuruvilla pays particular attention to the contrast between the established residents and the 'incomers' as manifested in everyday practices in public spaces. While for the former, the streets, squares, and parks have become mere spaces of transit, the new arrivals are making productive use of these as social spaces, particularly in the summer months when North Africans, Chinese, Filipinos, South Americans, Romanians, Bangladeshi, Indians, Sri Lankans all go outdoors, "i bambini giocano nei cortili, le donne chiacchierano sui ballatoi e gli uomini si incontrano per strada" (children play in the yards, women chat on the balconies and men meet on the street).[80] In this way, these neighbourhoods represent what Massey calls the "contemporaneous existence of a plurality of trajectories, a simultaneity of stories-so-far,"[81] and constitute urban "space as the sphere of the possibility of the existence of multiplicity in the sense of contemporaneous plurality."[82] It can, though, also be the space of conflict, of coexisting inequalities, and of practices of forced cohabitation.[83]

Polylingual Spaces

The dual nature of neighbourhoods characterized simultaneously by the 'dynamics of village' and by the 'dynamics of global relations,' where the global flow of international goods and the daily routines of elderly people and families come together, is encapsulated in the neighbourhood on Via Paolo Sarpi. Known as Milan's 'Chinatown,' it consists of a "dedalo di stradine in cui ci si perde [...], situato poco lontano dal Duomo [...] ma è come [essere] nel centro di Pechino" (maze of streets where you get lost [...], located not far from the Cathedral [...] but it is like [being] in the centre of Beijing).[84] The endogenous point of view is provided by Stefania, a Milanese self-employed photographer and painter, whose photographs document the popular perception of the Chinese living in Milan as a closed, silent, introverted and isolated community: they rarely speak Italian with the locals and pass quickly through the streets "come se fossero qui ma si trovassero altrove: ancora in Cina, forse. E in Cina probabilmente siamo" (as if they were here, but find themselves somewhere else: still in China, perhaps. And we probably are in China).[85] In a mixture of standard Italian and Milanese dialect, Stefania reflects on how native Italians are excluded from the intimate, individual Asian topography of the neighbourhood:

> tu che sei italiano non ci capisci nulla, di quello che leggi e di quello che senti, degli ideogrammi e del mandarino: tanto che par che te set anda a scoeula de giuvedì. E un tempo le scuole, il giovedì, erano chiuse.

[you who are Italian don't understand anything of what you read and what you hear, the ideograms and Mandarin: so much so that it's as if you only attended school on Thursdays. And in the past, schools were closed on Thursdays.][86]

While Stefania's narrow viewpoint fails to take into account that any non-Mandarin speaker is similarly excluded, her remark serves as a re-minder that

> the linguistic landscape [...] provides a unique perspective on the coexistence and competition of different languages and their scripts, and how they interact and interfere with each other in a given place.[87]

Indeed, public and commercial signs can be used to reinforce a collective identity, or as Ben-Rafael puts it, they may be designed to assert "their actors' particularistic identities, i.e. 'who they are' in front of 'who they are not,' exhibiting thereby a priori commitment to a given group within the general public."[88]

A specular view of the localized use of language (from an auditory rather than a visual perspective) is presented by Wadia in an episode of *Amiche per la pelle* in which the novel's migrant characters go on a group excursion and, on the bus, encounter an elderly Triestine couple who only speak in dialect. The use of Triestine dialect in this episode re-inforces the cultural and linguistic distance between the autochthonous citizens of Trieste and the immigrants. However, it also reminds us that Italy, while sharing a common standard language, presents in its daily use a variety of dialects and regional variants that identify speakers as belonging to a certain linguistic and cultural region. Wadia highlights the linguistic heterogeneity that has always been present in Italian cul-ture and draws attention to the widespread use of polylingual practices in everyday contexts by both 'natives' and 'immigrants.' In using local accents, both writers effectively explore new directions in the challenge to linguistic normativeness, countering the prevalent misconception of vernacular variants as essentialized markers of ethnicity. 'Dialect' is just as learnable, they demonstrate, as any other form of language: "Oramai il dialetto lo riesco a seguire. È essenziale per la sopravvivenza" (By now I can understand dialect. It's essential to survive).[89] It is important to note that, in Italy, in order to gain access to 'the place of speech,' mi-grants need to master not only standard Italian but also the local dia-lects, which, as the languages spoken by their users in everyday practices, provide the most effective means of cementing their translational assimi-lation to Italian culture. In these novels, the complex intersections of the 'local' and the 'global' that occur in this highly stratified multi-ethnic society are reflected in the characters' everyday language practices.

Their language use is influenced by varieties of English and global youth subcultures, while traces of Milanese or Triestine dialect coexist with inflections and words from the immigrants' own ethnic languages. This is a process of creolization that not only highlights the difficulty of thinking about 'local' and 'global' as separate entities, but also, through the constant fragmenting and recombination of linguistic elements, compels us to rethink the relationship between 'native' and 'non-native' speakers in terms of "diversalism" rather than 'otherness.'[90] In other words, we must put to one side a "sense of language or knowledge that attempts to dominate or comprehend (in the sense of 'grasping' that which is Other) and adopt one that is shared."[91]

In the multilingual neighbourhoods depicted by Kuruvilla, speakers do not confine themselves to using languages separately, but rather they translanguage as they make meaning. For example, each of Kuruvilla's characters has a distinct idiolect, a way to express themselves laden with personal connotations: Samir speaks Italian mixed with Arabic; Stefania regularly cites Milanese idioms; Anita Patel's old-fashioned Italian infused with proverbs and clichés learned from her mother evokes a strong sense of unresolved tension between her Italian and Indian heritage: "né vecchiabianca né giovanenera" (neither oldwhite nor youngblack), she embodies duality and ambiguity;[92] but the most representative of the linguistic and ethnic creolization that is taking place in Italy, and in Milan in particular, is Tony. His entire personality is characterized by his translanguaging practices: his speech is configured by the Neapolitan dialect, because his family is from Naples, and the Milanese dialect learned in the suburban area of Corvetto, where there is still a strong sense of Milanese identity ('milanesità'), but where nowadays one also encounters a profusion of English slang along with Jamaican patois. Tony belongs to a large family that lives in a tiny, overcrowded apartment. The municipality has been promising for years that they would be moved to a new area and larger premises but, in Tony's colourful words: "a promise is a comfort to a fool, una promessa è una comodità per uno sciocco. An wi nuh bawn back a cow: e noi non siamo stupidi, lo sappiamo che nisciuno c'aiuta" (a promise is a comfort to a fool. I wasn't born yesterday and we're not stupid; we know no one will help us).[93] In order to convey the full extent of his disillusionment with local government, Tony uses all of the linguistic codes at his disposal: from reggae lyrics (Gregory Isaacs' "a promise is a comfort to a fool") and Jamaican patois to standard Italian and Neapolitan vernacular. The depiction of the polylingualism characteristic of multi-ethnic neighbourhoods invites readers to reflect on how the symbolic intersection between different languages and cultures redefines the forms of multiculturalism. In other words, the translanguaging practices deployed by Kuruvilla and Wadia's characters in response to their environment correspond to the view of translation as "a sensory activity"; a view "that develops, phenomenologically, out of living experiences of direct perception—that is, out of the full synaesthesia of 'being present' to the throbbing disorienting dimensions of a new, strange environment."[94] Conceptualizing translation in this way enables us to see how everyday practices and identities are rooted in the trajectories of the transcultural communities to which individuals belong, and how differences become fluid in the process of cultural transformation.[95]

Concluding Remarks

Wadia and Kuruvilla's literary representations of how immigrants in Trieste and Milan conceptualize and perform their identities through polylanguaging practices emphasize the translation–migration nexus and contest the notion of languages as 'bounded entities.' Suggesting a multifocal and multisensory remapping of transcultural encounters, their polyphonic narratives of mobility create a literary space in which a human element is added to the often highly politicized discussions of immigrants and their place in the nation. The mix of languages and fluidity of interactions presented in the novels reflect the new strategies of interpersonal communication and cultural literacy that are being developed in everyday life as people speaking different languages and dialects of Italian interact with each other. As mentioned above, the form of polyphony adopted by both authors is one that reflects the intricate relationship between language, mobility, and space in transcultural urban environments. It is important to stress that it is not only what the characters say that conveys certain understandings of self and environment. It is also how they speak—from translanguaging practices (not only switching between languages but also the ways they structure their discourse) to the use of strategies of translational assimilation—that contributes to their means of making identity claims. It seems to me that this form of polyphony, with its emphasis on polylingual soundscapes, which is both the artistic principle of composition and a central theme in both novels, provides a more useful model to understand the complex configurations of contemporary urban societies than the more traditional representations of multilingual/multicultural spaces, which tend to privilege a rather self-contained notion of language/culture as discrete systems.

To better comprehend difference we need to recognize the plurality of voices and lives that intersect and shift and that cannot be aggregated into one identity. Even where the city is represented as a space of segmentation or regimentation—like the Corvetto neighbourhood in which immigrants only have access to the first floor of the Bowling Centre where the slot machines are located, or the Sherazad café where all the clients speak Arabic or French and Italians are not welcome—it remains a space of cultural translation.[96] Both the psychological and political spaces of the "cultural borderland" are to be found in the morphology of transcultural urban localities like the fictional via Ungaretti and the real Via Padova.[97] In these "sites of creative cultural creolization [...] where the residents often refuse the geopolitical univocality of the lines,"[98] new heterogeneous identities are formed while the intersections between polyvocal perspectives demonstrate the power of language to recompose the difficult, but not impossible, coexistence of different worlds. By celebrating the multiplicity of perspectives and by juxtaposing multiple voices "that correct, nourish, and mutually enrich each other,"[99] Wadia and Kuruvilla demonstrate how the encounter with other cultures and languages creates a path to reciprocal knowledge. Their "highly personal detailed readings" of the diversified linguistic spectrum in multi-ethnic urban spaces provide insight into "larger structures of coherence."[100] The articulation of multiple points of view expressed through the polyphony of individual utterances leads to a better understanding of the cultures of 'translation zones' as a locus of intersections, contacts, tensions, and relationships and generates a polyphonic epistemology that redefines and diversifies prevailing structures of meaning and knowledge.[101] Translingual/transcultural writers like Wadia and Kuruvilla shift the emphasis from the "transnational to the *translocational*,"[102] and, by situating themselves at the intersection of the local and the global, show how "local knowledge can motivate conversations between different localities, answering questions that transcend one's own borders,"[103] thus concretely contributing to the making of a more multifaceted, changing and connected city: a city whose identity is constantly reshaped and transformed by multiple flows and encounters.

Notes

1 Doreen Massey, "A Global Sense of Space," *Marxism Today* 38 (1991): 24–9.
2 Bertrand Westphal, *Geocriticism: Real and Fictional Spaces*, trans. Robert T. Tally Jr. (Basingstoke: Palgrave Macmillan, 2011).
3   From 1970 until today, the foreign citizens with regular residence permits in Italy have increased tenfold, and the rhythm of growth seems to be unstoppable. In 2003, following the last act of regularization, almost 700,000 non-EU workers were legalized. This figure, when added to the one and a half million aliens who were already living on the Italian peninsula, increases the total foreign population to two and a half million people, including minors. These substantial figures outline a complex situation, characterized by immigrant flows from more than 191 countries, especially Central Eastern Europe [...], Northern Africa [...], China and the Indian subcontinent.

   IDOS, ed. *The Impact of Immigration on Italy's Society* (Rome: Edizioni Centro Studi e Ricerche, 2004), 7.
4 The term transcultural is used here as a critical perspective that sees cultures as relational webs and acknowledges their transitory, confluential, and mutually transforming nature. According to German philosopher Wolfgang Welsch, cultures are today characterized internally by a pluralization of identities and externally by border crossing patterns. Previously

homogeneous and separate cultures have assumed a new form, "which is to be called *transcultural* insofar that it *passes through* classical cultural boundaries." Wolfgang Welsch, "Transculturality: The Puzzling Form of Cultures Today," in *Spaces of Culture: City-Nation-World*, ed. Mike Featherstone and Scott Lash (London: Sage, 1999), 204.

5 The body of works written in Italian by foreign-born writers is often referred to as 'Italophone' or 'migrant' literature. Scholars are increasingly challenging the use of these terms with reference, for instance, to the definition of 'first- and second-generation migrant' and 'native' writer. See, in particular, Graziella Parati, *Mediterranean Crossroads: Migration Literature in Italy* (Madison, NJ: Fairleigh Dickinson University Press, 1999) and *Migration Italy: The Art of Talking Back in a Destination Culture* (Toronto, ON: University of Toronto Press, 2005); Rita Wilson, "Cultural Mediation through Translingual Narrative," *Target* 23 no. 2 (2011): 235–50.

6 Armando Gnisci, "Editorial." *Kumà. Creolizzare l'Europa* 13, www.disp. let.uniroma1.it/kuma/editoriale13.html.

7 Homi K. Bhabha, *The Location of Culture* (London: Routledge, 1994), 37.

8 Bhabha, *Location of Culture*, 37; Emily Apter, "On Translation in a Global Market," *Public Culture* 13 no. 1 (2001): 1–12.

9 Tim Cresswell, *On the Move. Mobility in the Modern Western World* (London: Routledge, 2006).

10 Iain Chambers, "Interview for V° Convegno Nazionale di Culture e Letteratura della Migrazione," www.librialice.it/news/primo/paesaggimigratori. htm.

11 Mary Louise Pratt, *Imperial Eyes: Travel Writing and Transculturation* (London: Routledge, 1992).

12 Giuliana Benvenuti, "La letteratura costruisce luoghi inediti: il protagonismo dello spazio," (2009), http://isintellettualistoria2.myblog.it/2009/07/15/ giuliana-benvenuti-il-protagonismo-dello-spazio/. All translations from Italian are mine unless otherwise indicated.

13 Benvenuti, "La letteratura costruisce luoghi inediti."

14 Michael Cronin, "Babel's Standing Stones: Language, Translation and the Exosomatic," *Crossings* 2 no. 1 (2002): 1–7.

15 Nikos Papastergiadis, *The Turbulence of Migration: Globalization, Deterritorialization and Hybridity* (Malden, MA: Blackwell Publishers Inc., 2000), 129.

16 Salman Rushdie, *Imaginary Homelands: Essays and Criticism 1981–1991* (London: Granta Books, 1991), 277–8.

17 Arjun Appadurai, *Modernity at Large: Cultural Dimensions of Globalization* (Minneapolis: University of Minnesota Press, 1996).

18 Andrew Geddes, "Il rombo dei cannoni? Immigration and the centre-right in Italy," *Journal of European Public Policy* 15 no. 3 (2008): 349–61.

19 Alessandro Dal Lago, *Non-Persone* (Milan: Feltrinelli, 1999).

20 Giovanni Spadolini, *Nazione e nazionalità in Italia: dall'alba del secolo ai nostri giorni* (Rome and Bari: Laterza, 1994).

21 Parati, *Mediterranean Crossroads*.

22 Melita Richter, "Women Experiencing Citizenship," in *Common Passion, Different Voices: Reflections on Citizenship and Intersubjectivity*, ed. E. Skaerbæk et al. (York: Raw Nerve Books, 2006), 45.

23 Parati, *Migration Italy*, 13.

24 Parati, *Mediterranean Crossroads*.

25 Mikhail Bakhtin, *Problems of Dostoevsky's Poetics*, trans. C. Emerson (Minneapolis: University of Minnesota Press, 1984), 6.

26 Hugo Letiche, "Polyphony and Its Other," *Organization Studies* 31 no. 3 (2010): 262.

27 "Questo processo è ancora più visibile per coloro che attraversano i diversi contesti geografici e culturali" (Melita Richter, "Essere stranieri," in *Sguardi e parole migranti*, ed. Melita Richter and L. Dugulin (Trieste: Co-ordinamento delle associazioni e delle comunità di immigrati della provincia di Trieste, 2005), 20.

28 Richter, "Women Experiencing Citizenship," 38–9.

29 Massimo Canevacci, *La città polifonica: saggio sull'antropologia della comunicazione urbana* (Rome: Editore SEAM, 1993), 15–17.

30 Massey, "A Global Sense of Space."

31 Henri Lefebvre, *La Production de l'Espace* (Paris: Anthropos, 2000 [1974]).

32 Born in Bombay, Lily-Amber Laila Wadia moved to Italy to study and has lived in Trieste for 20 years, where she currently works at the University of Trieste as an English language expert. To date, she has published two short stories in the best-selling anthology, *Pecore nere* (Laterza, 2005); two short story collections *Il burattinaio e altre storie extra-italiane* (Cosmo Iannone, 2004), *Se tutte le donne* (Barbera, 2012); an ironic memoir *Come diventare italiani in 24 ore* (Barbera, 2010); and edited a food-themed collection of short stories by translingual writers, *Mondo pentola* (Cosmo Iannone, 2007).

33 Born in Milan to an Indian father and an Italian mother, Gabriella Kuruvilla has a degree in architecture and is a freelance professional journalist. In 2001, under the pen name of Viola Chandra, she published the novel *Media chiara e noccioline* (DeriveApprodi). In 2005, the anthology *Pecore Nere*, published by Laterza, included two of her short stories. She is also an artist: mainly producing works in sand and fabric that have been exhibited both in Italy and abroad.

34 Both authors adopt what Cronin has defined as the analytic component of the politics of microspection, that is, "the proper investigation of places and their inhabitants through methods and practices which reveal the full, fractal complexity of human habitation." Michael Cronin, *The Expanding World. Towards a Politics of Microspection* (Winchester & Washington: Zero Books, 2012), 65.

35 Sherry Simon, *Cities in Translation: Intersections of Language and Memory* (London: Routledge, 2011).

36 Laila Wadia, *Amiche per la pelle* (Rome: Edizioni e/o, 2007), 7–8.

37 Kuruvilla's work, too, bears testimony to the new kinds of segmentation that have been reshaping the face of Italian urban landscapes. For more on this, see, for example, the collective volume, edited by Asher Colombo, Antonio Genovese and Andrea Canevaro, that gathers results of several sociological and anthropological studies in which the impact of immigration on Italian urban spaces has been analysed empirically. Asher Colombo, Antonio Genovese, and Andrea Canevaro, eds., *Immigrazione e nuove identità urbane. La città come luogo di incontro e scambio culturale* (Trento: Edizioni Erickson, 2006).

38 Simon, *Cities in Translation*.

39 Glenda Sluga, "Italian National Identity and Fascism: Aliens, Allogenes and Assimilation on Italy's North-Eastern Border," in *The Politics of Italian National Identity: A Multidisciplinary Perspective*, ed. Gino Bedani and Bruce Haddock (Cardiff: University of Wales Press, 2000), 163.

40 In Victor Turner's definition "a state or process which is betwixt-and-between the normal, day-to-day cultural and social states and processes of getting and spending, preserving law and order, and registering structural

status." Victor Turner, "Frame, Flow and Reflection. Ritual and Drama as Public Liminality," *Japanese Journal of Religious Studies* 4 (1979): 465–6.

41 Turner, "Frame, Flow and Reflection," 466.
42 Bhabha, *Location of Culture*, 38.
43 In an interview, Wadia explicitly evokes the notion of "transculturalism" to account for her decision to reside in Italy. Carlotta Caroli, "Intervista a Laila Wadia. L'ironia come arma di istruzione di massa," http://donna. immigrazioneoggi.it/25062011/primopiano/wadia.html.
44 Bakhtin, *Problems of Dostoevsky's Poetics*, 6.
45 Simon, *Cities in Translation*, 157.
46 Wadia, *Amiche per la pelle*, 46, 60, 74, 145.
47 Cronin, *The Expanding World*, 21.
48 Wadia, *Amiche per la pelle*, 46–7.
49 Walter Mignolo, *Local Histories/Global Designs* (Princeton, NJ: Princeton University Press, 2000), 65.
50 Wadia, *Amiche per la pelle*, 53.
51 Ibid., 53.
52 Antonello Petrillo, *La città delle paure: per un'archeologia delle insicurezze urbane* (Avellino: Sellino Editore, 2003); Marinella Belluati, *L'in/sicurezza dei quartieri. Media, territorio e percezioni d'insicurezza* (Milan: Franco Angeli, 2004).
53 Alison Phipps, "Travelling Languages? Land, Languaging and Translation," *Language and Intercultural Communication* 11 no. 4 (2011): 368, 365.
54 Michael Cronin, *Translation and Identity* (London: Routledge, 2006), 52.
55 Cronin, *Translation and Identity*.
56 Ibid., 54.
57 Doreen Massey, *For Space* (London: Sage, 2005).
58 Marc Augé, *Non-Places: Introduction to an Anthropology of Supermodernity*, trans. John Howe (London: Verso, 1995).
59 J. Normann Jørgensen et al., "Polylanguaging in Superdiversity," *Diversities* 13 no. 2 (2011): 23–37. *Multilingualism* 5 no. 3 (2008).
60 Translanguaging includes notions of hybrid language use in which aspects of each language are merged by the bi- or multilingual language user, as well as code-switching and other manifestations of languages in contact. See Ofelia Garcia and Li Wei, *Translanguaging. Language, Bilingualism and Education* (New York: Palgrave Macmillan, 2013).
61 Massey, *For Space*.
62 Massey, "A Global Sense of Space," 28.
63 Wadia, *Amiche per la pelle*, 39.
64 Ibid., 9.
65 Jorg Durrschmidt, *Everyday Lives in the Global City: The Delinking of the Locale and the Milieu* (London: Routledge, 2000), 1.
66 Wadia, *Amiche per la pelle*, 39.
67 Parati, *Migration Italy*, 71.
68 Talja Blokland and Mike Savage, "Social Capital and Networked Urbanism," in *Networked Urbanism*, ed. Talja Blokland and Mike Savage (Aldershot: Ashgate, 2008), 1–20.
69 Antonio Tosi, *Abitanti: Le nuove strategie dell'azione abitativa* (Bologna: Il Mulino, 1994).
70 As Westphal points out,

the bipolar relationship between otherness and identity is no longer governed by a single action, but by interaction. The representation of space comes from a reciprocal creation, not simply a one-way activity of

> a gaze looking from one point to another, without considering the other, reciprocating gazes.

Westphal, *Geocriticism*, 113.

71 Itamar Even-Zohar, "Interference in Dependent Literary Polysystems," *Poetics Today* 11 no. 1 (1990): 88.

72 Gabriella Kuruvilla, *Milano, fin qui tutto bene* (Rome and Bari: Laterza, 2012), 17.

73 Kuruvilla, *Milano, fin qui tutto bene*, 6.

74 Ibid., 7–8.

75 Westphal., *Geocriticism*, 48.

76 Itamar Even-Zohar, "Polysystem Theory," *Poetics Today* 11 no. 1 (1990): 11. Even-Zohar defines a literary system as "the network of relations that is hypothesized to obtain between a number of activities called 'literary,' and consequently these activities themselves observed via that network." Itamar Even-Zohar, "The 'Literary System,'" *Poetics Today* 11 no. 1 (1990): 28. Other cultural/social systems are defined along the same lines.

77 Édouard Glissant, *Poetics of Relation*, trans. Betsy Wing (Ann Arbor: University of Michigan Press, 1997), 141–57.

78 The endogenous point of view characterizes an autochthonic vision of space. Normally resistant to any exotic view, it limits itself to familiar space. [...] The exogenous point of view, however, reflects the vision of the traveller; it exudes exoticism. [...] Finally, the allogeneous point of view lies somewhere between the other two. It is characteristic of those who have settled into a place, becoming familiar with it, but still remaining foreigners in the eyes of the indigenous population.

See also Westphal, *Geocriticism*, 128.

79 See L'Asterisco Dimezzato—G. Kuruvilla: pastiche linguistico e culturale, "Milano, fin qui tutto bene," www.youtube.com/watch?v=xBhMJV3BH64, Published 10 Oct 2012.

80 Kuruvilla, *Milano, fin qui tutto bene*, 77.

81 Massey, *For Space*, 12.

82 Ibid., 9.

83 Bruno Riccio, "Transnazionalità e interazioni urbane. Un'esperienza etnografica oltre il 'globalismo' e l''ibridismo,'" in *Immigrazione e nuove identità urbane. La città come luogo di incontro e scambio culturale*, ed. Asher Colombo, Antonio Genovese, and Andrea Canevaro (Trento: Edizioni Erickson, 2006), 37.

84 Kuruvilla, *Milano, fin qui tutto bene*, 97.

85 Ibid., 98.

86 Ibid., 106.

87 Peter Backhaus, *Linguistic Landscapes. A Comparative Study of Urban Multilingualism in Tokyo* (Clevedon: Multilingual Matters, 2007), 145.

88 Elizier Ben-Rafael, "A Sociological Approach to the Study of Linguistic Landscapes," in *Linguistic Landscape: Expanding the Scenery*, ed. E Shohamy and D Gorter (New York: Routledge, 2009), 46.

89 Wadia, *Amiche per la pelle*, 89.

90 Glissant, *Poetics of Relation*.

91 Sandra Bermann, "Translation as Relation and Glissant's Work," *CLCWeb: Comparative Literature and Culture* 16 no. 3 (2014). doi:10.7771/1481-4374.2516.

92 Kuruvilla, *Milano, fin qui tutto bene*, 13.

93 Ibid., 159.

94 Phipps, "Travelling Languages?" 369.
95 Papastergiadis, *The Turbulence of Migration*.
96 Kuruvilla, *Milano, fin qui tutto bene*, 156 and 58.
97 Douglas E. Foley, *The Heartland Chronicles* (Philadelphia: University of Pennsylvania, 1995). The psychological space is the one in which border crossers struggle with their bicultural identities. The political space is created as ethnic groups actively fuse and blend their culture with the mainstream culture, thus achieving a form of cultural creolization.
98 Smadar Lavie and Ted Swedenburg, eds., *Displacement, Diaspora and Geographies of Identity* (Durham, NC: Duke University Press, 1996), 15.
99 Westphal, *Geocriticism*, 113.
100 Ibid., 37–8.
101 Henri Lefebvre, *The Production of Space*, trans. Donald Nicholson-Smith (Oxford: Blackwell-Wiley, 1991), 184; Massey, *For Space*.
102 Cronin, *The Expanding World*, 39.
103 A. Suresh Canagarajah, "Reconstructing Local Knowledge, Reconfiguring Language Studies," in *Reclaiming the Local in Language Policy and Practice*, ed. A. Suresh Canagarajah (Mahwah, NJ: Lawrence Erlbaum Associates, Publishers, 2005), 20.

Bibliography

Appadurai, Arjun. *Modernity at Large: Cultural Dimensions of Globalization.* Minneapolis: University of Minnesota Press, 1996.

Apter, Emily. "On Translation in a Global Market." *Public Culture* 13 no. 1 (2001): 1–12.

Augé, Marc. *Non-Places: Introduction to an Anthropology of Supermodernity.* Translated by John Howe. London: Verso, 1995.

Backhaus, Peter. *Linguistic Landscapes. A Comparative Study of Urban Multilingualism in Tokyo.* Clevedon: Multilingual Matters, 2007.

Bakhtin, Mikhail. *Problems of Dostoevsky's Poetics.* Translated by Caryl Emerson. Minneapolis: University of Minnesota Press, 1984.

Belluati, Marinella. *L'in/sicurezza dei quartieri. Media, territorio e percezioni d'insicurezza.* Milan: Franco Angeli, 2004.

Ben-Rafael, Elizier. "A Sociological Approach to the Study of Linguistic Landscapes." In *Linguistic Landscape: Expanding the Scenery*, edited by Elana Shohamy and Durk Gorter, 40–54. New York: Routledge, 2009.

Benvenuti, Giuliana. "La letteratura costruisce luoghi inediti: il protagonismo dello spazio." (2009). Published electronically 15 July. http://isintellettualistoria2.myblog.it/2009/07/15/giuliana-benvenuti-il-protagonismo-dello-spazio/.

Bermann, Sandra. "Translation as Relation and Glissant's Work." *CLCWeb: Comparative Literature and Culture* 16 no. 3 (2014). doi:10.7771/1481-4374.2516.

Bhabha, Homi K. *The Location of Culture.* London and New York: Routledge, 1994.

Blokland, Talja, and Mike Savage. "Social Capital and Networked Urbanism." In *Networked Urbanism*, edited by Talja Blokland and Mike Savage, 1–20. Hampshire: Ashgate, 2008.

Canagarajah, A. Suresh. "Reconstructing Local Knowledge, Reconfiguring Language Studies." In *Reclaiming the Local in Language Policy and Practice*, edited by A. Suresh Canagarajah, 3–24. Mahwah, NJ: Lawrence Erlbaum Associates, 2005.

Canevacci, Massimo. *La città polifonica: saggio sull'antropologia della comunicazione urbana*. Rome: Editore SEAM, 1993.

Caritas/Migrantes. "Sommario: Immigrazione Dossier Statistico 2009." Rome: IDOS Centro Studi e Ricerche, 2009.

Caroli, Carlotta. "Intervista a Laila Wadia. L'ironia come arma di istruzione di massa." http://donna.immigrazioneoggi.it/25062011/primopiano/wadia.html.

Chambers, Iain. "Interview for Vº Convegno Nazionale di Culture e Letteratura della Migrazione," www.librialice.it/news/primo/paesaggimigratori.htm.

Colombo, Asher, Antonio Genovese, and Andrea Canevaro, eds. *Immigrazione e nuove identità urbane. La città come luogo di incontro e scambio culturale.* Trento: Edizioni Erickson, 2006.

Cresswell, Tim. *On the Move. Mobility in the Modern Western World*. London: Routledge, 2006.

Cronin, Michael. "Babel's Standing Stones: Language, Translation and the Exosomatic." *Crossings* 2 no.1 (2002): 1–7.

———. *Translation and Identity*. London and New York: Routledge, 2006.

———. *The Expanding World. Towards a Politics of Microspection*. Winchester and Washington, DC: Zero Books, 2012.

Dal Lago, Alessandro. *Non-Persone*. Milan: Feltrinelli, 1999.

Durrschmidt, Jörg. *Everyday Lives in the Global City: The Delinking of the Locale and the Milieu*. London: Routledge, 2000.

Even-Zohar, Itamar. "Interference in Dependent Literary Polysystems." *Poetics Today* 11 no. 1 (1990): 79–83.

———. "The 'Literary System.'" *Poetics Today* 11 no. 1 (1990): 27–44.

———. "Polysystem Theory." *Poetics Today* 11 no. 1 (1990): 9–26.

Foley, Douglas E. *The Heartland Chronicles*. Philadelphia: University of Pennsylvania, 1995.

Garcia, Ofelia, and Li Wei. *Translanguaging. Language, Bilingualism and Education*. New York: Palgrave Macmillan, 2013.

Geddes, Andrew. "Il rombo dei cannoni? Immigration and the centre-right in Italy." *Journal of European Public Policy* 15 no. 3 (2008): 349–61.

Glissant, Édouard. *Poetics of Relation*. Translated by Betsy Wing. Ann Arbor: University of Michigan Press, 1997.

Gnisci, Armando. "Editorial. Kumà. Creolizzare l'Europa 13," www.disp.let.uniroma1.it/kuma/editoriale13.html.

IDOS, ed. *The Impact of Immigration on Italy's Society*. Rome: Edizioni Centro Studi e Ricerche, 2004.

Jørgensen, J. Normann, Martha Karrebæk, Lian Malai Madsen, and Janus Spindler Møller, "Polylanguaging in Superdiversity." *Diversities* 13 no. 2 (2011): 23–37.

Kuruvilla, Gabriella. *Milano, fin qui tutto bene*. Rome and Bari: Laterza, 2012.

Lavie, Smadar, and Ted Swedenburg, eds. *Displacement, Diaspora and Geographies of Identity*. Durham, NC: Duke University Press, 1996.

Lefebvre, Henri. *The Production of Space*. Translated by Donald Nicholson-Smith. Oxford: Blackwell-Wiley, 1991.

———. *La Production de l'Espace*. 1974. Paris: Anthropos, 2000.

Letiche, Hugo. "Polyphony and Its Other." *Organization Studies* 31 no. 3 (2010): 261–77.

Massey, Doreen. "A Global Sense of Space." *Marxism Today* 38 (1991): 24–9.

———. *For Space*. London: Sage, 2005.

Mignolo, Walter. *Local Histories/Global Designs: Coloniality, Subaltern Knowledges, and Border Thinking*. Princeton, NJ: Princeton University Press, 2000.

Papastergiadis, Nikos. *The Turbulence of Migration: Globalization, Deterritorialization and Hybridity*. Malden, MA: Blackwell Publishers, 2000.

Parati, Graziella. *Mediterranean Crossroads: Migration Literature in Italy*. Madison, NJ: Fairleigh Dickinson University Press, 1999.

———. *Migration Italy: The Art of Talking Back in a Destination Culture*. Toronto, ON: University of Toronto Press, 2005.

Petrillo, Antonello. *La città delle paure: per un'archeologia delle insicurezze urbane*. Avellino: Sellino Editore, 2003.

Phipps, Alison. "Travelling Languages? Land, Languaging and Translation." *Language and Intercultural Communication* 11 no. 4 (2011): 364–76.

Pratt, Mary Louise. *Imperial Eyes: Travel Writing and Transculturation*. London: Routledge, 1992.

Riccio, Bruno. "Transnazionalità e interazioni urbane. Un'esperienza etnografica oltre il 'globalismo' e l'ibridismo.'" In *Immigrazione e nuove identità urbane. La città come luogo di incontro e scambio culturale*, edited by Asher Colombo, Antonio Genovese and Andrea Canevaro, 35–45. Trento: Edizioni Erickson, 2006.

Richter, Melita. "Essere stranieri." In *Sguardi e parole migranti*, edited by Melita Richter and L. Dugulin. Trieste: Coordinamento delle associazioni e delle comunità di immigrati della provincia di Trieste, 2005.

———. "Women Experiencing Citizenship." In *Common Passion, Different Voices: Reflections on Citizenship and Intersubjectivity*, edited by E. Skaerbæk, D. Duhaček, E. Pulcini and Melita Richter, 36–48. York: Raw Nerve Books, 2006.

Rushdie, Salman. *Imaginary Homelands: Essays and Criticism 1981–1991*. London: Granta Books, 1991.

Simon, Sherry. *Cities in Translation: Intersections of Language and Memory*. London: Routledge, 2011.

Sluga, Glenda. "Italian National Identity and Fascism: Aliens, Allogenes and Assimilation on Italy's North-Eastern Border." In *The Politics of Italian National Identity: A Multidisciplinary Perspective*, edited by Gino Bedani and Bruce Haddock, 163–90. Cardiff: University of Wales Press, 2000.

Spadolini, Giovanni. *Nazione e nazionalità in Italia: dall'alba del secolo ai nostri giorni*. Rome and Bari: Laterza, 1994.

Tosi, Antonio. *Abitanti: Le nuove strategie dell'azione abitativa*. Bologna: Il Mulino, 1994.

Turner, Victor. "Frame, Flow and Reflection. Ritual and Drama as Public Liminality." *Japanese Journal of Religious Studies* 4 (1979): 465–99.

Wadia, Laila. *Amiche per la pelle*. Rome: Edizioni e/o, 2007.

Welsch, Wolfgang. "Transculturality: The Puzzling Form of Cultures Today." In *Spaces of Culture: City–Nation–World*, edited by Mike Featherstone and Scott Lash, 194–213. London: Sage, 1999.

Westphal, Bertrand. *Geocriticism: Real and Fictional Spaces.* Translated by Robert T. Tally Jr. Basingstoke: Palgrave Macmillan, 2011.

Wilson, Rita. "Cultural Mediation through Translingual Narrative." *Target* 23 no. 2 (2011): 235–50.

Zincone, G., and M. Basili. "Country Report: Italy, EUDO Citizenship Observatory." Florence: European University Institute, 2009.

5 "Ah'm the man ae a thoosand tongues"

Multilingual Scottishness and Its Limits

Rachael Gilmour

This chapter works from the coordinates of contemporary Glasgow—specifically, Scottish-Asian writer Suhayl Saadi's Glasgow-set debut novel, *Psychoraag* (2004)—in order to think about how literature can register the language diversity which is at the same time an everyday fact of contemporary global modernity, and a challenge to conventions of literary language and form. It considers Scotland's position as 'semi-periphery': part of the UK, a centre of global literary production in the pre-eminent language of cultural and economic power, English, and yet at the same time, peripheral to both.[1] Saadi's novel traces the networks that define the quotidian linguistic localism of working-class Pakistani Glasgow within global flows of language and culture that are not necessarily routed via London. Indeed, it is critical of the dominance of London as a hub of cultural and publishing power, with its demand for certain kinds of "hyper-ironic" cultural product: "Very London," muses Saadi's protagonist-narrator Zaf at one point, "Straight faces, stiff lips. Mind the Gap! Ooh sooo coooooool."[2] Oriented, instead, between Glasgow and Lahore, *Psychoraag* is in critical dialogue with literary models of language diversity and vernacularity that emerge from Scotland on the one hand and South Asia on the other, each of which has posed influential and well-known challenges to the literary dominance of 'English' as colonial legacy and contemporary world language. Saadi's linguistic pyrotechnics have drawn comparison with Salman Rushdie, whose writing has become, in many ways, definitive of prevailing postcolonial literary models of linguistic cosmopolitanism. Nevertheless, he has distanced himself in interviews from what he terms Rushdie's elite metropolitan, "Oxford educated upper class English" perspective,[3] and aligns himself far more willingly with the vernacular writing of Scottish novelists, in particular James Kelman, which challenges the hegemony of Standard English under the signs of class and nation, addressing the material, social, cultural, and historical conditions of linguistic marginalization.[4] At the same time, his writing engages critically with homogenizing models of vernacular 'authentic' Scottishness, perpetuated not least through literature, as implicitly white, masculine, and working class. Perhaps in part as a consequence of the novel's idiosyncratic and assertively local/global Glaswegianness, *Psychoraag* has been lauded in the Scottish press, but almost entirely ignored south of the border. As Ali Smith observes: "the critical silence that met it down south is an interesting reaction in itself to a book about race and invisibility, voice and silence, whose central theme is the question of whether anyone out there is actually listening."[5]

Psychoraag's Glasgow is asynchronous and uneven, defined by its past as an imperial metropolis as well as by its histories of colonization and resistance to English rule, and structured in the present as much by US-led global capitalist culture as by the ongoing dominance of London. Simultaneously realist and phantasmagoric, its uncanny language effects serve not only to compress distances of space and time, but to collapse distinctions between inside and outside, authentic and inauthentic, like and unlike. As the Warwick Research Collective have recently and resonantly written of the formal qualities of "world-literature" within the modern capitalist world-system, *Psychoraag* dramatizes at the level of language "discrepant encounters, alienation effects, surreal cross-linkages, unidentified freakish objects, unlikely likenesses [...]— the equivalent of umbrellas meeting sewing machines on (animated) dissecting tables."[6] Drawing on formal models that include the earliest Calcutta sound recordings, the writing of James Joyce and T.S. Eliot, and the South Asian musical form of *raag* from which the novel's title derives, *Psychoraag*'s self-conscious modernist experimentalism is global and anti-metropolitan in formation. Deeply invested in the radical potential of synthetic vernaculars and multilingual inventiveness, it is nevertheless highly sceptical of the idea of language diversity as a progressive given.[7] Multilingualism, like any other language practice, is never immune from regressive politics of class, race, or gender; it may be exoticized, commodified, or institutionalized. And yet, in *Psychoraag* it is everyday experiences of linguistic and cultural difference—and surrender to them—that hold the key to an open, expansive vision of Scottish belonging.

A devolved nation within the wider United Kingdom, with a highly visible resurgent nationalist politics, evident in the current dominance of the Scottish National Party (SNP) within the Scottish Parliament even after the recent (2014) referendum vote against full Scottish political independence, Scotland's politics, including its language politics, could be argued to be oriented primarily in relation to the dominance of England and English. The Gaelic and Scots languages, with their histories of marginalization, suppression, and survival, serve in certain forms of Scottish cultural nationalism both as 'native' symbols of Scottish exceptionalism, and as markers of Scotland's history of colonial oppression and resistance. Postcolonial theory has, since the 1980s, served as a key tool for interpreting the unequal power relations between England and Scotland.[8] Yet at the same time, as Graeme Macdonald has argued,

Scottish colonial history has also had to take account of "the role of Scots and Scotland in the British empire"—from providing the economic theories and moral and philosophical reasoning which underpinned and legitimized it, to the machinery and personnel which helped it to run— and of the "duplicitous, conflicting status of Scotland as both (internal and external) colonising *and* colonised nation."[9] The unevenness and ambivalence of Scotland's relationship to colonialism and imperialism, to processes of dominance and subordination, persists into the present. Tom Nairn argues in "Break Up: Twenty-Five Years On," that as Britain has become a "new type of colony" in relation to the US, so Scotland has become "the subordinate [...] of a subordinate state." In Nairn's analysis, Scotland's only means of escape from "self-colonization" is to find ways to define itself beyond Britain's ambit.[10] At odds with atavistic kinds of cultural nationalism, rooted in invocations of blood-and-soil Scottishness—with their language–political correlates in certain kinds of Scottish linguistic 'authenticity'—stand remodelled, civic ideas of Scottish belonging that stress diversity and inclusivity, at least in theory, and internationalism.[11]

It is by now almost a commonplace that in the vacuum of political self-determination, literature and the arts provided a space for the imagining of the diverse cultural meanings and coordinates of 'Scottishness,' in which the creative and political potentialities of Scotland's distinctive linguistic diversity have occupied a vital place.[12] Following Scotland's devolution from Britain in the late 1990s, the "reconstruction of a national literary field" saw Scots and Gaelic as well as English occupy a significant place in the resurgent institutions of Scottish national literature: in independent publishing, academic production, literary festivals, and prizes.[13] Rural Scots and Gaelic carry associations of historical cultural purity, prized within certain kinds of nationalist discourse. Nevertheless, it is textual representations of urban working-class Scots speech—forms of language associated with economic and social deprivation, and long stigmatized—which have come, in the writing of Tom Leonard, James Kelman, or Irvine Welsh, to serve as markers of Scottish distinctiveness from England and its dominant literary conventions, as well as conduits for often highly self-conscious, resistant engagements with the politics of language, class, and nation.[14] In an interview from 1985, Kelman describes the underlying language–political assumptions of Standard English narration as

> a wee game going on between reader and writer and the wee game is 'Reader and writer are the same' and they speak in the same voice as the narrative, and they're unlike these fucking natives who do the dialogue in phonetics [...]. In other words, the person who speaks is not as [...] intellectually aware as the writer or reader.[15]

Kelman's assessment of the language politics of the English literary establishment was amply borne out in English journalist Simon Jenkins' notoriously vicious response to the former's 1994 Booker Prize-winning novel *How Late It Was, How Late*, with its Scots vernacular narration. In an article in *The Times*, Jenkins accused Kelman of "literary vandalism," and likened the experience of reading his novel to being accosted on a train by an aggressive Scottish drunk:

> My reeking companion demanded attention like a two-year-old. He told me his so-called life story, requested money with menaces, swore and eventually relieved himself into the seat.[16]

Thus there is a strongly resistant, radical dimension to the central role played by varieties of urban Scots, exploiting "the interplay between the traditions of written English and the orality of working-class Scots speech," in contemporary Scottish fiction.[17] At the same time, Kirstin Innes rightly suggests, there is a problem with the way that this kind of literary language—influenced in particular by the runaway success of Irvine Welsh's 1993 novel *Trainspotting*, "the most widely global-ised representation of contemporary Scottishness," with its distinctive working-class Edinburgh vernacular—has become "standardized as *the* authentic Scottish voice."[18] As Innes argues, *Trainspotting* is in fact concerned not only with the politics of language and class, but with how its protagonist Renton is "continually pulled back by the implicit codes of the language he speaks": a language whose speakers' sense of marginalization and disenfranchisement on grounds of nation and class is displaced through references to "poofs," "pakis," and "cunts." Nevertheless its effect, paradoxically, has been to help to entrench these codes as the literary hallmarks of a raw, genuine Scottishness.[19] This priz-ing of a particular vision of 'authenticity' in Scottish writing as white, working-class, masculine, androcentric, speaking a language punctu-ated not only with obscenities but also, certainly in the case of Welsh and his imitators, the lexis of homophobia, misogyny, and racism, works to the obvious exclusion of other voices that might signal a more open and capacious Scottishness. Berthold Schoene, for one, also points out the irony that "these days globalisation might actually come in the guise of the kind of bestselling Scottish writing most fêted for its local authen-ticity."[20] Alongside the 'tartan warrior' *Braveheart* vision of history, *Trainspotting* and its iconic 1996 Danny Boyle-directed film adaptation (the film's supposedly impenetrable Edinburgh Scots dialogue subtitled for US audiences) have come to dominate as globally marketed visions of the Scottish 'local.'

Yet a more inclusive, 'postethnic' Scottishness, which Schoene suggests emphasizes "voluntary over involuntary affiliations, balances an ap-preciation for communities of descent with a determination to make room for new communities, and promotes solidarities of wide scope that incorporate people with different ethnic and racial backgrounds," may equally be imagined through language.[21] James Kelman has argued that the inherently polyglot nature of urban Scots (in his case, Glasgow Scots) makes it not a pure, autochthonous marker of Scottish exceptionalism,[22] but quite the opposite: irreducibly plural, equally local and global in its orientations, and not so much uniquely 'Glaswegian' as a metonym of late-modern urban experience.

> There is nothing about the language used by folk in and around Glasgow [...] that makes it generally distinct from any other city in the sense that it is a language composed of all sorts of particular influences, the usual industrial or post industrial situation where different cultures have intermingled for a great number of years. In the case of my own family we fit neatly into the pattern, one grandparent was a Gaelic speaker from Lewis, another was from a non-Gaelic speaking family in Dalmally [...] My wife is Welsh, but her people are Irish and Irish Canadian stock including some whose first language is French. All of these are at play in my work, as filtered in through my own perspective that, okay, is Glaswegian, but in these terms 'Glaswegian' is a late twentieth century construct.[23]

For Kelman, Glasgow Scots is always-already multiple, both rural and urban, national and transnational. As such, it stands for a roomy vision of Scottishness, whose inherent linguistic pluralism resists, even as it is sometimes invoked to shore up, hegemonic or cultural nationalist visions of the nation. Indeed, it is notable that Kelman's models for his experiments with vernacular literary language, and his consciousness of the relationship between language and power, come from postcolonial as well as Scottish writing; in particular, the 'rotten English' narrative experiments of Nigerian novelist, poet, and activist Ken Saro-Wiwa, as well as the earlier, ground-breaking work of Amos Tutuola.[24] Scotland's current Makar or poet laureate, the Glasgow-raised black Scottish poet and novelist Jackie Kay, has also written of how the Scots language provides a "flexibly suggestive political resource."[25] In her poem "Where it Hurts," Kay uses the expressive power of Scots as the starting point for reflection on densely interconnected global histories of marginalization, poverty, material suffering, and violence, and their relationship to linguistic disenfranchisement.[26] Poet, playwright, and multimedia artist Raman Mundair, who was born in India and grew up in Manchester in northern England before moving to Scotland, has also written extensively in Shetlands Scots, reflecting on her own status as a Shetlands "incomer" and her relationship to and love for a form of language which she associates closely in her poetry with the islands' distinctive landscape.[27] Both Kay's and Mundair's poetry reflects an investment in the relationship of varieties of Scots language to particular histories, landscapes, and social contexts, alongside a belief in its mutability and openness, in relation to a sense of Scottishness which might prove under pressure to be similarly inclusive.

In an essay titled "Being Scottish," Suhayl Saadi argues for just such a vision of Scottishness, which "mistrust[s] walls, stridency and final definitions" in favour of "all things polyglot, musical and oceanic":

> I celluloid my forehead and hastily scribble: SCOTTISH. But that is inadequate, so I add: English, British, Pakistani, Indian, Afghan, Sadozai, Asian, European, Black (-ish), Minority Ethnic, Male, Non-resident, 21st Century person, 15th Century being, Glaswegian, middle-class, Writer, Seeker, Lover, Physician, Agha Jaan, Son, English-speaking, Music-loving, Left-leaning...until I run out of space and time and ink. Scottishness becomes a metaphor through which I perceive other things.[28]

In another essay, "Infinite Diversity in New Scottish Writing," Saadi emphasizes 'diversity' as a longstanding and defining characteristic of Scottish literature, inflected both by Scotland's internal heterogeneity, and global processes of cultural exchange that also recall its long relationship to empire. At the same time, he underlines the particular contexts—social, creative, and material—that are necessary for the entry of certain *kinds* of 'diversity' into literature. He describes, for example, his own founding of the Pollokshields Writing Group for ethnic minority writers in the predominantly working-class Pollokshields area of Glasgow. He also discusses the publishing initiative New Writing Scotland, which provides support for Gaelic, Scots, and minority ethnic writers, with a policy of "maximum inclusiveness."[29] Here and elsewhere, Saadi is concerned to lay bare the mechanisms by which writing gets written and published: the role of arts funding, arts councils, publishers, university curricula, and critics, in shaping the field of literature. In particular, he has written scathingly of the literary market dominance of what he terms "safe multiculturalism": novels with "Orientalist covers—a sari-clad henna-daubed Indian woman pirouetting on a pyramid of spices," in which a thrilling but ultimately safe sense of "difference"—including linguistic difference, through an exotic scattering of foreign words—does not trouble the stability of "normative absolutes."[30]

Saadi's own poetry, prose, and short stories have been published by independent Scottish publishers or in online forums, and he has written of his difficulties in finding publishers for his more linguistically experimental work.[31] *Psychoraag*, dwelling on the politics, practices, and affective experience of language diversity in Glasgow's Pakistani community, is largely written on a continuum between Standard Scottish English and Glaswegian Scots. In addition, the novel performs a more pyrotechnic multilingualism, incorporating not only Urdu lexis, but also fragments of multiple other languages, different font sizes and styles, fragments of Arabic script, capitalization, upside-down text, right-left reversal of English words, as well as images and fragments of maps. Saadi recounts how an anonymous reader for a UK publisher reported of *Psychoraag* that "the use of unusual words and foreign words is a difficulty" and "they seem to be drawn from such a broad range of languages and traditions that their impact and meaning became lost." Of this, he remarks sardonically:

> Signalling acute (partly sexual) anxiety at the dissolution of old boundaries, this kind of response is no less than fundamentalist monocultural rearguard action disguised as a sensible plea for decorum and aptitude.[32]

In fact, laudatory reviews in the Scottish press particularly emphasized the novel's polyphony, as well as its distinctive Scottish–Asian perspective. In reviews used in the novel's cover blurbs, *Scotland on Sunday* describes how in *Psychoraag* "Glasgow is made simultaneously strange and familiar [...] Saadi's imagination has produced a novel as polyglot [...] pacey and audacious as the city itself." The *Scotsman* describes it as "the first-ever Asian-Scottish novel." Placing the novel into a particular comparative frame, both Scottish and Asian, of vernacular writing and linguistic experimentalism, the *Sunday Herald* calls the novel "not just *Midnight's Children*-meets-*Trainspotting*, because Saadi is more thoughtful than Welsh or Rushdie."[33]

Psychoraag is set in an Asian community radio station in Glasgow, Radio Chaandi (moonlight radio), on its final night on air. It follows Zaf, the station's night-shift DJ, through the last-ever broadcast of his *Junuune Show* (*junuune* meaning "madness, a trance-like state" according to the novel's glossary (425); in Urdu, Hindi, Arabic, and Persian), from midnight to 6 a.m. Zaf's on-air persona is flamboyantly multilingual, mixing Glaswegian Scots and English with a plethora of fragments of other languages; while the novel's free indirect narration also tacks between English and Glaswegian Scots, with a scattering of languages including Urdu, Punjabi, Gaelic, and Arabic. The night's hour-by-hour progression is followed chapter-by-chapter, and through Zaf's music playlist; yet both the narrative's linear order and the sequencing of Zaf's playlist are subject to disruption and doubling throughout the long night of the novel. The narrative travels analeptically to tell the story of Zaf's parents' illicit love affair in Lahore, Pakistan in the late 1950s, and their subsequent journey to Glasgow. It is also disrupted by Zaf's own memories, of his parents and his childhood, but particularly of his relationships—on the one hand, with his current partner Babs, pale, blonde, Galloway-born, and "bona fide Scottish, blue and white down to the marrow" (30); and on the other, recalling his Glaswegian-Pakistani ex-girlfriend Zilla and her descent into heroin addiction. The narrative mimics, at times, the psychically disordering effects of absinthe and heroin, both of which Zaf (probably) ingests over the course of the night. Midway through, it splits into two distinct, hallucinatory, parallel narrative realities: one version of Zaf remaining within the confines of the radio station DJ booth, the other journeying out into the city at night. The novel probes the operations and disjunctures of race, class, national, and transnational belonging, and it explores these themes not least through a disorientating narrative of linguistic, sensory, and experiential breakdown and recombination.

In view of the novel's emphasis on polyglot disorientation and undecidability, it is worth noting Saadi's, perhaps surprising, typographic concession to his eventual publisher, the independent Edinburgh-based Chroma, who insisted on the italicizing of 'foreign' words in the text—words from languages other than English, Scots, and Gaelic.[34] Thus romanized Urdu, Punjabi, Arabic, and so forth are italicized, while switches between English and Scots or Gaelic remain typographically unmarked. Saadi has indicated his initial resistance to this strategy, the obvious effect of which is to mark a visible separation between endogamous/exogamous or Scottish/foreign—precisely the kind of distinction which, at the level of narrative, the novel works hard to unpick.[35] In the novel's extensive glossary, this distinction is at least partly undone: alphabetically arranged, incorporating words and phrases from Scots and Gaelic in amongst Urdu, Punjabi, Arabic, French, Mexican Spanish, and others, Saadi's glossary suggests resonances and homophonies between them, a heterogeneous collation of global language. Nevertheless, as Saadi himself has acknowledged, the inclusion of a glossary also risks being read as a "regressive linguistic-political statement," as modelling a relationship both of difference and of simple lexical equivalence between 'native' and 'foreign,' and in terms of what it thereby suggests about the status of a multilingual text and the strategies required to read one.[36] However, *Psychoraag* includes a series of appendices—not only the glossary, but also a playlist and a discography—each of which offers a different hermeneutic frame to make sense of the novel's fragmented narrative, and each of which could be said to raise as many questions as it answers. The playlist reassembles the sequence of music Zaf plays over the course of the night, which becomes increasingly obscure both to the reader and Zaf himself as the novel progresses. Yet its chronological sequencing, following the forward temporal motion of the narrative, has no way to account for its complex analepses and narrative doubling. The alphabetized discography gives the impression of flicking through Zaf's CD collection, yet shorn of any sense of the complex connections and associations that govern his relationship to the music it contains. And the glossary, while it offers a superficial sense of 'translatability' to the narrative, is also a multivalent text demanding interpretation in its own right. As Saadi himself has argued,

> the glossary in *Psychoraag* represents both a hypertextual, etymological exposition and a creative deviance from the psychological intensity of the narrative itself. For example, *hijaab*, the Arabic word for a woman's headscarf (but metaphysically speaking also the term for a protective spiritual 'covering') sits next to *hijerah*, the Urdu word for 'transvestite.' Similarly, *khotay ka lun* (Punjabi for 'you're a donkey's prick') nestles up alongside *Khuda hafez*, which is Persian/Urdu for 'God go with you,' and *khuserah*, the Urdu term for 'effeminate homosexual.' I did not intend to be outrageous; these juxtapositions are alphabetical and I have picked them at random. None the less, the effect is subversive and egalitarian: *Psychoraag* becomes an homage to the work of Diderot's encyclopedists.[37]

Saadi here presents *Psychoraag*'s glossary as a creative endeavour in its own right. Both diverting from and reflecting on the narrative itself, it beckons the reader into a backwards-and-forwards movement between main narrative and translational paratext, with new meanings being created through relations both of "exposition" and "deviance" between them. He paints the glossary as a heterogeneous and "egalitarian" space of intimate juxtaposition and homophonic "nestling," likened to "the work of Diderot's encyclopedists"—recalling Diderot's encyclopaedia not least in its refusal of the distinction between sacred and secular.[38] The examples Saadi chooses are obviously salient: reinstituting nuance to the Arabic "*hijaab*," so commonly reduced in mainstream British discourses on Islam; while at the same time provocatively underscoring a phonological similarity (and perhaps implying a ghostly etymological connection) to "*hijerah*." Other neighbouring pairs make equally interesting connections: Ali Smith, for example, in a review article in *The Guardian*, notes the juxtaposition of "Gaidhealtachd" and "Ganga Jumna."[39] And yet the glossary also raises discomforting questions. For one thing, how these words "nestle up alongside" each other, and seem to resemble one another, is itself a function of the glossary's romanization and its imposition of the Latin alphabet as an organizing principle. The invocation of Diderot also recalls the relationship of European Enlightenment thought to racial theories (not least, in the hands of Scottish Enlightenment philosophers) underpinning slavery and empire, which the encyclopaedists' celebratory eclecticism did nothing to challenge. Thus the construction and ordering of knowledge, even in the seemingly "subversive and egalitarian" space of *Psychoraag*'s glossary, should always be subject to scrutiny. Equally, as Saadi suggests in his glossing of "*khuserah*" as "the Urdu term for 'effeminate homosexual,'" *all* languages, not only English, can be tools of oppression.

Psychoraag's Glasgow is, and has always been, a multilingual city, where the contemporary sounds of Glaswegian Scots, English, Urdu, Punjabi, Gujarati, Kashmiri, Swahili, and Pashto (60) are continuous with the ghostly polyphonic voices of the city's past. It is "haunted," not just by dominant, Scottish nationalist versions of its past—"the Young Pretender and all that," "Rabbie Burns"—but by the empire that built the city, global from the start: the "Tobacco Barons" (21), the "great sailin ships which had been built by the bonnie banks of the Clyde" (199), and "the sound of marchin boots. The 70 wars of the British Empire which had been fought with Scottish soldiery in the van" (21). Listening to the city, Zaf hears long-ago Irish Gaelic songs of the navvies who built much of Glasgow, which "still slunk about the walls—they had been intoned so often in strange, polyphonic choruses that their notes had become inspissated into the grains" (271), and the voices of Jewish immigrants, with their "fading, twirling mazurkas" (233). Reversing Herderian romantic nationalist models of language as an emanation of a specific place and landscape, Zaf imagines languages becoming "inspissated" where they are spoken, their words and rhythms embedding in and altering the city's very material fabric. Saadi's Glasgow is multi-voiced, imagined via the polyphonic crackle of radio transmission; as Zaf observes, "the whole thing wis one big hi-fi system" (75). Both transmitter and receiver in global flows of language, the city's multilingualism is at the same time highly localized. In the language of the Scottish-Pakistani "Kinnin Park Boys," for example—a gang of violent criminals and savvy entrepreneurs, whose fathers took over from the Kinning Park area's Protestant sectarian "Orange gangs" in the 1980s—are embedded the unacknowledged, transnational histories of working-class experience:

> They were the sons and grandsons ae the *kisaan* who had powered the buses, the underground trains, the machines of the sweatshop underwear-manufacturers. [...] [T]hey had clothed the lily-white bodies of whole generations of Scots and then, later, they had filled their stomachs too. You eat what you are. If that was the case, then Glasgae wis Faisalabad a hundred times over. But their sons and daughters had gone in the opposite direction and become Scots. Right down to their gangs and their dancin and their chip-bhatti *sahib* footba tops, they had sipped of the waters of the Clyde and had become cold killers. And they were swearin at him and Ruby in a mixture of Glaswegian and Faisalabadi.

> "*Maa di pudhi!*"
> "Fuckin *gandu!*"
> "Oh, *chholae!*"
> "*Teri maa di lun!*"

> (242–3)

The history of Glasgow's transformation through Pakistani culture is quite literally submerged here—underground, beneath Glaswegians' clothes and in their bellies, while, in an equally unacknowledged set of processes, Pakistani culture has been remade through the filter of Glaswegianness. Along the way, two working-class urban speech forms, Glaswegian Scots, and Faisalabad-inflected Urdu, have been transnationally recombined, together with "stock phrases" from "East Coast gangsta" culture and American films (253). The outcome, however, is no kind of liberating hybridity, but a hyper-masculine vernacular in which the oppressive codes of an implicitly Irvine Welsh-esque localized white working-class urban Scots—that of the "Orange gangs" of Kinning Park—are spliced with Urdu homophobic and misogynistic obscenities, and the "stock phrases" of an implicitly violent, sexist, commodified "East Coast gangsta" culture. Thus, for all its heterogeneous, apparently improvisatory form, this is a language that combines codes which are equally regressive in compensating for marginalization through an aggressive masculinity, and which offer a brutal riposte to any easy celebratory account of hybridity as necessarily progressive.

Zaf, himself Glasgow-born, has "never learned his own mother tongue," Punjabi: "not properly so that he would have been able to converse in it, to construct meanin from chaos" (246). His parents, speaking Punjabi between themselves, used English with him "except when they were angry or upset or when they had forgotten" (162). The living antithesis of the supposedly linguistically unified, self-identical speaking subject, fully 'at home' neither in English nor in Punjabi, he articulates his own self-understanding through the motif of musical sampling:

> He liked samples, felt comfortable with them. He was a sample of Pakistan, thrown at random into Scotland, into its myths. And, in Lahore, he had felt like a sample of Glasgow [...].
>
> (227)

At a willed level, Zaf's is a playful linguistic polymorphism: languages are resources from which he is free to sample at will, and he self-consciously opposes monologisms of all kinds, whether the supposedly unassailable purity of 'Standard English,' the hermeticism of certain strands of Scots nationalism, or the "people who live in *halaal* universes" as means to stave off the fear of change (199). In his on-air radio persona, calling himself "the man ae a thoosand tongues," he greets his listeners in a plethora of languages:

> Hi there, *samaeen. Sat sri akaal, namaste ji, salaam alaikum. Bonjour, Buongiorno, Subax wanaagsan, Nee-haa, Günaydin, Buenos días, Dobro jutro, Làbas rytas, Bom dia, Mirëmëngjes, Guten morgen, Maidin mhaith dhuit, Molo, Boker tov, Shubh subah, Kalai vanakkam, Go Eun A Chim.* Hiya in fifty thousand

tongues! Zero wan five or five meenuts past wan. Bet ye thought Ah wis skimmin doon a phrase book. But, naw, you'd be wrong. Ah've goat loads ae tongues in ma heid—thu're aw there, wagglin away, almost singin. A babble.

(66)

Zaf's multilingual performance here is characteristically ambivalent. On the one hand, branching out from Punjabi, Hindi, and Arabic, he offers greetings in the languages of the city's immigrant communities old and new, from Hebrew to Somali, Irish to Albanian, beaming out a sound-sample of polyglot Glasgow over the airwaves, which, he tells his listeners, corresponds to the "babble" of the "tongues in ma heid." On the other, Zaf's "fifty thousand tongues" represent a superficial multilingualism that can progress no further than saying "hiya": a market-friendly, unthreatening performance of Glasgow's inclusivity. It is, in this sense, cut from much the same cloth as the rumoured new "'Commonwealth Tartan' that anyone could wear, a pretty blue-and-white woollen skin to wrap around yourself at football matches" (109). His radio persona both ironizes and at times partakes in this kind of superficial, self-congratulatory 'multiculturalism.'

Zaf revels in the flamboyant performativity of his on-air multilingualism and draws attention to its commodified artificiality: "Hey, wu're multilingual oan this station," he tells his listeners: "Polyethylene ethnic" (384). Even his on-air Glaswegian Scots is not strictly 'authentic': he slips into and out of it, adopting it as part of his radio performance. He is playfully neologistic: "Farangoid" (170), he portmanteau-terms his lifestyle, which is too much like that of a farangi/white man to please his mother; he provocatively coins the hybrid "Wahabi Calvinist" (58) to denote a mindset antithetical to the idea of hybridity.[40] Yet Zaf's carefully curated multilingualism is not always fully under his control, and even at times threatens its own dissolution. When he announces "Ah'm Zaf-Zaf-Zaf and Ah'm yer ghost. Host, Ah mean, host" (60), the partial erasure of "host" by "ghost" lends a spectral flimsiness to his exuberant on-air persona. Later, drunk on absinthe, his English words begin a kind of disorderly breakdown: "I just felt a bit faint. Must be that drink. That buggery blue stuff—green, I mean. Mean I green. Whatever" (260). While his omnivorous language practices serve to disrupt apparent distinctions between authenticity and artifice, they are not straightforwardly either playful or progressive. His use of Glaswegian Scots, for example, is a marker of solidarity with his listeners, but it is also a protectively self-ironizing performance that is kept carefully separate from the rest of his linguistic praxis. Off-air, Glaswegian is a source of shame to him: inadvertently slipping "intae a broad Glaswegian," he immediately feels "like kickin himself in the shins" (70). Later he admonishes himself, "Get yerself thegether! Get yourself together, straighten out your words, down among the lush chords" (104–105): in Zaf's mind the 'straight' words, the proper words, are still English. His internalized prejudices about race, as well as class, emerge in language. At one point, on air, he is tempted to use a "fake Indian accent" (132); later, listening to his mother's Punjabi English, he finds "he had constantly to resist the temptation to stereotype" her (274). Zaf's internalized linguistic racism reveals his upbringing in a late twentieth-century Britain in which, as I have discussed elsewhere, the racist mimicry of using a "fake In-dian accent" was part of the cultural mainstream in film, television, and radio comedy, and central to the construction of the meanings of "Asianness" within the dominant culture.[41] This is further complicated by Zaf's sense of the voicelessness of Pakistanis within Scotland and more widely in Britain, in which Pakistan is not only seen "completely differently" from the rest of Asia (notably, from India) but "most of the time, it wasn't seen at all." It is "perceived as bein a repository of the dirty, the oppressed, the smelly, the cunning and the inscrutable," its people "pictured as nameless, liquid hordes that would pour in" (73). Above all, "Pakistanis had remained completely inaudible. They had no music, no voice, no breath" (74). A projection of this vision of Paki-stan and Pakistanis can be seen in Zaf's negatively distorted and often highly racialized and sexualized view of his ex-girlfriend Zilla: "like a tree charred black by lightning," she "could've been an *Asian Babe* if she'd wanted but she'd had other demons to ride" (90). Zilla is a silenced presence: as Pittin-Hedon notes, she is "a figure of the suppressed, in-audible voice" (91), whose final emergence into the narrative, in a vio-lent, hallucinatory sex scene, "provokes an explosion of language, which scatters words on the page as so much shrapnel."[42] By contrast, Zaf sees his white Scottish girlfriend Babs as embodying a full relationship between language and subjectivity: she "never had to think before she felt, before she spoke. The words just came out like a river—clear and rushin and confident. He envied that" (12). He associates Babs with a romanticized, apparently authentic Scottishness rooted in language and land, with "clarsach spaces and bodhrán mountains, unchangin in their unimaginable antiquity" (31).

In *Psychoraag*, multilingualisms of all kinds, whether official or un-official, national or transnational, part of literary discourse or the lived everyday, must be probed for their politics. No kind of language practice has a given and self-evident value, and Saadi reserves a particular sus-picion for what the novel casts as superficial, commodified, or exoticist celebrations of 'diversity.' Meanwhile, it is largely at the levels of analogy and metaphor that the novel explores more radical possibilities of linguis-tic recombination and connectivity—in particular, through the practices and formal properties of music. Sampling is a governing metaphor in the novel, in which recorded sound, like language, is approached not as one integrated whole but as a sequence of disarticulable components subject to appropriation, layering, and recontextualization. Sampling, as a fragment of one sound recording is repurposed into another, both plays on and self-consciously distorts its 'original' signification. Sampling in the novel stands for the never-authentic, for identities fragmenting, travelling, and recombining in a postcolonial, globalized reality. In musical terms, as Russell Potter puts it, sampling makes sounds "anything but what they were," replicating "a ghostly aurality" that at the same time makes the sound signify in new ways, as "an element in a far more complex discursive structure."[43] This is true, too, of the musical technique of counterpoint, which is a structuring principle of the novel as a whole: counterpoint refers to the polyphonic relationship between voices that differ from each other rhythmically and melodically, while working together harmonically, combining into a whole distinct from, and greater than, the sum of their parts. Both sampling and counterpoint stand as metaphors for language as unstable and non-linear, subject to constant, improvisatory recombination into new forms.

Over the course of one long, hot summer's night, Zaf plays an eclectic mix of vocal tracks, with an emphasis on unexpected fusions and connections, and spanning "the whole of recording history" (5). He begins with the 1990s British–Asian political electronica of Asian Dub Foundation, going on to play everything from 1960s American psychedelic folk to the Beatles and the Yardbirds, to Scottish folk and Glaswegian indie rock, to Bollywood playback artists, to Algerian raï, back to the earliest, turn-of-the-twentieth-century recordings of Indian *tawaïf* singers. While on the one hand, the novel's playlist and discography give chronological and alphabetical order respectively to its musical contents, Saadi's narrative itself is just as concerned with the distorting, disruptive, space-annihilating, time-bending properties of sound recording, playback, and broadcast technology. Sometimes tracks blend into one another, overlap, or emerge in multiple versions; at certain moments, it becomes unclear whether they are playing forwards or backwards. Music and language provide extensions of one another in the novel's insistently heteroglot exploration of the power of fragmentation and recombination.

The novel's interest in fragmentation and recombination over notions of purity and wholeness play out, too, in typographic and visual–textual experimentation and bricolage. These strategies disrupt the apparent linear transparency of the novel's text and, specifically, they seem to offer a fleeting equivalence in the English text to the experience of multilingual disruption—for example in right-left reversal which makes English conform to the directionality of written Arabic or Hebrew. The obvious association of these typographic techniques to the methods and concerns of Euro-American modernism is evident, and self-consciously so. At one point, for example, Zaf plays Stravinsky's *Rite of Spring*, a piece of music associated more than any other with high European modernism. The music is apt, in a section of the novel that concerns itself with women's sacrifice, but the reference is oblique: Zaf himself cannot remember what the piece is called, never mind what it is about (although readers can consult the playlist at the back of the book and find out). Instead, he improvises an audaciously appropriative title, calling the piece "Ode to my Father" (283):

> It wis classical—Western classical. Some kind of polytonal thing. Modern. Well, not more than a hundred years old, at most. That wis modern. [...] The swirlin wind produced by the instruments would have been strong enough to have blown the iron needle right out of its groove, even the strongest of the dancers off the stage, the night clean out of its time.
>
> (282)

Zaf's response to the power of the music captures its sense of 'newness' anew, extracted from its longstanding modernist associations, while at the same time sampling, in the word "iron," T.S. Eliot's famous review of the *Rite*:

> [I]t did seem to transform the rhythm of the steppes into the scream of the motor horn, the rattle of machinery, the grind of wheels, the beating of iron and steel, the roar of the underground railway, and the other barbaric cries of modern life; and to transform these de-spairing noises into music.[44]

Euro-American modernism, in other words, is subject to the kind of improvisation and recombination signalled by the *raag* of the novel's title, a South Asian musical form distinguished, as the glossary defines it, by the "interplay of prescribed melodic movement and on-the-spot composition" (428). European modernism's polyphonic models provide important intertexts for *Psychoraag*'s multilingualism—the novel repeatedly evokes James Joyce, in particular *Ulysses*—but only as part of a constellation of works of multilingual art to which it responds. For example, the early Calcutta sound recordings of Armenian-Indian *tawaif* singer Gauhar Jan:

> The impossibly distant and yet somehow knowing voice of Gauhar Jan, singer-songwriter and polylingual diva, lasered out from Deck A, through the twisted metal of the Radio Chaandni Community Asian Radio Station, out into the cracks of the dawn and beyond. 'Bhairavi.' The vocal cords of Erevan transplanted to Kolkata and the brass horns and thick wax of the Gramophone and Typewriter Company.
> [...]

It seemed as though the words were issuin from several of Gauhar Jan's eleven languages at once. But, more than that, the singin style wis archaic, open throated, somethin from the deep past that lay beyond livin memory. Voices which only the insane could hear, issuin from the trees. Voices strainin with the bonded freedom of words and convention. Wild voices.

(345–6)

Zaf hears in Gauhar Jan's singing voice something which crosses both time and space and goes beyond sense or signification. The song is incomprehensible to Zaf not because it is not linguistic, but because it represents an excess of language—"several of Gauhar Jan's eleven languages at once"—in which meaning appears to be transcended by the voice as sound. Polyphonic and plurilingual to the point of incomprehensibility, it is singing which, to use Mladen Dolar's terms,

brings the voice energetically to the forefront, on purpose, at the expense of meaning. [...] Singing takes the distraction of voice seriously, and turns the tables on the signifier; it reverses the hierarchy—let the voice take the upper hand, let the voice be the bearer of what cannot be expressed by words.[45]

In Zaf's interpretation, this voice appears to be able to go beyond language, to travel in time and space, to cross the boundaries between human and non-human nature, even if this transcendence is ultimately illusory. As he himself acknowledges, voice may "strain" for freedom but ultimately remains "bonded" to language.[46]

What is significant is not only the sound of Gauhar Jan's "wild voices" themselves, but their survival and reproducibility, through the material processes of sound recording and reproduction, from "brass horns and thick wax" to laser disc, and the capacity of radio broadcasting to transmit them, a century after their recording and thousands of miles away, "out into the cracks of the dawn and beyond." Radio transmission is capable, in the novel, of crossing distances of time as well as space: voices of the past cross over with songs yet to be played. Across the airwaves, sounds meld, distort, and recombine, while at the same time, it is often implied, none ever truly disappear:

Well, let me ask ye this: Whit happens tae a particular wavelength aifter a radio station hus stopped usin it? Where dae aw the wurds go? Eh? Does it jis fade away or does it refuse tae disappear? Does it grab the invisible air an take oan a life ae its ane so that, even aifter the radio station's door hus been closed an bolted, the voice goes oan?

(378)

In such endless, multidirectional flows, relations of speaker and addressee, transmitter and receiver are not straightforward. Zaf, hearing his own voice "falling deep into the night," "over the airwaves, spiralling into the darkness of space" (8), wonders whether anyone is actually listening; at other times, he fantasizes about reversing the direction of flow: "Ah'll put my ear up tae the mike. Don't all answer at wance" (2). Voices transmitted via the radio may be lost to static, and tuning to a particular frequency easily slips. As the narrative travels analeptically to the moment of Zaf's parents' first meeting in 1950s Lahore, a radio emits a sub-audible hum in the background:

> Over in one corner, in the window recess, the Bakelite volume control on a wooden radio had been turned down just after he arrived. But, though it had not been switched off, it seemed to have lost its tuning because he was sure that, underneath everything, he could make out the low, dissonant sound of static.
>
> (51–2)

Right at the end of the novel, the same old valve radio sits in Zaf's father's hospital room:

> [Zaf] tried again and, this time, the set began to emit a low-pitched hum. A faint green light began to glow from behind the glass of the frontage, began to illuminate the tables that ran vertically over its surface and which delineated the frequency wavebands all the way from Thirteen Meters to Long Wave, from the Light Programme to Tangier to Kalundberg, Ankara, Tel Aviv, Tehran, and then back again to the Third Programme. And, unmarked, somewhere out over the dark ocean, the remembered voices of Lahore, Karachi, Delhi, Agra. Most of the stations on Jamil Ayaan's radio were long defunct and the wavelengths, which they once had occupied, were now filled with the bark and chatter, the strange burzakh hyper-speak of the disc jockeys with their rhythm-heavy fanfares.
>
> (418)

This radio stands both for lost communication, and for the possibility of its coming into being. The sound of static is "dissonant": lacking musicality, made up of multiple, discordant sub-sounds. It is unsettling, unmelodious, and without meaning; yet it also signifies an open channel along which a new signal may be transmitted. On the radio voices are lost, but may also be found. At the novel's end, finally, it is through the radio that Zaf seeks to communicate with his father, who is lost in dementia. Entering his father's disoriented linguistic realm, in which past and present merge and in which individuated selves lose their borders, he sings in his father's Punjabi and in the voice of his long-lost brother Qaisar:

> Zaf turned the volume up to full, pushed the fade switch back as far
> as it would go and then some. Leaned forwards into the microphone.
> Whispered. Sang. '*Haa ji*, Papa. Qaisar *hai*.'

(419)

These are the final words of Saadi's novel: we never discover whether
they reach their intended recipient. Amid *Psychoraag*'s hypertrophic
whirl of signs and patterns, of crisscrossing systems of meaning, it is in
fact never clear whether acts of communication are successful. At one
level, undoubtedly, the novel is driven by the urge to interpret, translate, make knowable, to complete the loop of communication—for example, through the relationship between main narrative and glossary.
In counterpoint, however, it suspends the circuits of communication:
voices circulate without being sure of reaching their hearers, or of being
understood if they do so. It also thereby, and perhaps more profoundly,
dramatizes a surrender to *unknowing*, to the *inability* to understand, as
a locus of a different kind of revelation. Thus, as Zaf plays the Algerian
raï of singer Chaba Fadela, for example, and attempts to continue with
annotating his increasingly illegible playlist,

> his writin resembled a hermeneutic form of shorthand, a kind of
> hidden Hebrew or mibbee a revealed Arabic. The syncopated
> quarter-tones of Chaba Fadela's voice cut in Kufic across the mornin,
> words transfigured from stone to music to air. It wis a duet with
> Cheb Sahraoui—a call-and-response thing—and, after a few bars,
> it became hard to distinguish between words and instrumentation
> so that the whole was like a flat-woven kilim or a rough woollen
> prayer rug. [...] And, somehow, this song, this risin, lyrical piece
> of raï, whose words Zaf had no hope of understandin, seemed to
> penetrate his brain, the muscles of his limbs, the lengthenin rubric
> of his bones, so that he felt, liftin inside him, the urge to dance or, at
> least, to move about, to do somethin purely physical. To abrogate his
> mind, his voice, and simply to lose himself in the Rif Berber fractals
> of the Maghrebian night.

(125–7)

The recording Zaf plays is, we should note, a commodity in a global
marketplace: Fadela's 1983 "N'sel Fik (You Are Mine)," sung with her
then-husband Cheb Sahraoui, was one of the first raï records to become
an international hit, via the Euro-American music industry's marketing
of so-called 'world music.' Thus, as for the majority of the track's audience as it travels globally, Zaf is a listener for whom the meaning of
its Arabic lyrics is inaccessible. Excluded from the song at the level of
linguistic signification, his experience—just as with Stravinsky's *Rite*—
dwells instead on its sounds, and the spiralling, ultimately uninterpretable

connections between systems of meaning which they convey to him. The textual "hermeneutic shorthand" of Hebrew and Arabic blends with the musical "syncopated quarter-tones" of Fadela's voice, whose words Zaf imagines as Kufic: an angular, calligraphic Arabic script, carved in stone, that is "transfigured" by her voice from "stone to music to air." Unable to understand the meaning of the words, to Zaf the human voices and instrumentation become indistinguishable parts of an acoustic field which, in turn, is likened to "a flat-woven kilim or a rough woollen prayer rug"—material objects which, in fact, also possess their own intricate systems of signification. Thus in this passage, *everything means*, from the carving of Kufic to the rubric of bones: inviting Zaf, and the reader, to an intricate decoding. Yet at the same time, their effect on Zaf is also the transcendence of meaning and a kind of sublime, synaesthetic surrender, abrogating "his mind, his voice" and calling him "simply to lose himself in the Rif Berber fractals of the Maghrebian night." This comes close, at least, to what Doris Sommer has characterized as the multilingual sublime: an experience of linguistic and cultural difference that is truly "foreign, even fearsome."[47] Moving beyond the fear or paralysis of being overwhelmed by difference, Sommer's sublime constitutes an ethical adjustment not only towards acceptance, but towards the pleasure of being unsettled by what one does not know or understand: a "disturbing sublime" which "offers more intense effects than does easily lovable beauty," and "offers a thrill of survival close to catharsis."[48] Such a move, Sommer argues, is a necessity under global capitalism, dependent on flows of migrant labour, yet haunted by "the fear of losing control, given the spectres of violence, scarce resources, or just clogged institutions." Facing the challenge, and the perceived threat, of difference and incomprehension, nevertheless Sommer argues that

> the enormity that makes any one of us feel small might look inviting, if we developed a taste for the sublime. On reflection, society would exceed any individual imagination; the complexities would excite awe and contemplation and our only partial understanding would safeguard the modesty that democracy depends on.[49]

In the end, *Psychoraag* refuses any absolute distinction between this kind of unsettling, vertiginous experience of the "multilingual" and its commodified, nationalist, instrumentalized, or institutionalized forms. The former can be experienced in the context of the latter: though the music, which provokes a sublime response in Zaf, has been commodified as "world music," he is still able to experience it in all of its unsettling, disturbing strangeness. Multilingualism's radical possibilities are not, therefore, exclusive to an elite and rarefied field of art, nor can they be kept pristine from the operations of capital. Linguistic diversity is fundamental, in the novel's imaginary, not only to the formation of individual subjectivity, nor to comprehending contemporary Glasgow, but also to an understanding of the world-system of which they are both products. In Glasgow, as synecdoche for urban late-modernity, forms of language mix and combine in a constellation of ways, while opening up new ways of making meaning for the "distinctly and intensely polyglot" late-modern urban subject.[50] In many ways, language becomes denaturalized in the process, or what Rey Chow calls "prostheticized": "whereupon even what feels like an inalienable interiority, such as the way one speaks is— dare I say it?—impermanent, detachable, and (ex)changeable."[51] Incomprehension and partial understanding become, increasingly, dimensions of everyday life. And so, too, does the corresponding experience of longing to interpret, to translate, to transcend barriers of language and to be able to understand, or say, everything. Thus in *Psychoraag*, for all of its scepticism, Saadi posits an open, expansive vision of Scottishness—and, by extension, of the global flows of contemporary language and culture, viewed from the 'semi-periphery' of Glasgow—that is routed through these conflicting and complementary processes, experiences, and urges; that is imagined through the experience of surrender to linguistic and cultural difference in the lived everyday.

Notes

1 On the formulation of "peripheral modernities" and Scotland's—specifically, Glasgow's—position therein, see Harry Harootunian, *History's Disquiet: Modernity, Cultural Practice, and the Question of Everyday Life* (New York: Columbia University Press, 2000), 62–3.
2 Suhayl Saadi, *Psychoraag* (Glasgow: Chroma, 2004). All subsequent references are to this edition and will be given in parentheses in the text.
3 Anna Battista, "Facts and Fictions: Interview with writer Suhayl Saadi," *Erasing Clouds*, www.erasingclouds.com/0714saadi.html.
4 Nick Mitchell, "Interview—Suhayl Saadi: *Psychoraag*," *Spike Magazine*, 1 April 2006, www.spikemagazine.com/0406-suhayl-saadi-psychoraag-interview.php.
5 Ali Smith, "Life Beyond the M25," *The Guardian*, 18 December 2004. Cited in Mitchell, "Interview."
6 Warwick Research Collective, *Combined and Uneven Development: Towards a New Theory of World-Literature* (Liverpool: Liverpool University Press, 2015), 17.
7 On the tendency to treat modernism as a phenomenon that radiates from metropolitan origins to implicitly belated and derivative colonial and post-colonial modernisms, see, for example, Warwick Research Collective, *Combined and Uneven Development*, 81–2.
8 See for example Berthold Schoene, "A Passage to Scotland: Scottish Literature and the British Postcolonial Condition," *Scotlands* 2 no. 1 (1995): 107–22; Michael Gardiner, "Democracy and Scottish Postcoloniality," *Scotlands* 3 no. 2 (1996): 24–41; Liam Connell, "Modes of Marginality: Scottish Literature and the Uses of Postcolonial Theory," *Comparative Studies of South Asia, Africa and the Middle East* 23 no. 1–2 (2003): 41–53; Graeme Macdonald, "Postcolonialism and Scottish Studies," *New Formations* 59 (2006): 115–31.

9 Macdonald, "Postcolonialism and Scottish Studies," 116–18.

10 Tom Nairn, *"Break-Up:* Twenty-Five Years On," in *Scotland in Theory,* ed. Eleanor Bell and Gavin Miller (Amsterdam and Philadelphia, PA: Rodopi, 2004), 17–34.

11 For example, the Scottish Government's current "race equality campaign," as part of their *One Scotland* initiative, aiming to promote an inclusive civic vision of Scottishness, Onescotland.org.

12 Cairns Craig, "Scotland and Hybridity," in *Beyond Scotland: New Contexts for Twentieth-Century Scottish Literature,* ed. Gerard Carruthers, David Goldie and Alastair Renfrew (Amsterdam: Rodopi, 2004), 234. The founding critical text in many respects is Robert Crawford, *Devolving English Literature* (Oxford: Clarendon, 1992).

13 Macdonald, "Postcolonialism and Scottish Studies," 122. See also Johann Wolfgang Unger, *The Discursive Construction of the Scots Language: Language, Education, Politics and Everyday Life* (Amsterdam and Philadelphia, PA: John Benjamins, 2013), 17.

14 Cairns Craig, *The Modern Scottish Novel: Narrative and National Imagination* (Edinburgh: Edinburgh University Press, 1999), chapter 5.

15 Duncan McLean, "James Kelman interviewed," *Edinburgh Review* 71 (1985): 64–80. See Macdonald, "Postcolonialism and Scottish Studies"; Ellen-Raïssa Jackson and Willy Maley, "Celtic Connections: Colonialism and Culture in Irish-Scottish Modernism," *Interventions: International Journal of Postcolonial Studies* 4 no. 1 (2002): 68–78; Nairn, *"Break-Up:* Twenty-Five Years On," 17–34.

16 Simon Jenkins, "An Expletive of a Winner," *The Times,* 15 October 1994, 20.

17 Craig, "Scotland and Hybridity," 235.

18 Kirstin Innes, "Mark Renton's Bairns: Identity and Language in the Post-*Trainspotting* Novel," in *The Edinburgh Companion to Contemporary Scottish Literature,* ed. Berthold Schoene (Edinburgh: Edinburgh University Press, 2007), 301.

19 Innes, "Mark Renton's Bairns," 301. See also Jürgen Neubauer, *Literature as Intervention: Struggles over Cultural Identity in Contemporary Scottish Fiction* (Marburg: Tectum Verlag, 1999), 151.

20 Berthold Schoene, "Going Cosmopolitan: Reconstructing 'Scottishness' in Post-Devolution Criticism," in *The Edinburgh Companion to Contemporary Scottish Literature,* ed. Berthold Schoene (Edinburgh: Edinburgh University Press, 2007), 13.

21 David Hollinger, *Postethnic America: Beyond Multiculturalism* (New York: Basic Books, 1995), 3; cited in Schoene, "Going Cosmopolitan," 10.

22 See for example Gavin Miller, who takes to task the tendency of some linguists and writers to represent Scots as "a magical language which is directly connected to the world of things, feelings, and actions—a language in which one can directly hear meaning." Gavin Miller, "'Persuade without Convincing... Represent without Reasoning': The Inferiorist Mythology of the Scots Language," in *Scotland in Theory: Reflections on Culture and Literature,* ed. Eleanor Bell and Gavin Miller (Amsterdam: Rodopi, 2004), 205.

23 James Kelman, *Some Recent Attacks: Essays Cultural and Political* (Edinburgh: A K Press, 1992), 84.

24 Iain Lambert, "This is Not Sarcasm Believe Me Yours Sincerely: James Kelman, Ken Saro-Wiwa and Amos Tutuola," in *Scottish Literature and Postcolonial Literature,* ed. Michael Gardiner and Graeme Macdonald (Edinburgh: Edinburgh University Press, 2011), 198–209.

25 Schoene, "Going Cosmopolitan," 11.

26 Jackie Kay, "Where It Hurts," in *Off Colour* (Newcastle: Bloodaxe, 1998), 1–4.
27 Raman Mundair, *A Choreographer's Cartography* (Peepal Tree Press, 2007); Raman Mundair, *Incomers: Some Shetland Voices*, www.shetlandamenity. org/the-incoming-project.
28 Suhayl Saadi, "Being Scottish," http://sarmed.netfirms.com/suhayl/NEW/ articles_essays/being_scottish/index.htm.
29 Suhayl Saadi, "Infinite Diversity in New Scottish Writing," http://asls.arts. gla.ac.uk/SSaadi.html.
30 Suhayl Saadi, "In Tom Paine's Kitchen: Days of Rage and Fire," in *The Edinburgh Companion to Contemporary Scottish Literature*, ed. Berthold Schoene (Edinburgh University Press, 2007), 28–33. The most influential critique of this kind of linguistic exoticism remains Graeme Huggan, *The Postcolonial Exotic: Marketing the Margins* (London: Routledge, 2001).
31 Saadi's 2001 short story collection *The Burning Mirror*, for example, written in Glaswegian Scots mixed with standard Scottish English and Urdu, was published by independent Edinburgh publisher Polygon. He also publishes essays and other writing online, on his own and a range of other websites. "Glaswegian-ish" ("first") and English ("second") versions of his short story "Extra Time in Paradise," for example, are published online as part of the Stirling University/Newcastle University *Devolving Diasporas* project, www.devolvingdiasporas.com/writing_02.htm.
32 Saadi, "In Tom Paine's Kitchen," 31.
33 All review quotations are taken from cover blurbs, Saadi, *Psychoraag*.
34 Mitchell, "Interview." See for example Saadi, *Psychoraag*, 13, 31.
35 Ibid.
36 Saadi, "In Tom Paine's Kitchen," 29.
37 Ibid., 29–30.
38 Doris Sommer has termed the elision of the sacred and secular itself as a kind of "bilingualism." Doris Sommer, *Bilingual Games: A New Sentimental Education* (Durham, NC: Duke University Press, 2004), xx
39 Ali Smith, "Life Beyond the M25," *The Guardian*, 18 December 2004. Cited in Mitchell, "Interview."
40 Zaf here echoes the poet Imtiaz Dharker, a contemporary of Saadi's, who has called herself a "Scottish Muslim Calvinist." British Council, "Imtiaz Dharker." https://literature.britishcouncil.org/writer/imtiaz-dharker.
41 Rachael Gilmour, "Punning in Punglish, Sounding 'Poreign': Daljit Nagra and the Politics of Language," *Interventions: International Journal of Postcolonial Studies* 17 no. 5 (2015): 689–90.
42 Marie-Odile Pittin-Hedon, *The Space of Fiction: Voices from Scotland in a Post-Devolution Age* (Glasgow: Scottish Literature International, 2015), 91–2.
43 Russell Potter, *Spectacular Vernaculars: Hip-Hop and the Politics of Postmodernism* (New York: SUNY Press, 1995), 35–6.
44 Thomas Stearns Eliot, "London Letter," *The Dial* 71 no. 4 (1921): 452–5.
45 Mladen Dolar, *A Voice and Nothing More* (Cambridge, MA: MIT Press, 2006), 30.
46 Ibid.
47 Sommer, *Bilingual Games*, xxiv.
48 Ibid.
49 Ibid., 128–9.
50 Jan Blommaert, Sirpa Leppänen, Massimiliano Spotti, "Endangering Multilingualism," in *Dangerous Multilingualism: Northern Perspectives on Order, Purity and Normality*, ed. Jan Blommaert, Sirpa Leppänen,

Päivi Pahta and Tiina Räisänen (Basingstoke: Palgrave, 2012), 9. See also, for example, Jens Normann Jørgensen et al., "Polylanguaging in Superdiversity," *Diversities* 13 no. 2 (2011), www.mmg.mpg.de/fileadmin/user_upload/Subsites/Diversities/Journals_2011/2011_13-02_art2.pdf.
51 Rey Chow, *Not Like A Native Speaker: On Languaging as a Postcolonial Experience* (New York: Columbia University Press, 2014), 14–15.

Bibliography

Alim, H. Samy, Awad Ibrahim, and Alastair Pennycook. *Global Linguistic Flows: Hip Hop Cultures, Youth Identities, and the Politics of Language.* London and New York: Routledge, 2009.

Battista, Anna. "Facts and Fictions: Interview with writer Suhayl Saadi." *Erasing Clouds* www.erasingclouds.com/0714saadi.html.

Bell, Eleanor, and Gavin Miller, eds. *Scotland in Theory: Reflections on Culture and Literature.* Amsterdam: Rodopi, 2004.

Bissett, Alan. "The 'New Weegies': The Glasgow Novel in the Twenty-First Century." In *Edinburgh Companion to Contemporary Scottish Literature*, edited by Berthold Schoene, 59–67. Edinburgh: Edinburgh University Press, 2007.

Blommaert, Jan. "Commentary: A Sociolinguistics of Globalization." *Journal of Sociolinguistics* 7 no. 4 (2003): 607–23.

Blommaert, Jan, Sirpa Leppänen, and Massimiliano Spotti. "Endangering Multilingualism." In *Dangerous Multilingualism: Northern Perspectives on Order, Purity and Normality*, edited by Jan Blommaert, Sirpa Leppänen, Päivi Pahta and Tiina Räisänen, 1–21. Basingstoke: Palgrave, 2012.

British Council. "Imtiaz Dharker." https://literature.britishcouncil.org/writer/imtiaz-dharker.

Chow, Rey. *Not Like A Native Speaker: On Languaging as a Postcolonial Experience.* New York: Columbia University Press, 2014.

Connell, Liam. "Modes of Marginality: Scottish Literature and the Uses of Postcolonial Theory." *Comparative Studies of South Asia, Africa and the Middle East* 23 no. 1–2 (2003): 41–53.

Craig, Cairns. *The Modern Scottish Novel: Narrative and National Imagination.* Edinburgh: Edinburgh University Press, 1999.

———. "Scotland and Hybridity." In *Beyond Scotland: New Contexts for Twentieth-Century Scottish Literature*, edited by Gerard Carruthers, David Goldie, and Alastair Renfrew, 229–53. Amsterdam: Rodopi, 2004.

Crawford, Robert. *Devolving English Literature.* Oxford: Clarendon, 1992.

Dolar, Mladen. *A Voice and Nothing More.* Cambridge, MA: MIT Press, 2006.

Eliot, Thomas Stearns. "London Letter." *The Dial* 71 no. 4 (1921): 452–5.

Gardiner, Michael. "Democracy and Scottish Postcoloniality." *Scotlands* 3 no. 2 (1996): 24–41.

Gilmour, Rachael. "Punning in Punglish, Sounding 'Poreign': Daljit Nagra and the Politics of Language." *Interventions: International Journal of Postcolonial Studies* 17 no. 5 (2015): 686–705.

Harootunian, Harry. *History's Disquiet: Modernity, Cultural Practice, and the Question of Everyday Life.* New York: Columbia University Press, 2000.

Huggan, Graeme. *The Postcolonial Exotic: Marketing the Margins*. London: Routledge, 2001.

Innes, Kirstin. "Mark Renton's Bairns: Identity and Language in the Post-*Trainspotting* Novel." In *The Edinburgh Companion to Contemporary Scottish Literature*, edited by Berthold Schoene, 301–309. Edinburgh: Edinburgh University Press, 2007.

Jackson, Ellen-Raïssa, and Willy Maley. "Celtic Connections: Colonialism and Culture in Irish-Scottish Modernism." *Interventions: International Journal of Postcolonial Studies* 4 no. 1 (2002): 68–78.

Jenkins, Simon. "An Expletive of a Winner." *The Times*, 15 October 1994.

Jørgensen, Jens Normann, M. S. Karrebæk, L. M. Madsen, and J. S. Møller. "Polylanguaging in Superdiversity." *Diversities* 13 no. 2 (2011). www.mmg.mpg.de/fileadmin/user_upload/Subsites/Diversities/Journals_2011/2011_13-02_art2.pdf.

Kay, Jackie. *Off Colour*. Newcastle: Bloodaxe, 1998.

Kelman, James. *Some Recent Attacks: Essays Cultural and Political*. Edinburgh: A K Press, 1992.

Lambert, Iain. "This is Not Sarcasm Believe Me Yours Sincerely: James Kelman, Ken Saro-Wiwa and Amos Tutuola." In *Scottish Literature and Postcolonial Literature*, edited by Michael Gardiner and Graeme Macdonald, 198–209. Edinburgh: Edinburgh University Press, 2011.

Macdonald, Graeme. "Postcolonialism and Scottish Studies." *New Formations* 59 (2006): 115–31.

———. "Scottish Extractions: 'Race' and Racism in Devolutionary Scotland." *Orbis Litterarum* 65 no. 2 (2010): 79–107.

McLean, Duncan. "James Kelman Interviewed." *Edinburgh Review* 71 (1985): 64–80.

Mignolo, Walter. *Local Histories/Global Designs: Coloniality, Subaltern Knowledges, and Border Thinking*. Princeton, NJ: Princeton University Press, 2000.

Miller, Gavin. "'Persuade without Convincing... Represent without Reasoning': The Inferiorist Mythology of the Scots Language." In *Scotland in Theory: Reflections on Culture and Literature*, edited by Eleanor Bell and Gavin Miller, 197–209. Edinburgh: Edinburgh University Press, 2004.

Mitchell, Nick. "Interview—Suhayl Saadi: *Psychoraag*." *Spike Magazine*, 1 April 2006. www.spikemagazine.com/0406-suhayl-saadi-psychoraag-interview.php.

Mundair, Raman. *A Choreographer's Cartography*. Leeds: Peepal Tree Press, 2007.

———. *Incomers: Some Shetland Voices*. www.shetlandamenity.org/the-incoming-project.

Nairn, Tom. "*Break-Up*: Twenty-Five Years On." In *Scotland in Theory*, edited by Eleanor Bell and Gavin Miller, 17–34. Amsterdam: Rodopi, 2004.

Neubauer, Jürgen. *Literature as Intervention: Struggles over Cultural Identity in Contemporary Scottish Fiction*. Marburg: Tectum Verlag, 1999.

Potter, Russell. *Spectacular Vernaculars: Hip-Hop and the Politics of Postmodernism*. Albany, NY: SUNY Press, 1995.

Rodríguez González, Carla. "The Rhythms of the City: The Performance of Time and Space in Suhayl Saadi's *Psychoraag*." *Journal of Commonwealth Literature* 51 no. 1 (2016): 92–109.

Saadi, Suhayl. *The Burning Mirror.* Edinburgh: Polygon, 2001.
———. *Psychoraag.* Edinburgh: Chroma, 2004.
———. "In Tom Paine's Kitchen: Days of Rage and Fire." In *The Edinburgh Companion to Contemporary Scottish Literature*, edited by Berthold Schoene, 28–33. Edinburgh: Edinburgh University Press, 2007.
———. "Being Scottish." http://sarmed.netfirms.com/suhayl/NEW/articles_essays/being_scottish/index.htm.
———. "Infinite Diversity in New Scottish Writing." http://asls.arts.gla.ac.uk/SSaadi.html.
———. "Extra Time in Paradise—English Version"/ "Extra Time in Paradise—Glaswegian-ish Version." *Devolving Diasporas.* www.devolvingdiasporas.com/writing.htm.
Schoene, Berthold. "A Passage to Scotland: Scottish Literature and the British Postcolonial Condition." *Scotlands* 2 no. 1 (1995): 107–22.
———. "Going Cosmopolitan: Reconstituting 'Scottishness' in Post-Devolution Criticism." In *The Edinburgh Companion to Contemporary Scottish Literature*, edited by Berthold Schoene, 7–16. Edinburgh: Edinburgh University Press, 2007.
Scottish Government. "One Scotland." http://onescotland.org.
Unger, Johann Wolfgang. *The Discursive Construction of the Scots Language: Language, Education, Politics and Everyday Life.* Amsterdam and Philadelphia, PA: John Benjamins, 2013.
Upstone, Sarah. *British Asian Fiction: Twenty-First-Century Voices.* Manchester: Manchester University Press, 2010.
Warwick Research Collective. *Combined and Uneven Development: Towards a New Theory of World-Literature.* Liverpool: Liverpool University Press, 2015.

6 Language Choices in Belizean Literature

The Politics of Language in Transnational Caribbean Space

Britta Schneider

Introduction

To consider language as straightforwardly indexing cultural membership and territorial belonging is unsatisfactory where globalizing processes have made relationships between languages and borders more and more complicated. These complications have troubled old certainties, and yet they have also opened up new perspectives on language as a social semiotic. Focusing on the politics of language and linguistic difference in multilingual literature, it is crucial to consider the symbolic powers of language that are beyond referential and denotational meaning, where the inclusion of perspectives from both literary studies and sociolinguistics can produce valuable insight.

Language, particularly in written form,[1] appears in *languages*, which are media of communication but at the same time are historical cultural symbols that in Western contexts developed in times of modernism, nationalism, and colonialism,[2] and which today function in a global cultural marketplace. *Languages* are dialectically interwoven with social and cultural borders, which however, do not coincide only with national or ethnic ones.[3] Nevertheless, the national narrative of the coherence of ethnic and linguistic boundaries, despite having always been a myth, has had a strong impact on epistemological approaches to languages, which are typically understood as indices for territorially bounded communities. Yet, what kinds of social boundaries do languages produce in an age of transnational social interconnections and local linguistic diversity?

As a discipline that focuses on language variation and its meanings and operations, sociolinguistics gives central insights into the study of language and its relationships to the social, cultural, economic, and political realms. Sociolinguistics that understands language as an entry point to apprehend the social world—and does not merely map varying linguistic patterns[4]—has demonstrated language to be a central means of constructing, performing, and potentially renegotiating conceptions of society or community. This recognition of the socially performative power of language is crucial for investigating literature in a transnational cultural marketplace, and literary studies can take advantage of the insights of sociolinguistics into the social embeddedness of language.

On the other hand, sociolinguists have traditionally focused on oral language and have conceived of speech as primary, whereas an interest in written language has come to the fore only recently.[5] An understanding of the relevance of written language reveals the study of literary texts as an important source for insight into the social functions of language. Literature that makes use of multilingual resources allows us to study discourses and social borders that particular 'languages' imply. Languages, as central elements of the discourses that bring into being the groups that speak them, have symbolic meanings whose roots lie in their cultural histories. To illustrate this point, we may have a look at Latin, which clearly bears connotations of religious and social elitism; or think of the symbolic meaning of English, which cannot be understood without making reference to histories of colonialism and economic dominance; or consider a language like Jamaican Creole, which has associations with cultures of political resistance and postcolonial independence. Overall, the choice for or against a particular written code in literature is necessarily embedded in the social, political, local, national, and transnational context in which narratives take place and have been produced. Choices are at the same time informed by political and economic interest and a potential appeal to cosmopolitan spheres as an audience beyond national borders may be targeted.[6] In using multilingual literature as a kind of sociolinguistic corpus, we may gain insight into the non-referential functions of language beyond ethnic indexicalities and a deeper understanding of the symbolic capacities of language, where the complexity of the literary text and its often transnational distribution makes a simple *one language—one ethnic group* interpretation of symbolic meanings of language choice unlikely.

To this end, I study language choices in literature from Belize, a context where multilingualism has an established tradition. While many other places are multilingual, Belize is particularly interesting, due to its not always easy transnational connections within the Latin American region, to West African countries, to the UK, the US, and to the Caribbean, and due to its high degree of interethnic mixing. National language ideology, the idea that one nation uses one (and only one) language, is a meaningless concept in the Belizean case, whose interethnic complexity additionally has the effect of destabilizing conventional conceptions of language—how can we determine the 'borders' of a language if we cannot determine the community that speaks it?[7] The central aim of this chapter is to illustrate that languages, while typically remaining stable entities in literary texts, have multiplex symbolic meanings and can be analysed with regards to their local, national, and transnational socio-economic, political, and historical significations that are clearly beyond a simple *language and ethnicity* nexus.

Sociolinguistics and Literature: Approaching Language Choice as an Index of Heteroglossic Discourse

Following Mikhail Bakhtin, we can observe that literature is heteroglossic in nature: "The novel can be defined as a diversity of social speech types (sometimes even diversity of languages) and a diversity of individual voices, artistically organized."[8] Literature involves linguistic transformations, between different tones and different registers, high and low, formal and informal, and this is perhaps one of literature's defining characteristics.[9] Studying the use of several languages (obviously understood as discursive constructs) in a literary text, it is worthwhile to take a look at linguistic approaches to multilingual language use. The study of speakers' language choices has a prominent place in linguistics and sociolinguistics, where, due to Anglo-American dominance in the field, this is most commonly referred to as *code-switching*.[10] Its study has predominantly focused on conversational data.[11] Studies on conversational code-switching cannot be applied directly to multilingual literature. Interactional aspects between speaker and listener differ from the relationship between a writer and a reader, and written language is based on more conscious choices. Yet there are obvious overlapping points of interest.

Myers-Scotton's "markedness model" is prominent;[12] it defines as matrix language "the language that the speaker would normally be expected to use in that context, while the other language (normally the embedded language) is regarded as the marked language."[13] This has been critically debated, as in spoken language it is not always possible to determine the matrix language. Peter Auer's typology of different kinds of bilingual speech takes into account more intricate forms of language mixing, ranging from broader-level code-switches to mixed languages and fused lects. The former is defined by speakers perceiving the use of different codes as a "locally meaningful event."[14] This is not necessarily the case in the latter two, where grammatically fused structures range from less to more standardized, without speakers necessarily being aware of these forms originally deriving from different languages.

In the interpretation of literary texts, I concentrate on what Auer calls code-switching. In the texts I analyse, it is easily possible to define an 'unmarked' language, which is here English, over a 'marked' language. This effect comes into being through the particular use and positioning of language in the text—the unmarked language is typically used in narration, whereas the marked language may be used to refer to a particular topic, or only used in direct speech, or only by characters who are depicted as unable to speak other languages. Such instances of code-switching necessarily express non-referential information about the sociolinguistic economy in which the narration takes place.

The extraconversational knowledge indexed by code-switching usually implies references to group boundaries,[15] but in sociolinguistic research such extraconversational knowledge is often equated with assuming that particular languages index particular ethnic groups. While ethnic identity may well be important, it is vital to question whether that is indeed the only or most crucial category that is negotiated in strategies of code-switching. It is also relevant to consider what ethnic categories mean with reference to other social categories and histories. Linguistic anthropologist Susan Gal argues that "differences in code-switching practices of bilingual ethnic groups are symbolic responses to the ways in which these ethnic communities are differentially situated within regions of the world capitalist system."[16] Although the system has obviously changed since the publication of Gal's text, it may be even more important today to consider that people are aware of the economic and political positioning of their community in a global context. Thus, a "larger context is crucial in shaping the nature of interactions between and within ethnic groups, the permeability of boundaries, the definitions and evaluations of actions and resources and the nature of competition across boundaries."[17] Code-switching can therefore be interpreted as a symbolic practice that indexes sociopolitical positions in which ethnicity is a construction that interacts with other social, political, and economic factors. Ultimately, this leads to an understanding that any linguistic act is informed by larger social contexts:

> acts of speaking are ideologically mediated, since those acts necessarily involve the speaker's understanding of salient social groups, activities, and practices, including forms of talk. Such understandings incorporate evaluations and are weighted by the speaker's social position and interest. They are also affected by differences in speakers' access to relevant practices. Social acts, including acts of speaking, are informed by an ideologized system of representations, and no matter how instrumental they may be to some particular social goal, they also participate in the 'work of representation.'[18]

Languages are of course important in this "ideologized system of representation," as they traditionally index territorial and political entities and function as metonyms for larger, geographically locatable speech communities. As displayed in multilingual contexts like Belize and discussed in recent sociolinguistic theory, such established links between forms of speech and ethnic affiliations are the *outcome*, and not the precondition, of complex social interactions.[19] Today, due to linguistic/indexical resources becoming globally available, additional, non-ethnic, and transnational affiliations with languages have become more apparent.[20]

Applying these insights to the study of literary texts means to scrutinize the social, political, and historical discourses on which language choices in written language are based, and despite all the important caveats in relation to the concept of *language*, I use it as an analytical category.

I analyse switches between codes if there are indications that these are "locally meaningful events"[21] within the text, and I am interested in the discourses that inform these choices as a kind of 'window' into relationships of people and of social discourses. I argue that, due to discursive complexities grounded in intricate sociopolitical histories and in territorial ties on different levels, local to global, complex, and finally heteroglossic meanings of language symbolism emerge. It needs to be noted that my own writing, of course, also indexes a particular position where my European background, Anglo-influenced academic gaze, use of English, and field trips to Belize have to be considered, and are unavoidably reflected in my perception of Belizean discourses.

Language and Ethnicity in Multilingual Belize

Belize has a contested history in which, amongst others, Maya peoples, Spanish colonists, British buccaneers, enslaved and free people from Africa, and Mexican Mestizo refugees from the Caste War contributed to a complex social and linguistic makeup.[22] Despite claims to the territory by Spanish and later Guatemalan governments since the seventeenth century, the country became 'British Honduras' in 1862 and independent Belize in 1981. The political elite, since the 1950s dominated by the African-European Creole population, affiliates with British and American cultural values, and Belize has English as its official language. English is used in government publications and is the official medium of education in Belizean schools. Radio and television stations broadcast predominantly in relatively standardized forms of Caribbean English (there are some programmes in Spanish, and in-calling listeners and advertising may use more creolized forms of English). In written genres, English predominates, and in school curricula,[23] it is hardly possible to discern the highly multilingual makeup of the population. While it has been claimed that English is no one's native language in Belize,[24] Maya Yucatec, Queqchi Maya, Mopan Maya, Belizean Kriol, Spanish, Garifuna (an Arawakan Creole language of predominantly Carib and African descent, originally developed in St. Vincent[25]), Hindi, German, Arabic, and different varieties of Chinese contribute to the diverse linguistic composition of the country, which has only about 360,000 inhabitants.[26] Interethnic mixing within families is common and most Belizeans grow up speaking at least three languages.[27] Due to immigration from Mexico during the nineteenth century and, since the 1980s, from Guatemala, El Salvador, and Honduras,[28] Spanish has become demographically dominant. Nevertheless, it is Belizean Kriol that has the function of the country's lingua franca and that is seen as indexing Belizean identity.[29] Given that Creole languages usually do not carry overt prestige,[30] and given that these are languages predominantly used in informal and oral domains, this may come as a surprise. It is the socio-historical context and, to a certain extent, transnational cultural discourses that explain the status of the language. Whether or not to regard Kriol as having *overt* or *covert* prestige—a concept that is central in traditional sociolinguistics[31]—is a difficult decision and perhaps the distinction here is inappropriate.

Due to geographical and political conditions, Belize did not develop into a plantation colony. The British Crown showed little interest in making the muddy terrain of Belize into one, and the main source of income of the first British settlers was pirating,[32] which was given up after negotiations between the British and the Spanish crowns. Buccaneers were forced to find new sources of income, amongst which the mahogany trade was central.[33] For support in the hard labour of woodcutting, British settlers bought African slaves from Jamaican ports,[34] whose presence has been recorded since the beginning of the eighteenth century. Belizean Kriol is based on the language that was brought along by Jamaican slaves and further developed due to contact between European settlers and their slaves within Belize. A popular account of the logwood cutting practices that may contribute to the status of Kriol is that British settlers and their slaves worked side-by-side and never developed a relationship as alienated as reported for other slave societies. Although this does by no means imply that slaves in Belize had significantly greater rights than in other Caribbean slave societies,[35] it is worth mentioning that Belizeans take pride in presumably less disunited social ties between Europeans and Africans. This culminates in the yearly celebration of the Battle of St. George's Caye in 1798, where the British and their slaves supposedly fought together to defend their land against attacks from the Spanish (who by this time no longer supported slavery).

A second explanatory factor for the role of Kriol is Belize's hostile relationship to Guatemala. In 1862, it was British settlers, threatened by Guatemalan claims, who "ask[ed] Britain to lay formal claim on Belize as a colony."[36] As a cultural and linguistic minority in the region, Belizeans feel a strong need to differentiate themselves from their Spanish-speaking neighbours. The border between Belize and Guatemala remains a contested territory, the result of different interpretations of official agreements from the seventeenth century. As recently as 2014, the bilateral relationships between Belize and Guatemala remain difficult and Belizeans still fear annexation by Guatemala, which has not officially recognized Belize's full nation status.[37]

In trying to understand the prestigious status of Kriol, it is also worth mentioning that the British Crown, due to Belize's low potential for economic exploitation and the problematic status of the settlers' claim to the territory, had little interest in it. For this reason, there were a low number of British in Belize and thus an already fused population with British and African ancestry before independence in 1981, and parts of the African-European Creole population had gradually gained middle-class status even before that date. Political activities during the 1950s towards national independence were headed by Creoles (Creole is the term used for people of mixed European and African heritage, while Kriol is the term used for the language), who had been prominent in political positions as lawyers or journalists.[38] Political influence from Jamaican Garveyism and the US Black Panther movement, brought to the public by political activists such as Evan X Hyde,[39] and a Governor General who was trained as a sociolinguist by Robert Le Page and worked on Belizean Kriol in education,[40] added to the prestige of the language. Today, the *National Kriol Council* has created a standardized orthography and supports Creole culture, music, and language.[41] At the same time, these more recent activities also have to be understood in relation to the fact that Creoles have lost their status as the demographic majority.[42]

The reasons why Kriol plays an important role in the sociolinguistic economy in Belize are clearly linked to the sociopolitical history of the nation, which also involves the threat of losing political autonomy to Spanish-speaking neighbours. The language and its emerging relationship to ethnic identity[43] is illustrative for developmental cultural processes that must have taken place elsewhere but have been "erased"[44] under ideological discourses of nationalism since the nineteenth century. After all, each standard *language* is the result of historical sociopolitical struggles where, typically, the existence of a national language was regarded as crucial to legitimate the existence of an independent nation, and where, however, the status of this 'language' was often far from obvious (consider for example the cases of Standard Italian—previously a dialect from Tuscany, or Standard German, originally a dialect from northern Germany used in Luther's Bible translations). It is interesting that ethnic and linguistic categories come into being *because of* and not *despite* contact, in the case of Belize with internal difference, and with Guatemala, Mexico, Jamaica, and the UK.[45]

It is finally worth mentioning that transnational ties that impact on symbolic functions of Kriol are not only of a historical nature. A large segment of the Belizean population has migrated to the US, and the Belizean diaspora plays an important role in Belizean politics, music, and the media.[46] American English is frequently heard in broadcasting and also impacts on local varieties of English and Kriol. The local value of Kriol furthermore links to Jamaica particularly because of Reggae and Dancehall music. Through popular music in general, we find linguistic-cultural links to the Afro-Caribbean space, to Latin American traditions, or to contemporary commercial US styles, and different blends of these.

Multilingual Indexing in Belizean Literature

The sociolinguistic makeup of Belize, then, is internally highly diverse and the result of complex cultural-linguistic processes that mirror sociopolitical and economic histories. This renders the country an interesting example to study the politics of language in literature, in relation both to multilingual practices and transnational literary markets. Here, I will offer a brief overview of language choices in Belizean literature and proceed to a detailed interpretation of a Belizean novel, Zee Edgell's *Beka Lamb*.[47] It was the first book to be published in the independent nation of Belize and the first to gain an international audience.[48] Although the book was published in the early 1980s, I have selected *Beka Lamb* due to its multilingual practices and its central place in Belizean literature. An analysis of symbolic functions of language choice here illustrates how language indexes sociopolitical discourses and how this can be made relevant in interpreting fictional writing. Today, *Beka Lamb* continues to play a vital role in Belizean school curricula, is known by basically everyone in Belize, and is generally considered to be *the* Belizean novel. It thus functions as a model text for Belizean multilingual literacy.

Overall, due to the small size and the economically marginal situation of the country, Belizean literature is neither well distributed nor well funded. Yet, considering the size of the population, lower than that of a middle-sized city elsewhere, the number of publications is relatively high. The Ibero-American Institute in Berlin, which hosts the largest collection of publications from Latin American nations and the Caribbean in Europe, maybe the largest of Belize worldwide, at the time of writing contains about 45 Belizean novels and anthologies of short stories and poems published since the year 2000.[49] The absolute majority of texts are written in English, which is not surprising as Belizeans acquire literacy more or less only in English. Being the official language of Belize, English is the unmarked language in written form.

Kriol is the second most commonly used language. There are a few publications completely in Kriol, which have all been published by the National Kriol Council and whose publication is motivated by a desire to support Kriol as a literary language.[50] Some poetry is written entirely in Kriol, yet in anthologies, these poems invariably constitute only a small selection.[51] There is also an anthology of plays in both Kriol and in English.[52] Yet more commonplace, and despite a strong trend towards Standard English, are the strategies of many authors in putting some local Kriol 'flavour' in their otherwise English texts.[53] Some of these texts even use Kriol in their title as, for example, in the anthology of folktales *If Di Pin Neva Ben*[54] and other publications of the *Belizean Writers Series*.[55] In these novels and short stories, Kriol is usually not used in the narration but in direct speech, and various strategies are employed to ensure Kriol features do not become unintelligible to the English speaker. In the short stories in *Shades of Red*, for example, the author explains Kriol words that may be unfamiliar to the non-Belizean reader in footnotes;[56] others use predominantly expressions whose meaning an

English-speaking reader can deduce (as for example in Edgell's writings). Similar strategies are found when languages other than Kriol are used. One story, in an anthology edited by Gay Wilentz, makes use of Garifuna in direct speech, to which an English translation is provided.[57] The poem collection *The Poems Vinland Barranco* uses Garifuna words in bilingual English–Garifuna poems, which are translated in a glossary at the end of the book.[58] Thus, overall, in Belizean literature, there seems to be hardly any "aggressive" code-switching, which would be language use unintelligible to parts of the audience.[59] This enforces the status of English as an unmarked language, as it is predominantly the representation of oral speech that appears in other codes.

A striking aspect of Belizean language choices in literature is the invisibility of Spanish. It demonstrates the role of Kriol in indexing Belizean identity and the fact that the societal elite associates with Creole culture, although, demographically speaking, Spanish is the dominant language. There are only very few exceptions; one is the 2007 *Anthology of Belizean Literature*, which includes texts in English, Kriol, Spanish, and Garifuna.[60] The editor maintains that Spanish is the language of the Belizean Maya and Mestizo population, and he therefore includes texts in the language.[61]

The general trend is clear—English is the unmarked language, Kriol appears regularly as an addition where spoken language is represented or in poetry, while Garifuna is used rarely. The almost complete absence of Spanish is striking. Maya languages are also absent, but this is less surprising as Maya-speaking communities are culturally isolated, generally have different literacy cultures and often have shifted to Spanish.[62] Interestingly, despite the linguistic complexity of Belize, I have not found instances of conversational code-switching being represented in written texts. There are, however, cases of representations of spoken language where it is difficult to determine whether English or Kriol is used, as the languages exist in a continuum from basilectal to acrolectal forms.[63] It is questionable whether this constitutes a *switch*, in Auer's sense, namely a "locally meaningful event." Some representations of spoken language are thus closer to what Auer calls "fused lects." A more fine-grained analysis of selected passages in *Beka Lamb* helps us achieve a better understanding of these intricacies.

Heteroglossic Indexicalities of Language in *Beka Lamb*

Beka Lamb is the coming of age story of Beka, a Creole girl who attends a Catholic convent school in Belize City in the 1950s. Her best friend is Toycie, who becomes pregnant, is expelled from school, develops a psychotic disorder and eventually dies. In the novel, all main characters are female, and gender inequality is a central topic. The story takes place against a backdrop of political changes in Belize at a time when the Belizean independence movement was emerging. Beka's coming of age, involving her winning the first prize in an essay contest by writing a historical account of Belize, develops in parallel with political changes, where the nation of Belize similarly 'matures' in the course of the story. Beka is, in this sense, a metonym for the nation of Belize.[64]

The narration is written in Standard English, whereas in direct speech, there are many instances of creolized forms of English. Overall, English and Kriol are in a complementary relationship in the text, where English represents formal language and thought whereas Kriol represents spoken, vernacular language. As will become clear in the following analysis, Kriol at the same time has links to gender identity, social closeness, community values, and a developing Belizean national identity. Uses of Kriol are not visually set apart from the rest of the text; they are not italicized or translated. They are thus part of the 'normal' text and a translation is unnecessary for Anglophone readers as most forms are very similar to English. As has been noted, sometimes it is impossible to infer whether an acrolectal, closer to standard form of Kriol or an informal register of English is used.

Already on the first page of the novel, there is an example of this, where Beka's grandmother says: "Befo' time [...] Beka would never have won that contest" (1). The expression *before time* relates to a time when the non-white population had no access to power or education. In the representation of phonology, it is impossible to tell from the lack of the letters <re>[65] in the word *before* whether this relates to a non-rhotic pronunciation of English, as common in many contexts, or to a particular local feature. The lack of an accepted written form of Kriol hinders the representation of potential phonetic differences. Although there is now a written version of Kriol,[66] it is (still?) not generally known; moreover, it has not been widely accepted because of its phonetic character (which makes its links to English, valued by many speakers, hardly visible) and is rarely used, except by activists (based on information gained from personal communication and ethnographic fieldwork). Yet, as the rest of the sentence includes a complex verbal phrase ("would never have") and a representation of an inter-dental fricative (<th>), which is generally uncommon in Caribbean Creoles, it is at least problematic to interpret this as creolized speech and it would be partial to regard such forms as representations of code-switches. It is worth noting that some features of Creole Englishes historically derive from dialectal varieties of British English,[67] and it can thus be challenging to decide when or whether to interpret forms as culturally 'different.' The symbolic value of this rather seems the inclusion of oral, informal speech in a written genre.

In many instances in *Beka Lamb*, however, we find clearly distinguishable Kriol forms. These can be single lexical items embedded in sentences that are otherwise English. Beka's grandmother, for example, continues her previously presented utterance by saying "But things can change fi true" (1). The multi-functional particle *fi*, common to many Caribbean Creoles, arguably stemming from the West African language Twi,[68] here used as a preposition, is embedded in a sentence that is in Standard English, which is again detectable from the inter-dental fricative, represented by <th>. The sentence is not actually a Kriol sentence but an English sentence in which one element has been substituted by a Kriol form. Similar uses of Kriol forms occur regularly throughout the novel, as in direct speech by Beka, Toycie, and other family members; for example, when Beka says: "I'm so sleepy now Toycie gial" (6), the word *girl* is substituted by the Kriol form *gial*, representing the Kriol pronunciation [gjial].[69] Single lexical items in Kriol in direct speech represent the speakers in the novel as authentic Creole Belizeans and mark an otherwise English text as linked to the local context of Belize.

Particularly in the beginning of the novel, Kriol also impacts on more structural levels of language. "Flies really bad at waterside" (3), says Toycie's aunt: a sentence that stands out for the lack of a complement form, also a feature highly typical of Creole languages in general. It is noticeable that more creolized forms that impact on syntax or phonology represent speech by more uneducated speakers, which indicates that 'broader' or basilectal forms of Kriol intersect with class, which is of course typical for non-standardized languages.[70] Yet, the uses of Kriol do not generally challenge the English-speaking reader. Such practices have been called "extrinsic";[71] it is nevertheless inadequate to claim that the text therefore is directed at an external readership. Belizeans may not speak English in their private lives, but many are English-readers and -writers. It is, however, of course difficult to estimate the actual population's literacy rate. In official statistics, "persons who have completed at least Standard Five at primary school are considered literate" and the corresponding rate was 88.1 per cent in 2010;[72] yet enrolment does not necessarily mean attendance or acquisition of literacy skills, particularly in a context where the quality of education tends to be problematic. Language culture in multilingual contexts is different to monolingual ones and *languages* may here be less of an index of ethnic belonging and more one of social context. In the examples above, it is clearly the difference between orality and literacy, which intersects with education and class, that is represented through such language choices. The use of Kriol in *Beka Lamb* thus has non-referential functions, but the whole spectrum of symbolic meanings does not entirely unfold by looking at single instances only. Comparing the representation of speech throughout the novel is enlightening too.

Representations of more acrolectal Kriol speech appear frequently in Beka's and Toycie's speech. It is salient that Kriol features appear much more often in their conversations in the beginning of the novel, when the two friends experience happy times before Toycie becomes pregnant, which is also the period during which Beka still refuses to meet the expectations of the US-managed Catholic convent school. As is typical for non-standard languages, Kriol here indexes social closeness and intimacy; at the same time, within the context of the unfolding of the narration, it is Creole community values and gender identity that play a role in understanding the indexical value of Kriol, where it is women who are "custodians of an oral tradition" in this postcolonial society.[73]

Considering this as a bildungsroman, we may interpret the declining use of Kriol as the story progresses as indicating the parallel processes of Beka's maturation and her subordination to the rules of her middle-class father and the teachers at the school. The indexical function of Kriol is not simply to represent ethnicity but is linked to class status, to age, which intersects with educational status, to the type of social relationship characters have, and to the dilemma the postcolonial subject faces in striving for social ascendancy: to give up Kriol and to use English, which we see in Beka's increased use of English in the middle parts of the text.

Yet in spite of these patterns, the novel remains ambivalent with regards to the prestige of Kriol. A narrative description of Belize City runs as follows:

> It was a relatively tolerant town where at least six races with their roots in other districts of the country, in Africa, the West Indies, Central America, Europe, North America, Asia, and other places, lived in a kind of harmony. In three centuries, miscegenation, like logwood, had produced all shades of black and brown, not grey nor purple or violet, but certainly there were few people in town known as red ibos. Creole regarded as a language to be proud of by most people in the country, served as a means of communication amongst the races.
>
> (11–12)

The role of Kriol as a lingua franca amongst the highly diverse population here serves as an explanatory factor for its overt prestige in Belize, which presumably is one of the reasons why Kriol eventually has developed into an index of 'Belizean' identity in real-life everyday interaction too. In this respect, it is similar to European national *languages*, despite its lack of a written standard. Although the text is almost exclusively written in English, it is Kriol that is, in the passage above, declared as the means of communication and thus vital in the creation of national unity, where diversity and mixing—"miscegenation"—is what unites Belizeans. We see this mixing in linguistic terms where English mixes with West African languages, and the passage above even constructs this as analogous to biological 'mixing.' Although Kriol is used rather cautiously in *Beka Lamb*, its symbolic meaning is crucial in Belize becoming a nation—a nation that regards mixing and not purity as constitutional.

Moreover, the use of Kriol in the novel interacts with Beka's appropriation of colonial discourse. In the second half of the novel, Beka starts to accept the past and the tragic history of Toycie, and begins to behave as a responsible and hard-working pupil.[74] She then succeeds in winning the essay contest where the task is to present an aspect of Belize's history—the history of the *Sisters of Charity*, the rulers of the convent school, and their workings within Belize. Although the act of writing a historical account of the *Sisters* is very much based on cultures of colonialism and imperialism, it is vital that it is here not someone from outside—someone from Great Britain or the US—who writes and produces a text that constructs Belize as a nation. It is the Creole girl Beka who is presented as having the power to define discourse. Her essay-writing defines Belize as a cultural entity and the American *Sisters of Charity* as outsiders. The colonial institution of the Catholic Church is not destroyed and not even called into question as an institution of power. The novel never makes mention of the content of the essay, nor does it mention in which language it is written—the unmarked status of English for written language is beyond question. And yet, with Beka writing history, the perspectives have changed: the colonial object becomes a writing subject. The act of essay-writing and winning the essay contest can thus be interpreted as Belizean Creoles beginning to appropriate colonial power structures, which are changed "according to the articulations of desire and the social field."[75] This is a central element of the novel, which, we should remember, states on its first page: "Befo' time [...] Beka would never have won that contest" (1).

Beka has started to create her own normativity, adapting to the colonizers' values but also appropriating them where she presents her views of history in the essay. And despite the essay being written in English (implicitly, and thus all the more naturalized), the novel dramatizes a return to Kriol. While Kriol is used in the beginning as a language of informality and social closeness, often between two female friends who oppose their colonial upbringing, the later passages of the novel construct the formerly stigmatized language as becoming a more legitimate way of expression, also in public realms. A central scene in this regard is the celebration of a visit of the Mother Principal of the convent that directs the school. Beka is asked to put together a medley of folk songs, which are sung during the Mother's visit. One of the songs she chooses is a Creole folk song:

> 'Kean't work da mi plantaish, Kean't work deh at all, 'the entire school was bellowing the chorus,
> 'Pinqwing juk me, pinqwink juk me, kean't work deh at all!'[76]
>
> (164)

The song talks about slave culture in referring to plantation work. As slave plantations seem to never have existed in Belize, it remains unclear whether the song is originally from Jamaica, or whether it is perhaps a Belizean reference to other slave societies that constructs Belize as a 'slave-friendly' place. In any case, we have to assume from the celebratory context in the narration that the singing of the song expresses positive feelings and it is vital to note that, although sung in Kriol, it is performed in a public and very official context. The Mother Principal afterwards recounts a parable of a Moslem mullah travelling to another country where the mullah is asked "Now, tell me, mullah, did you learn the language of that country?" and the mullah eventually has to admit he did not (165). Kriol is here indirectly constructed as the *language of that country*, the language of Belize. Interestingly, it is not a Belizean who defines Kriol as the language of Belize, it is the perspective of the transnational 'other' that recognizes the indexical value of Kriol as Belizean, which allows for the language becoming *a language*—which is, however, also presented as the language of the former slaves of Belize.

Thus, despite the relatively optimistic outlook that Edgell constructs, a postcolonial ambivalence, of course, persists as Creole culture and Kriol language still draw on slave culture and the colonized past and "only such a language and such symbols are seen as adequate for synthesizing the often antagonistic ethnic and class differences that define the new nation."[77] Antagonistic tendencies become visible in Edgell's use of Spanish, which indexes interethnic class hostilities. The author has been accused of demonstrating her own "leaning" in "favour of her own race" as a member of the Creole community.[78] Given that Spanish has been a widely spoken language in Belize for a long time,[79] it is significant to consider the few passages where Spanish is used. The use of names for certain characters, together with their use of Spanish as represented in direct speech, mirror the tendency of public discourse in Belize to construct Spanish as 'other' and Hispanization as a 'threat.' We may infer from his name that Toycie's boyfriend, Emilio Villanueva, who impregnates her without marrying her, is Hispanic. His mother is depicted as a *nouveau riche* woman who thinks herself superior to Creoles (64–5). Hispanic shop-owners are presented as more business-minded and economically successful than Creoles (82).

Interestingly, Spanish is also associated with an attitude of servility. Beka herself uses Spanish in one instance, where she says "Inmediatamente, nino" [*sic*] (21) after her little brother has told her to wash the dishes. As the only female offspring in the family, it is Beka who is responsible for household duties. Her reply in Spanish, in a situation where she has to show obedience to her younger brother, associates it with obsequiousness. The language politics of *Beka Lamb* are consistent with the current situation in Belize, insofar as Kriol continues to carry the indexical load as the 'language of Belize' and negative attitudes to Spanish persist, which indeed today lead to discrimination against Spanish-speakers, indicated by tendencies to language shift.[80] On the basis of ethnographic observation, I can confirm that such perceptions are dominant in present-day Belize even amongst those who use Spanish at home.

Summarizing, English is the unmarked language in *Beka Lamb* and constructed as the norm through its use in narrating the entire story. Kriol has indexical functions that simultaneously relate to class, to gender, to traditional community values, to kinds of social relationships, to age, to emotional states, to forms of conduct, and to forming boundaries with surrounding groups so as to create a legitimate status as a nation, where the language and culture of former slaves is presented as being able to appropriate colonizers' institutions of power. Relationships to other nations and cultures contribute to Kriol's indexical meanings, where Spanish represents the 'other within,' as it links to the surrounding Hispanic nations and is used to index class and social attitudes, and where English remains predominant in written and formal language, while it is an American nun who is the first to say that Kriol is *the language of that country.*

Language Symbolism in Transnational Markets

Overall, we can clearly maintain that in *Beka Lamb*, multilingual resources have multiplex symbolic functions. An overly simple interpretation of language as indexing ethnicity "erases"[81] the intricate histories and conflicts of language that develop in local, national, and transnational interaction and discourse. Ethno-linguistic boundaries are the outcome of social opposition and cultural contact where linguistic and social categories, counter-intuitively, evolve through transcultural social processes. Multilingual literature can give access to the politics of language that has always been transnational in this respect. As illustrated in the relationship of English and Kriol in *Beka Lamb*, languages as symbols transcend social and cultural borders and gain their meaning through contact and interaction, rather than through isolation.

Considering the local but interconnected histories through which cultural categories of language and their indexical functions evolve, the role of language and translation in contemporary transnational contexts and multilingual literary marketplaces becomes fascinating but difficult to grasp. Questions of translatability will remain at the forefront of debates, and, considering Apter's notion of untranslatability,[82] it is questionable whether it is possible to translate the local cultural symbolism of a language, as its local connotations do not necessarily transmit in its words. Quite logically, literature "communicates fully to readers who have learnt in more specific detail about the language and culture in which it is grounded."[83]

A brief look into the German version of *Beka Lamb* confirms the complex and difficult nature of the translation of non-referential meaning.

What a close reading of language choices in the German translation primarily shows is that the language ideologies of the language culture into which a text is translated add to the complexity of symbolic meanings of languages in transnational literary markets. The German version of *Beka Lamb* has only standardized German in direct speech; the linguistic diversity of the original text is invisible. Interestingly, some English terms are kept so that the grandmother is called *gran* (German = *Grossmutter*, *Oma*), the female neighbour is *Miss Eila* (Frau Eila), and male characters are referred to with *Mr.*, including those who carry Spanish names, as for example the father of Toycie's boyfriend, who is *Mr. Villanueva* (Herr Villanueva). The use of standard language in direct speech indicates the very dominant role of standard language in Germany, where the use of non-standard German forms would be perceived as ridicule. A translation into Swiss or Austrian German might have been different, as non-standard speech here has a more prestigious status. The use of English terms in the German translation demonstrates positive attitudes towards English and the language's dominance in German public life, as it is expected that a German audience is familiar with terms that are probably used to increase the cultural authenticity of the text, yet function in perhaps an unintentionally ironic way (English is, after all, the language of the colonizers and not the dominant oral code of most of the protagonists of *Beka Lamb*). A *German vs. English* dichotomy is all that remains from multilingual heteroglossic meanings of the original text, where English in German discourse is typically associated with higher education and upper-middle-class prestige.[84] Linguistic and discursive resources are "easily but not unproblematically detachable from their traditional symbolic meanings,"[85] and it is questionable what kind of culture is evoked for a German reader through the use of English terms and difficult to even define what is here a 'traditional' symbolic meaning.

Where, through transnational social interaction, 'other' languages are not erased but reproduced in environments where they have not been used before, these need to be embedded in existing fields of meaning. It requires a process of discursive establishment to make meanings locally available and, where new symbolic meanings of languages emerge, these are typically "emblematic of spatial stratification in the political and economic local–global order."[86] It is not accidental that Creole languages or creolized Englishes play an important role in marking globally distributed music styles such as Reggae or Hip Hop as expressing resistance. Knowledge of European languages often continues to symbolize social mobility, for example in representing cosmopolitan values.[87] Certain symbolic meanings of languages seem to have become globally available. English is probably the prime example of this, ideologically mediated as 'up-to-date,' as indexing (commercial) success, cultural evolution, and educational advance.[88] The language choice of this very chapter—academic English, by a non-native English-speaking European writing about Central American literature—indexes and contributes to the global stratification of language, meaning and power, which will continue to enable and to complicate the analysis of language in global literary markets.

Conclusion

This chapter has illustrated that the analysis of symbolic functions of language can be applied to the study of literature. An elaboration on sociolinguistic theory that conceptualizes multilingual language use has shown that switches between languages can be made relevant to analyse written literary texts, as these are indexical of social, political, and cultural discourses that are on the one hand constructive of ethnic boundaries, and on the other hand reach beyond these, particularly in an age of globalization. As the example of Belizean literature has shown, the choice of particular languages in the text is informed by political and cultural contexts, and language is associated with internal and external boundaries in multiplex ways. Ambivalences emerge as it seems impossible to translate symbolic meanings of languages into other languages, but at the same time language and discourse are appropriated into local systems of meaning and potentially diversify. The meanings that unfold can be global and extremely local at the same time. A range of widely different factors comes into play—from idiosyncratic, to local, national, to broadscale and maybe global discourse, from referential to symbolic, from ethnic to class and transnational cultures—if we want to interpret meaning and what it means to speak and write in a particular language, where we finally may have to accept the insoluble opaque aspects of language. Yet even if we are unable to produce overall transparent translations and interpretations, what the above analysis has shown is that an application of sociolinguistics understanding of language as an effect of social discourse to the study of literary text can give fruitful and important insights into the complexities of language in transnational literary markets.

Acknowledgements

This work has been made possible by the DFG, Deutsche Forschungsgemeinschaft. I want to thank the editors and reviewers of this volume for very helpful, inspiring, and invaluable comment on an earlier draft of this paper.

Notes

1 See also Meir Sternberg, "Polylingualism as Reality and Translation as Mimesis," *Poetics Today* 2 (1981).
2 See, for example, Joseph Errington, *Linguistics in a Colonial World: A Story of Language, Meaning and Power* (Malden, MA: Blackwell, 2008); Rachael

Gilmour, *Grammars of Colonialism: Representing Languages in Colonial South Africa* (Basingstoke: Palgrave Macmillan, 2006); Sinfree Makoni and Alastair Pennycook, "Disinventing and Reconstituting Languages," in *Disinventing and Reconstituting Languages*, ed. Sinfree Makoni and Alastair Pennycook (Clevedon: Multilingual Matters, 2007); Britta Schneider, *Salsa, Language and Transnationalism* (Bristol: Multilingual Matters, 2014).

3   See Chapter 4.

4   Jan Blommaert, "Sociolinguistic Scales," *Intercultural Pragmatics* 4 (2007): 3.

5   See, for example, Theresa Lillis and Carolyn McKinney, ed. "Special Issue: Writing," *Journal of Sociolinguistics* (2013) 17.

6   On the problematic figure of the 'cosmopolitan' or 'metropolitan' reader, see Sarah Brouillette, *Postcolonial Writers in the Global Literary Marketplace* (Basingstoke: Palgrave Macmillan, 2007); Graham Huggan, *The Postcolonial Exotic: Marketing the Margins* (London: Routledge, 2001).

7   On translingualism, see Chapter 2.

8   Mikhail M. Bakhtin, *The Dialogic Imagination: 4 Essays*, ed. Michael Holquist, trans. Caryl Emerson and Michael Holquist (Austin: University of Texas Press, 1981), 262.

9   Elizabeth Gordon and Mark Williams, "Raids on the Articulate: Code-Switching, Style-Shifting and Postcolonial Writing," *Journal of Commonwealth Literature* 33 (1998): 75.

10   See, for example, Carol Myers-Scotton, *Duelling Languages: Grammatical Structure in Codeswitching* (Oxford: Clarendon Press, 1993); J. Blom Poplack and John J. Gumperz, "Social Meaning in Linguistic Structure: Code-Switching in Norway," in *Directions in Sociolinguistics: The Ethnography of Communication*, ed. John J. Gumperz and Dell Hymes (New York: Holt, Reinhardt and Winston, 1972).

11   See, however, Carla Jonsson, "Functions of Code-Switching in Bilingual Theater: An Analysis of Three Chicano Plays," *Journal of Pragmatics* 42 (2010); Erica McClure, "The Relationship between Form and Function in Written National Language—English Codeswitching: Evidence from Mexico, Spain and Bulgaria," in *Code-Switching Worldwide*, ed. Rodolfo Jacobson (Berlin: Mouton de Gruyter, 1998); Mark Sebba, "Multilingualism in Written Discourse: An Approach to the Analysis of Multilingual Texts," *International Journal of Bilingualism* 17 (2013).

12   Myers-Scotton, *Duelling Languages: Grammatical Structure in Codeswitching* (Oxford: Clarendon Press, 1993).

13   Lawrie Barnes, "The Role of Code-Switching in the Creation of an Outsider Identity in the Bilingual Film," *Communicatio: South African Journal for Communication Theory and Research* 38 no. 3 (2012), 248.

14   Peter Auer, "From Codeswitching Via Language Mixing to Fused Lects: Toward a Dynamic Typology of Bilingual Speech," *The International Journal of Bilingualism* 3 (1999): 310.

15   See Susan Gal, "The Political Economy of Code-Choice," in *Codeswitching: Anthropological and Sociolinguistic Perspectives*, ed. Monica Heller (The Hague: Mouton de Gruyter, 1988), 247.

16   Susan Gal, "Codeswitching and Consciousness in the European Periphery," *American Ethnologist* 14 (1987); quoted in McClure, "The Relationship between Form and Function," 126.

17   Gal quoted in McClure, "The Relationship between Form and Function," 126.

18   Judith T. Irvine, "'Style' as Distinctiveness: The Culture and Ideology of Linguistic Differentiation," in *Style and Sociolinguistic Variation*, ed. Penelope Eckert and John R. Rickford (Cambridge: Cambridge University Press, 2001), 24.

19 See also Robert Brock Le Page and Andrée Tabouret-Keller, *Acts of Identity: Creole-Based Approaches to Language and Ethnicity* (Cambridge: Cambridge University Press, 1985).

20 On Spanish, see, for example, Britta Schneider, "'Oh Boy, ¿Hablas Español?'— Salsa and the Multiple Value of Authenticity in Late Capitalism," in *Indexing Authenticity. Sociolinguistic Perspectives*, ed. Véronique Lacoste, Thiemo Breyer, and Jakob Leimgruber (Berlin/New York: de Gruyter, 2014), 113–35.

21 Auer, "From Codeswitching," 310.

22 Assad Shoman, *A History of Belize in 13 Chapters* (Belize City: Angelus Press, 2011).

23 As, for example, in Ministry of Education and Youth. Policy and Planning Unit, "Belize Education Sector Strategy 2011–2016. Annex a – Policy Objectives" (Belmopan: Government of Belize, 2012). http://moe.gov.bz/index. php?option=com_content&view=article&id=189&Itemid=249.

24 Geneviève Escure, *Creole and Dialect Continua: Standard Acquisition Processes in Belize and China* (Amsterdam: Benjamins, 1997), 28.

25 See "Garifuna," Endangered Language Alliance. http://elalliance.org/projects/ languages-of-the-caribbean/garifuna/.

26 Statistical Institute of Belize, 2011. "2010 Population & Housing Census Belize. Main Results of 2010 Population and Housing Census."

27 Geneviève Escure, *Creole and Dialect Continua: Standard Acquisition Processes in Belize and China* (Amsterdam: Benjamins, 1997), 28.

28 Alan Twigg, *Understanding Belize. A Historical Guide* (Madeira Park, BC: Harbour Publishing, 2006), 15.

29 See, for example, Osmer Balam, "Overt Language Attitudes and Linguistic Identities among Multilingual Speakers in Northern Belize," *Studies in Hispanic and Lusophone Linguistics* 6 (2013).

30 Mervyn Morris, "Is English We Speaking," in *Is English We Speaking and Other Essays* (Kingston: Ian Randle Publishers, 1999).

31 William Labov, "The Social Stratification of (R) in New York City Department Stores," in *Sociolinguistics: A Reader and Coursebook*, ed. Nicolas Coupland and Adam Jaworski (London: Macmillan, 1997 [1972]), 168–78.

32 Twigg, *Understanding Belize*, chapter 4.

33 Nigel Bolland, *The Formation of a Colonial Society: Belize, from Conquest to Crown Colony* (Baltimore, MD: Johns Hopkins University Press, 1977).

34 Shoman, *A History of Belize*, chapter 3.

35 See Zee Edgell, *Time and the River* (London: Heinemann, 2007) for a literary approach to the topic.

36 Twigg, *Understanding Belize*, 119.

37 See, for example, Adele Ramos, "Guat Passport Offensive," *Amandala*, 24 October 2014, http://amandala.com.bz/news/guat-passport-offensive/. For the Guatemalan perspective, see Ministerio de Relaciones Exteriores de Guatemala, "Situación del diferendo territorial existente entre Guatemala y Belice y las perspectivas de solución al mismo," (Guatemala: 2010) www.minex.gob.gt/ADMINPORTAL/Data/DOC/20100929165035248 SintesisdelDiferendojunio2010.pdf.

38 Assad Shoman, "Reflections on Ethnicity and Nation in Belize," *Cuaderno de Trabajo AFRODESC/EURESCL* 9 (2010).

39 See the newspaper *Amandala* and *Krem* radio for his continuing impact on public discourse.

40 Colville Young, *Belize Creole: A Study of the Creolized English Spoken in the City of Belize, in Its Cultural and Social Setting* (York: University of York 1973); *Language and Education in Belize* (Belize City: C.N. Young, 1995).

41 See National Kriol Council, http://nationalkriolcouncil.org/.

42 Geneviève Escure, "Belizean Creole: Gender, Creole, and the Role of Women in Language Change," in *Gender across Languages. Volume 1*, ed. Marlis Hellinger and Hadumod Bußmann (Amsterdam: Benjamins, 2001), 58.

43 There is a fascinating account of the history of how Kriol became linked to Belizean identity in Le Page and Tabouret-Keller, *Acts of Identity*.

44 Judith T. Irvine and Susan Gal, "Language Ideology and Linguistic Differentiation," in *Regimes of Language: Ideologies, Polities and Identities*, ed. Paul V. Kroskrity (Santa Fe, NM: School of American Research Press, 2000).

45 A process discussed in Fredrik Barth, introduction to *Ethnic Groups and Boundaries. The Social Organization of Cultural Difference*, ed. Fredrik Barth (Bergen: Universitetsforlaget, 1969).

46 Escure, "Belizean Creole," 58.

47 Zee Edgell, *Beka Lamb* (Oxford: Heinemann, 1982). Subsequent references are to this edition and page numbers are given parenthetically in the text.

48 See *Beka: Ein Roman aus Belize*, Goridis, Uta (Berlin: Orlanda Frauenverlag, 1989) for a German translation.

49 See Online Catalogue, Ibero-American Institute, Berlin, http://iaiweb1.iai.spk-berlin.de/.

50 See for example Hilda Gentle, *Di Stoari a Hilda: (Wahn Chroo Chroo Stoari)* (Belize City: Belize Kriol Project, 2005); Naomi Glock, *Sohn Stoari Fahn Gaylz Paint (Malanti)* (Belize City: Belize Kriol Project, 2005); Oswald Sutherland, *Anansi an Di Domplin Chree* (Belize City: Belize Kriol Project, 2004).

51 See, for example, some of the poems in Kalilah Enriquez, *Shades of Red* (Belize City: Excellence Publishing, 2007); Ritamae Hyde, *Mahogany Whispers* (Belize City: Ramos Publishing, 2010); Carrie Fairweather-Belgrave, *Parchment Pages: Speak to Me in Poetry* (Belize City: Identity Publishing, 2010); Edward (Bunny) Panting, *My Poems* (Belize City: Angelus Press, 2008); John Alexander Watler, *De Works* (Belize City: Factory Books, 2002).

52 See Michael Phillips, *Ping Wing Juk Me* (Benque Viejo del Carmen: Cubola, 2006).

53 See, for example, the fictional writings by Colville Young, *Pataki Full: Seven Belizean Short Stories* (Benque Viejo del Carmen: Cubola, 1988).

54 Tim Hagerthy and Mary Gomez Parham, *If Di Pin Neva Ben. Folktales and Legends of Belize* (Benque Viejo del Carmen: Cubola, 2006). Interestingly, the collection of folktales from Creole, Mestizo, Garifuna, Maya and East Indian contexts in this book is mostly based on oral storytelling in Kriol and Spanish, but the narratives have been translated into English (10). The authors maintain that this is "[f]or the sake of uniformity" (11).

55 See *Belizean Writers Series*, Cubola Productions. www.cubola.com/product-catalogue/belizean-writers-series/.

56 Enriquez, *Shades of Red*, 67.

57 Jessie Nuñez Castillo, "Misiyoun," in *Memories, Dreams and Nightmares: A Short Story Anthology by Belizean Women Writers*, ed. Gay Wilentz (Benque Viejo del Carmen: Cubola, 2005).

58 Victor Joseph Nicholas, *The Poems Vinland Barranco* (Belmopan: University of Belize, 2004).

59 Gordon and Williams, "Raids on the Articulate," 83.

60 Víctor Manuel Durán, ed. *An Anthology of Belizean Literature. English, Spanish, Garifuna* (Lanham, MD: University Press of America, 2007).

61 Durán, 11. Inclusions of Spanish are also found in poems (Amado Chan, *Make the Monarch Blush* [Belize City: Factory Books, 2001]) and in some

cases in direct speech (David Nicolas Ruiz, *Under the Yax'ché Tree* [Benque Viejo del Carmen: Poustinia Foundation Project, 2010]. There are also a few appearances in short stories in Young, *Pataki Full*.

62 Durán, *Anthology of Belizean Literature*, 10–11.

63 On the Creole continuum, see Mark Sebba, *Contact Languages: Pidgins and Creoles* (London: Macmillan, 1997).

64 See Ervin Beck, "Social Insecurity in Beka Lamb by Zee Edgell," *Goshen College Website*, www.goshen.edu/academics/english/ervinb/beka-lamb/. For additional analyses of gender and decolonization in *Beka Lamb*, see Roger Bromley, "Reaching a Clearing: Gender Politics in *Beka Lamb*," *Wasafiri* 1 (1985); Heidi Ganner, "Growing up in Belize: Zee Edgell's *Beka Lamb*," in *Autobiographical and Biographical Writing in the Commonwealth*, ed. Doireann MacDermott (Barcelona: Editorial AUSA, 1984); Charles Hunter, "*Beka Lamb*: Belize's First Novel," *Belizean Studies* 10 (1982); Heather Smyth, "'She Had Made a Beginning Too': *Beka Lamb* and the Caribbean Feminist Bildungsroman," *Genre* 44 (2011).

65 Angled brackets represent letters.

66 Work on such an orthography started during the 1990s; see Ken Decker, "Orthography Development for Belize Creole," (National Kriol Council of Belize, 1995). The current version can be found in Yvette Herrera, Paul Crosbie et al. eds., *Kriol-Inglish Dikshineri. English-Kriol Dictionary* (Belize City: Belize Kriol Project, 2009).

67 See, for example, Christian Mair, *English Linguistics* (Tübingen: Narr, 2008), chapter 14.

68 Ken Decker, *The Song of Kriol. A Grammar of the Kriol Language of Belize.* (Belize City: Belize Kriol Projekt, 2013), 53. www.sil.org/system/files/reapdata/20/99/21/20992139271472124394945438780794345365/The_Song_of_Kriol_UnicodeElectronic2013.pdf.

69 Square brackets represent sounds.

70 See any introduction to sociolinguistics, as for example, Miriam Meyerhoff, *Introducing Sociolinguistics* (London: Routledge, 2006).

71 Compare Gordon and Williams, "Raids on the Articulate," 81.

72 See Statistical Institute of Belize, *Belize: Population and Housing Census. Country Report 2010* (Statistical Institute of Belize, 2010), 10. www.sib.org.bz/Portals/0/docs/publications/census/2010_Census_Report.pdf; see also UNICEF, "Belize. Statistics," *UNICEF*, 2015, www.unicef.org/infobycountry/belize_statistics.html.

73 Simon Gikandi, *Writing in Limbo: Modernism and Caribbean Literature* (Ithaca, NY: Cornell University Press, 1992), 201.

74 On capitalist middle-class values in *Beka Lamb*, see Beck, "Social Insecurity in *Beka Lamb*," n.p.

75 Gilles Deleuze and Felix Guattari, *Anti-Oedipus: Capitalism and Schizophrenia,* trans. Robert Hurley, Mark Seem, and Helen R. Lane, Preface by Michel Foucault (Chicago, IL: University of Minnesota Press, 1983), 62–3; quoted in Gikandi, *Writing in Limbo*, 225.

76 "Can't work at my plantation, can't work there at all, *Pinqwing juk me, pingwinq juk me*, can't work there at all."

77 Gikandi, *Writing in Limbo*, 201.

78 Ganner, "Growing up in Belize"; quoted in Beck, "Social Insecurity in *Beka Lam*," n.p.

79 See also Le Page and Tabouret-Keller, *Acts of Identity*.

80 See Balam, "Overt Language Attitudes."

81 Irvine and Gal, "Language Ideology and Linguistic Differentiation."

82 Here applied to a different level of language, see Emily Apter, *Against World Literature. On the Politics of Untranslatability* (London: Verso, 2013) and also Chapter 4.

83 Morris, "Is English We Speaking," 14.

84 Consider Helga Kotthoff, "Anglizismen sind das neue Imponier-Deutsch," *ZEIT*, 9 November 2011, www.zeit.de/wissen/2011-11/anglizismen-wissenschaftssprache.

85 Monica Heller, Adam Jaworski, and Crispin Thurlow, "Introduction: Sociolinguistics and Tourism – Mobilities, Markets, Multilingualism," *Journal of Sociolinguistics* 18 no. 4 (2014), 426.

86 Michael Silverstein, "Contemporary Transformations of Local Linguistic Communities," *Annual Review of Anthropology* 27 (1998): 401–26, quoted in Heller et al. "Introduction: Sociolinguistics and Tourism," 450.

87 On cosmopolitanism, see Ulf Hannerz, *Transnational Connections: Culture, People, Places* (London: Routledge, 1996). For French community discourses appropriated in Barcelona and London, see Maria Rosa Garrido, *Emmaus as a Transnational Imagined Community: Language, Interdiscursivity and Stratification in a Social Movement*. PhD thesis, Universidad Autònoma de Barcelona, 2014. www.tesisenred.net/handle/10803/285359.

88 On English and its cultural capital, see Brian Lennon, *In Babel's Shadow: Multilingual Literatures, Monolingual States* (Minneapolis: University of Minnesota Press, 2010), chapter 2.

Bibliography

Apter, Emily. *Against World Literature: On the Politics of Untranslatability.* London: Verso, 2013.

Auer, Peter. "From Codeswitching via Language Mixing to Fused Lects: Toward a Dynamic Typology of Bilingual Speech." *The International Journal of Bilingualism* 3 (1999): 309–32.

Bakhtin, Mikhail M. *The Dialogic Imagination: 4 Essays.* Edited by Michael Holquist. Translated by Caryl Emerson and Michael Holquist. Austin: University of Texas Press, 1981.

Balam, Osmer. "Overt Language Attitudes and Linguistic Identities among Multilingual Speakers in Northern Belize." *Studies in Hispanic and Lusophone Linguistics* 6 (2013): 247–77.

Barnes, Lawrie. "The Role of Code-Switching in the Creation of an Outsider Identity in the Bilingual Film." *Communicatio: South African Journal for Communication Theory and Research* 38 no. 3 (2012): 247–60.

Barth, Fredrik. "Introduction." In *Ethnic Groups and Boundaries: The Social Organization of Cultural Difference*, edited by Fredrik Barth, 9–38. Bergen: Universitetsforlaget, 1969.

Beck, Ervin. "Social Insecurity in Beka Lamb by Zee Edgell." *Goshen College.* www.goshen.edu/academics/english/ervinb/beka-lamb/.

Blommaert, Jan. "Sociolinguistic Scales." *Intercultural Pragmatics* 4 (2007): 1–19.

Bolland, Nigel. *The Formation of a Colonial Society: Belize, from Conquest to Crown Colony.* Baltimore, MD: Johns Hopkins University Press, 1977.

Bromley, Roger. "Reaching a Clearing: Gender Politics in Beka Lamb." *Wasafiri* 1 (1985): 10–14.

Brouillette, Sarah. *Postcolonial Writers in the Global Literary Marketplace.* Basingstoke: Palgrave Macmillan, 2007.

Chan, Amado. *Make the Monarch Blush.* Belize City: Factory Books, 2001.

Decker, Ken. "Orthography Development for Belize Creole." National Kriol Council of Belize, 1995.

———. *The Song of Kriol. A Grammar of the Kriol Language of Belize.* Belize City: Belize Kriol Projekt, 2013. www.sil.org/system/files/reapdata/ 20/99/21/209921392714721243949454387807943453651The_Song_of_ Kriol_UnicodeElectronic2013.pdf.

Deleuze, Gilles, and Felix Guattari. *Anti-Oedipus. Capitalism and Schizophrenia.* Translated by Robert Hurley, Mark Seem, and Helen R. Lane. Preface by Michel Foucault. Chicago, IL: University of Minnesota Press, 1983.

Durán, Víctor Manuel, ed. *An Anthology of Belizean Literature: English, Spanish, Garifuna.* Lanham, MD: University Press of America, 2007.

Edgell, Zee. *Beka Lamb.* Oxford: Heinemann, 1982.

———. *Beka: Ein Roman aus Belize.* Goridis, Uta. Berlin: Orlanda Frauenverlag, 1989.

———. *Time and the River.* London: Heinemann, 2007.

Endangered Language Alliance. "Garifuna." http://elalliance.org/projects/ languages-of-the-caribbean/garifuna/.

Enriquez, Kalilah. *Shades of Red.* Belize City: Excellence Publishing, 2007.

Errington, Joseph. *Linguistics in a Colonial World: A Story of Language, Meaning and Power.* Malden, MA: Blackwell, 2008.

Escure, Geneviève. "Belizean Creole: Gender, Creole, and the Role of Women in Language Change." In *Gender across Languages. Volume 1*, edited by Marlis Hellinger and Hadumod Bußmann, 53–84. Amsterdam: Benjamins, 2001.

———. *Creole and Dialect Continua: Standard Acquisition Processes in Belize and China.* Amsterdam: Benjamins, 1997.

Fairweather-Belgrave, Carrie. *Parchment Pages: Speak to Me in Poetry.* Belize City: Identity Publishing, 2010.

Gal, Susan. "Codeswitching and Consciousness in the European Periphery." *American Ethnologist* 14 (1987): 637–53.

———. "The Political Economy of Code-Choice." In *Codeswitching: Anthropological and Sociolinguistic Perspectives*, edited by Monica Heller, 245–64. The Hague: Mouton de Gruyter, 1988.

Ganner, Heidi. "Growing up in Belize: Zee Edgell's Beka Lamb." In *Autobiographical and Biographical Writing in the Commonwealth*, edited by Doireann MacDermott, 89–93. Barcelona: Editorial AUSA, 1984.

Garrido, Maria Rosa. "Emmaus as a Transnational Imagined Community: Language, Interdiscursivity and Stratification in a Social Movement." PhD thesis, Universidad Autònoma de Barcelona, 2014. www.tesisenred.net/ handle/10803/285359.

Gentle, Hilda. *Di Stoari a Hilda: (Wahn Chroo Chroo Stoari).* Belize City: Belize Kriol Project, 2005.

Gikandi, Simon. *Writing in Limbo: Modernism and Caribbean Literature.* Ithaca, NY: Cornell University Press, 1992.

Gilmour, Rachael. *Grammars of Colonialism: Representing Languages in Colonial South Africa.* Basingstoke: Palgrave Macmillan, 2006.

Glock, Naomi. *Sohn Stoari Fahn Gaylz Paint (Malanti)*. Belize City: Belize Kriol Project, 2005.

Gordon, Elizabeth, and Mark Williams. "Raids on the Articulate: Code-Switching, Style-Shifting and Postcolonial Writing." *The Journal of Commonwealth Literature* 33 (1998): 75–96.

Hagerthy, Tim, and Mary Gomez Parham. *If Di Pin Neva Ben: Folktales and Legends of Belize*. Benque Viejo del Carmen: Cubola, 2006.

Hannerz, Ulf. *Transnational Connections: Culture, People, Places*. London: Routledge, 1996.

Heller, Monica, Adam Jaworski, and Crispin Thurlow. "Introduction: Sociolinguistics and Tourism – Mobilities, Markets, Multilingualism." *Journal of Sociolinguistics* 18 no. 4 (2014): 425–58.

Herrera, Yvette, Paul Crosbie, et al., eds. *Kriol-Inglish Dikshineri. English-Kriol Dictionary*. Belize City: Belize Kriol Project, 2009.

Huggan, Graham. *The Postcolonial Exotic: Marketing the Margins*. London: Routledge, 2001.

Hunter, Charles. "Beka Lamb: Belize's First Novel." *Belizean Studies* 10 (1982): 14–21.

Hyde, Ritamae. *Mahogany Whispers*. Belize City: Ramos Publishing, 2010.

Ibero-American Institute, Online Catalogue. Berlin. http://iaiweb1.iai.spk-berlin.de/.

Irvine, Judith T. "'Style' as Distinctiveness: The Culture and Ideology of Linguistic Differentiation." In *Style and Sociolinguistic Variation*, edited by Penelope Eckert and John R. Rickford, 21–43. Cambridge: Cambridge University Press, 2001.

Irvine, Judith T., and Susan Gal. "Language Ideology and Linguistic Differentiation." In *Regimes of Language: Ideologies, Polities and Identities*, edited by Paul V. Kroskrity, 35–83. Santa Fe, NM: School of American Research Press, 2000.

Jonsson, Carla. "Functions of Code-Switching in Bilingual Theater: An Analysis of Three Chicano Plays." *Journal of Pragmatics* 42 (2010): 1296–310.

Kotthoff, Helga. "Anglizismen sind das neue Imponier-Deutsch." *ZEIT*. 9 November 2011. www.zeit.de/wissen/2011-11/anglizismen-wissenschaftssprache.

Labov, William. "The Social Stratification of (R) in New York City Department Stores." In *Sociolinguistics: A Reader and Coursebook*, edited by Nicolas Coupland and Adam Jaworski, 168–78. London: Macmillan, 1997 (1972).

Le Page, Robert Brock, and Andrée Tabouret-Keller. *Acts of Identity: Creole-Based Approaches to Language and Ethnicity*. Cambridge: Cambridge University Press, 1985.

Lennon, Brian. *In Babel's Shadow: Multilingual Literatures, Monolingual States*. Minneapolis: University of Minnesota Press, 2010.

Lillis, Theresa, and Carolyn McKinney, eds. Special Issue: Writing. *Journal of Sociolinguistics* (2013) 17.

Mair, Christian. *English Linguistics*. Tübingen: Narr, 2008.

Makoni, Sinfree, and Alastair Pennycook. "Disinventing and Reconstituting Languages." In *Disinventing and Reconstituting Languages*, edited by Sinfree Makoni and Alastair Pennycook, 1–41. Clevedon: Multilingual Matters, 2007.

McClure, Erica. "The Relationship between Form and Function in Written National Language—English Codeswitching: Evidence from Mexico, Spain and Bulgaria." In *Code-Switching Worldwide*, edited by Rodolfo Jacobson, 125–50. Berlin: Mouton de Gruyter, 1998.

Meyerhoff, Miriam. *Introducing Sociolinguistics*. London: Routledge, 2006.

Ministerio de Relaciones Exteriores de Guatemala. "Situación del diferendo territorial existente entre Guatemala y Belice y las perspectivas de solución al mismo." Guatemala, 2010. www.minex.gob.gt/ADMINPORTAL/Data/DOC/20100929165035248SintesisdelDiferendojunio2010.pdf.

Ministry of Education and Youth. Policy and Planning Unit. "Belize Education Sector Strategy 2011–2016. Annex a – Policy Objectives." Belmopan: Government of Belize, 2012. http://moe.gov.bz/index.php?option=com_content&view=article&id=189&Itemid=249.

Morris, Mervyn. "Is English We Speaking." In *Is English We Speaking and Other Essays*, 1–16. Kingston: Ian Randle Publishers, 1999.

Myers-Scotton, Carol. *Duelling Languages: Grammatical Structure in Codeswitching*. Oxford: Clarendon Press, 1993.

National Kriol Council. Accessed 6 July 2016. http://nationalkriolcouncil.org/.

Nicholas, Victor Joseph. *The Poems Vinland Barranco*. Belmopan: University of Belize, 2004.

Nuñez Castillo, Jessie. "Misiyoun." In *Memories, Dreams and Nightmares: A Short Story Anthology by Belizean Women Writers*, edited by Gay Wilentz, 26–9. Benque Viejo del Carmen: Cubola, 2005.

Panting, Edward (Bunny). *My Poems*. Belize City: Angelus Press, 2008.

Phillips, Michael. *Ping Wing Juk Me*. Benque Viejo del Carmen: Cubola, 2006.

Poplack, J. Blom, and John J. Gumperz. "Social Meaning in Linguistic Structure: Code-Switching in Norway." In *Directions in Sociolinguistics: The Ethnography of Communication*, edited by John J. Gumperz and Dell Hymes, 407–34. New York: Holt, Reinhardt and Winston, 1972.

Ramos, Adele. "Guat Passport Offensive," *Amandala*, 24 October 2014. http://amandala.com.bz/news/guat-passport-offensive/.

Ruiz, David Nicolas. *Under the Yax'ché Tree*. Benque Viejo del Carmen: Poustinia Foundation Project, 2010.

Schneider, Britta. "'Oh Boy, ¿Hablas Español?' – Salsa and the Multiple Value of Authenticity in Late Capitalism." In *Indexing Authenticity: Sociolinguistic Perspectives*, edited by Véronique Lacoste, Thiemo Breyer and Jakob Leimgruber, 113–35. Berlin/New York: de Gruyter, 2014.

———. *Salsa, Language and Transnationalism*. Bristol: Multilingual Matters, 2014.

Sebba, Mark. *Contact Languages: Pidgins and Creoles*. London: Macmillan, 1997.

———. "Multilingualism in Written Discourse: An Approach to the Analysis of Multilingual Texts." *International Journal of Bilingualism* 17 (2013): 97–118.

Shoman, Assad. "Reflections on Ethnicity and Nation in Belize." *Cuarderno de Trabajo AFRODESC/EURESCL* 9 (2010): 1–61.

———. *A History of Belize in 13 Chapters*. Belize City: Angelus Press, 2011.

Silverstein, Michael. "Contemporary Transformations of Local Linguistic Communities." *Annual Review of Anthropology* 27 (1998): 401–26.

Smyth, Heather. "'She Had Made a Beginning Too': *Beka Lamb* and the Caribbean Feminist Bildungsroman." *Genre* 44 (2011): 181–204.

Statistical Institute of Belize. *Belize: Population and Housing Census. Country Report 2010.* Statistical Institute of Belize, 2010. www.sib.org.bz/Portals/0/docs/publications/census/2010_Census_Report.pdf.

———. "2010 Population & Housing Census Belize. Main Results of 2010 Population and Housing Census," 2011.

Sternberg, Meir. "Polylingualism as Reality and Translation as Mimesis." *Poetics Today* 2 (1981): 221–39.

Sutherland, Oswald. *Anansi an Di Domplin Chree.* Belize City: Belize Kriol Project, 2004.

Twigg, Alan. *Understanding Belize: A Historical Guide.* Madeira Park, BC: Harbour Publishing, 2006.

UNICEF. "Belize. Statistics." UNICEF, 2015. www.unicef.org/infobycountry/belize_statistics.html.

Watler, John Alexander. *De Works.* Belize City: Factory Books, 2002.

Wilentz, Gay. *Memories, Dreams and Nightmares: A Short Story Anthology by Belizean Women Writers.* Benque Viejo del Carmen: Cubola, 2005.

Young, Colville. *Belize Creole: A Study of the Creolized English Spoken in the City of Belize, in Its Cultural and Social Setting.* York: University of York, 1973.

———. *Language and Education in Belize.* Belize City: C.N. Young, 1995.

———. *Pataki Full. Seven Belizean Short Stories.* Benque Viejo del Carmen: Cubola, 1988.

7 *We Need New Names*

Novel and Reading Publics as Conduits for Producing Contradictions

Carli Coetzee

Let no one be fooled by the fact that we may write in English, for we intend to do unheard of things with it.

—Chinua Achebe[1]

This chapter traces the diverse reception histories of the recent novel *We Need New Names* by Zimbabwean-born NoViolet Bulawayo.[2] Debates around the novel's circulation are representative of a trend in which novels written by diasporan African writers are sometimes criticized as products of a shallow transnationalism. Such a reading of the novel as opportunistically cosmopolitan elides other, more complexly layered ones, by readers familiar with the Zimbabwean literary tradition and its historically and linguistically coded references. In this chapter, the contribution to the larger project on multilingual currents is to show that a novel can be diverse (or translated) *within* itself, circulating as it does amongst diverse audiences and in multiple discursive spaces. The quotation from Achebe with which this chapter opens asserts that there is diversity *within* the English language, and Achebe's use of the phrase "unheard of things" references not only the rise of the novel in Africa, but also the innovative and adaptive uses made of English by its speakers on the African continent.

The argument of the chapter is that there are readers who are aware of multiple currents. These readers can hear the "unheard of" things in the text, but are also aware of more tone-deaf "transnational" readings, and incorporate these in their own contextual readings. In fact, the ability to read locally while also being aware of the transnational reception increases the reading pleasure for these readers, who can read the novel in multiple ways, attuned to how the "unheard of" things are overlooked elsewhere. My argument is in the first place that there is a multiplicity of englishnesses within the English of NoViolet Bulawayo's novel, and that in this sense English has multilingual currents within itself. The second strand of the argument pays particular attention to an untranslated song in *We Need New Names*, which is included in the novel in isiNdebele without English translation.[3] The song has histories that draw together musical practices from the Zimbabwean Chimurenga and South African anti-apartheid struggles and creates an intimate community of those readers who do not need an English translation. Its lyrics are about leaving the land of one's ancestors, but instead of simply confirming a story of diasporan departure, it functions in this novel to draw together those who remain connected through many currents and routes, maintaining identities informed by both home and elsewhere. Reading the novel with such an inflection, which shows that the local and the transnational are complexly interwoven rather than oppositional, can reveal the multilingual currents *within* the English of the novel, currents that flow within as well as between the spaces of writing and reading.

The opposition often posed between local and transnational is a metanarrative in which the transnational is anxiously invested. More useful than this approach, I suggest, is to develop a dynamic theorization of the relationship between the local and the transnational, and to view the relationship between these two imagined sites of reading instead like a pipeline with multiple points along its length, and constant (but not consistent) flows backwards and forwards. A suggestive example of such a theory is found in Ato Quayson's recent monograph *Oxford Street, Accra*.[4] Quayson writes about the density of information, found in slogans, on signboards, as well as on vehicles and buildings on Oxford Street in Accra, as a discursive ensemble of the "relay" between the transnational and the local.[5] In this way, the local is not made secondary to, or less significant than, the transnational. Instead, meaning is created precisely in the movements and currents between these spaces. Globalization is neither the demon of regress nor the angel of progress, writes Quayson: it is "a conduit for producing contradictions."[6] Depending on what, and how much, a reader understands, these contradictions can signify very differently. The contradictions can be the source of a certain kind of anxiety if the reader at the extreme monolingual and monocultural end of the pipeline suspects that there are "unheard" currents elsewhere that she cannot access or understand. These "conflicts" and contradictions can also provide a revolutionary impetus, and convene a sense of intimacy for readers who *are* able to interpret the restless relay of meanings.

Ashleigh Harris, in the 2014 issue of the *Johannesburg Workshop in Theory and Criticism Salon*, writes in a piece called "Awkward Form and Writing the African Present" about

> a steady turn in a significant amount of African writing away from everyday life on the continent towards immigrant and diaspora experience, which is occurring (unsurprisingly) in resonance with the emigration of many of Africa's top writers to the global north.[7]

In this reading, there is more traffic in one direction of Quayson's "conduit"; writers are more interested in the transnational as mode and as theme than they are in what one might call the local. Harris invokes Eileen Julien's influential description of such novels as "extroverted African novels,"[8] which Julien theorizes as novels that represent the local to the nonlocal reader. Harris's argument is clearly and strongly made that these novels are "not in dialogue with African everyday life and as such eliminate [...] Africa as one of the sites upon which form is (globally) contingent."[9]

NoViolet Bulawayo's novel *We Need New Names* (published in 2013 by Zimbabwean Weaver Press[10] and simultaneously by Chatto & Windus in international editions) is an excellent case study for testing the claim made by Harris. The novel seems to fall neatly into two halves, both narrated by someone called "Darling." In the first half of the novel, the child Darling and her gang maraud through a fictionalized Bulawayo, re-enacting scenes from news reports and TV shows, stealing guavas, and meeting a range of adults who are described from the child gang's point of view. In the second half of the novel, Darling is slightly older, and lives with her aunt in the USA. The novel's narrative thus seems to offer the familiar story of a bright young African who has gone somewhere north in search of an education. Bulawayo is representative of the trend Harris maps—she was a winner of the Caine Prize; she is beautiful, young, and gifted; she attended a writing programme at an American university; and the novel that is based on her prize-winning story has been nominated for many awards, including the Man Booker Prize and the Etisalat Prize for Literature (which, amongst many others, it won).

Harris remarks on what she calls the "odd structural break" in the middle of the text, and suggests that the novel reads as if it had been conceived of as "two stories written for creative writing class: the first driven by the content demands of 'writing what you know' as the member of the group bringing the high cultural pluralism into the group."[11] Harris continues that in the second half of the novel, where Darling makes her transition into a provisional life as an American teenager, the novel

> reads as the cinch in the deal of making this an American fiction: in writing the immigrant experience of the protagonist Darling, Bulawayo tethers her 'Africa' ('write what we expect you to know') to the American context ('write your American everyday') in a way that leaves both sections oddly unsatisfying.

So, she concludes, the awkward form is indicative of "a greater underlying awkwardness: the positioning of the African writer in and for America."[12]

Harris's insight that the novel's form is "awkward"[13] and the references to extrovertedness offer a compelling model for reading this text as an "awkward" text that interprets, in each of the two halves, a local scene to a transnational audience. This interpretation, however, itself replicates that which it means to expose. When one turns to what might be called the "local" (that is Zimbabwean, or more specifically Bulawayan) scenes of reception of the novel, there is in fact little sense of this anxiety or awkwardness. The perception of an awkwardness of form may instead be indicative of something else. Using Achebe's idea of the "unheard of" uses of English, and thinking of these unheard things alongside Quayson's "relay" between the local and the transnational, one might say that this reading of the novel "as" an American or trans-national novel is knowingly encoded in the novel. The reader who reads restlessly, up and down the pipeline, is aware of the reader who reads more statically and does not hear the "unheard" contradictions. The reader who reads the novel with an awareness of its multilingualism (in terms of multiple englishes) understands and can "hear" the mul-tiplicity that the awkward monolingual (in the sense of speaking and hearing only one English) reader cannot.

The most prominent transnational reception of Bulawayo's novel was in the UK newspaper *The Guardian*, which carried a number of discussions and reviews.[14] The novel was shortlisted for the Guardian First Book Award in 2013, and as part of a series each author on the shortlist was in-terviewed and invited to present extracts from the nominated book. During the same months, the novel was also shortlisted for the Man Booker prize. Philip Hensher commented anxiously on the opening up of the Guardian book prize to authors from the USA that year.[15] This new opening up beyond the region historically bounded by the UK and Commonwealth meant that the field would from now on, he thought, be dominated by "a superficial multicultural aspect" catering to a specifically North American taste.[16] He singled out Jhumpa Lahiri and NoViolet Bulawayo (ironically both eligible as members of the Commonwealth category, although then both based in the USA) as representative of this "superficial" multicultural trend. Bulawayo, he wrote, "dutifully covered all the external and societal concerns about African society that a creative writing student, or a de-voted viewer of CNN's nightly special, might believe significant—NGOs, exorcisms, corruption, the plight of the white Africans, etc."[17] Hensher's anxiety about the Man Booker's "Britishness" is certainly worthy of com-ment; but more striking is his certainty that Bulawayo's novel is "dutiful," "student-"like, and invested in the CNN version of Africa. His criticism of the novel's inclusion is that it is "too American," too "CNN." This reading of the novel is full of anxiety, but it is an anxiety that produces an almost incomprehensible level of misreading of the novel—emptying it out of its encodedness as a Zimbabwean novel, deeply invested in and intertextually connected to the great Zimbabwean literary tradition. This reading of the novel sees only the globalized reading scene, at the one end of the pipeline. The "conflict" here is between the USA and the UK (plus "its" Common-wealth); Zimbabwe or any of the many positions in between or beyond do not even rise to the surface.

The Kenyan author and cultural activist Binyavanga Wainaina had written in the same newspaper, two years before, a piece the fury and hilarity of which may well have been missed by most *Guardian* readers.[18] While the debate was about how African novels and authors are understood, Wainaina turned the question around in a characteristically provocative and ironic way. He bemoaned instead the indigestibility of *British* writers, his piece providing a contemporary riff on Ngũgĩ wa Thiong'o's seminal arguments in *Decolonising the Mind*.[19] Wainaina is a master craftsman of the parodic inversion of discourse, performing a position for the purposes of undermining it, as he did so well in his widely read "How to Write about Africa," in which he compiled a checklist of ways of writing about Africa, for the purpose of critiquing these very ways.[20] In the pages of *The Guardian* a few days later, NoViolet Bulawayo responded more soberly to write that all literatures are of course encoded, and all readings are always partial readings.[21] This version of the work done by any reader of any text (not only "African") is much closer to Quayson's understanding of cultural work as a conduit for producing contradictions, and places the reader in Bulawayo and the reader in London in parallel, rather than in oppositional, reading situations. The responses by Bulawayo and Wainaina thus redefine the discussion about "the" African novel into one where influence and ignorance can be distributed everywhere along the pipeline, and locate the anxiety of Hensher's reading at a position along the conduit of contradictions where only the northern circuits are heard and noticed.

The term anxiety appears also in Stephanie Bosch Santana's analysis of the debates around the Caine Prize, accused by many as peddling a certain ("CNN") brand of writing about Africa.[22] Writing about *We Need New Names* and countering accusations that the novel unselfconsciously uses stereotypes, Bosch Santana argues instead that it is "*meant to make us anxious, to make us think about the process of stereotyping and our own complicity in it.*"[23] So here the anxiety is not *caused* by the novel and its depiction of African people; the anxiety is in fact encoded in the novel itself. The reader in New York and in London is meant to be anxious, to experience anxiety; but the anxiety is performed self-consciously in and by the novel already. Darling's descriptions of life in what she calls "my America" have made many readers uncomfortable. Bulawayo's satirical descriptions, for example Aunt Fostalina's attempt to buy a bra from the "Angel Collection" over the telephone, exaggerate Darling's alienation. Aunt Fostalina practices her pronunciation before (and again after) she places her call, but the woman taking her order in the call centre is unable to understand her accented speech and the reader is witness to an excruciating call centre conversation which remains stuck on the unheard and misunderstood word (Aunt Fostalina's variant *pronunciation* of the word) "Angel."[24] In this commentary on the unheard English of Aunt Fostalina, the satire is also angry and judgemental of American society and its inability to 'hear' a different variety. And the crucial point here is that the reader who 'knows' Bulawayo, perhaps even knows NoViolet Bulawayo, incorporates that anxiety about being 'unheard' in her or his reading of the novel.

This is where I want to relocate attention, namely to investigate the complexly contradictory scenes of reception of the novel, and to show how the anxieties analysed above are understood in other locations. I offer some linked interventions, imagined from the vantage point of the "relay" between the transnational and the local. Many theorizations of "the African novel" can be seen as ways of revisiting awkwardness and re-examining the sources of anxiety. A particularly useful way of thinking about the anxiety of readership and location is provided by Simon Gikandi in a piece called "Reading the Referent: Postcolonialism and the Writing of Modernity."[25] Fortuitously for the Bulawayo-centred perspective here, Gikandi uses a Zimbabwean example to make his point.

Gikandi's paper is an inventive commentary on the ways in which postcolonial theory often ignores local knowledge. Gikandi uses here the same image as Quayson, namely the conduit, to talk about how postcolonial theory distorts the relationship between the local and the transnational. His concern is with the "absence of the postcolonial text, its readers and its referent from postcolonial theory."[26] To make his point, he provides a close reading of a paragraph from Zimbabwean writer Dambudzo Marechera's "The House of Hunger," where there is a reference to "Lobengula's letter to the Queen" and an allusion to a character in the story (a certain Philip), being like Shakespeare's Macbeth. Gikandi imagines two readers, for the sake of argument (although as we know, most readers are somewhere along the pipeline rather than at either end). One reader readily recognizes the Shakespeare referent, but simply ignores the name Lobengula as providing background atmosphere. Another reader, with different intellectual and experiential knowledge, knows that *this* is the reference that carries the most weight. Gikandi writes that, between the narrator and a certain kind of reader, there exists a "conspiratorial" universe of meaning and evaluations. But when a text like this enters a scene of reading, unable to hear the varieties of experience and locatedness, the first reference often simply falls out of view.[27]

Gikandi's allusion to a conspiratorial relationship between reader and author is perhaps the twin of the anxiety discussed above; for the conspiratorial reader there is instead an added pleasure in knowing that the anxious reader, the reader who reads in the more tone-deaf scene, has misread or perhaps not even heard at all. Speaking about pedagogies and institutional teaching cultures, Gikandi argues that there have to be "protocols of reading" that take into consideration both (I would prefer multiple) sets of intertextual referents and their historical contexts.[28] Gikandi's point is not a simple relativist one, suggesting that all readers are equal. Instead he insists that, in the metropolitan scene of reading, there is a responsibility to inform oneself of "what the text takes for granted that its ideal reader will know,"[29] and that the metropolitan reader of a text often is precisely *not* this ideal reader.

The conspiratorial reader who has heard and interpreted the many referents and currents is aware that the novel's many reading scenes act as a "conduit for producing contradictions," and the conspiracy between author and reader enhances and informs the pleasure of this restless reading. While the readers along the pipeline all read the novel in what seems like the same "English," some readers are aware of the tensions and contradictions, and aware of the unheard of meanings that flow up and down the currents of the many local-accented englishes.[30]

NoViolet Bulawayo's novel was the subject of a great deal of online and newspaper discussion in Zimbabwe and in Zimbabwe-centric news media. The dense discourses around the novel often incorporated comments on its reception and its transnational circulation. "Bookworm," the name used by Tinashe Mushakavanhu for his column in the Zimbabwean newspaper *The Standard*, published a few pieces in which the novel was discussed, as well as a review in his own name reprinted on the page of Weaver Press, Bulawayo's "local" publisher.[31] In a piece that appeared in February 2014, called "Treason against Literature," Mushakavanhu wrote:

> This lack of serious interest in our own [Zimbabwean] literature has invited foreign critics to dominate the shaping of Zimbabwean literature. They read and define us. It is time we not only declared our independence but seriously started reading our own writers.[32]

Interesting here is the language used, which clearly twins literary and cultural self-definition with political independence and colonial legacies. In his piece "Diaspora Influence on Zim Literature" of 2 March 2014, in *The Standard*, Mushakavanhu developed this argument:

> The experience of being 'restless' with terrible economic and socio-political conditions has not only been the driving force for ordinary Zimbabweans to keep moving, it has also been shaping an incredible creative force displayed in Brian Chikwava's debut, *Harare North*, Christopher Mlalazi's *Many Rivers* and recently NoViolet Bulawayo's book that straddles between home and exile.[33]

Mushakavanhu's columns offer an incisive analysis and a knowing critique of many of the issues that appear in the UK *Guardian* discussions under "anxiety." His responses aim to understand the meanings of what he calls Zimbabwean "restlessness."

Charting the histories of the Zimbabwean "diaspora novel," he argues that it is not a genre that is limited to the period after independence (a recurrent trope in CNN discourses about Zimbabwe is that Zimbabwe's crisis was caused solely by the Mugabe years, and that colonial legacies play no role). Instead,

> what is uniquely apparent is that the diaspora novel is becoming the dominant genre of contemporary Zimbabwean writing. Those writers who are giving a global face to Zimbabwean literature are ensconced outside, far from the madding crowds of Harare or Bulawayo, not witness to the buzz, the gossip, the scandals. Perhaps it doesn't mean anything.[34]

The point he makes is not about the Zimbabwean novel, but about the "global face" of the Zimbabwean novel, and the fact that the "restlessness" of Zimbabweans means that diaspora comes to seem the single story of Zimbabwe. This approach draws attention to the assumptions of the metanarrative which presents the global face as the only face. Another important sub-text of the columns is a rhetorical emphasis on Zimbabwe's colonial liberation; while many outside Zimbabwe ascribe all the concerns of contemporary Zimbabweans (especially the "born-free" generation to which both Bulawayo and Mushakavanhu belong) to Mugabe, his analysis has a longer historical reach.

"The" Zimbabwean narrative, in Mushakavanhu's argument, is not necessarily to be found in a novel that is read "at home" either because this novel is unavailable to buy, or because its face is turned away towards a different horizon and reader. This piece ends with the words: "Whatever the case may be, thanks to the diaspora for injecting life to an ailing literary culture. Our literature, Zimbabwean literature, is better off." While "the" Zimbabwean narrative may feed a transnational desire, it is not only that; in fact, that desire is a secondary concern.

NoViolet Bulawayo's novel is aware of these different traditions of reading "the" Zimbabwean novel, and the novel in fact can be understood, in part, as a commentary on these tensions. Future scholars will no doubt trace the explicit ways in which NoViolet Bulawayo's novel is intertextually linked to the great Zimbabwean novel tradition that includes Dambudzo Marechera, Chenjerai Hove, Yvonne Vera, and Tsitsi Dangarembga. Her novel quotes phrases, adopts stylistic elements and lifts characters from these novels, and at the same time it performs the entextualizing work done by readers and non-readers living in the geographical place known as "Zimbabwe," and more specifically "Bulawayo," but only to and for those readers who recognize these references and echoes.

The novel makes complex references to restless circulation and transnationalism, as if it knowingly wishes to pre-empt the anxiety of its metropolitan reception. The city Bulawayo in the text is, and at the same time is not, mappable onto the geographical Bulawayo. A reader who has walked the streets of Bulawayo will know that this is not a documentary creation, and it certainly is not attempting to be a CNN report. The world inhabited by the gang of children shares some features with the real Bulawayo (some street names, a general sense of familiarity); but a reader who knows Bulawayo will realize that the world in the novel is one made as much out of remembered and imagined geographical features as out of the Zimbabwean literary tradition.

Instead of a book about "Africa" (the place where some believe that things fell apart just at the moment that the colonizers happened to be leaving), NoViolet Bulawayo's book is a text that engages with and reflects on what she calls in a *Newsweek* piece published in 2011 the "weight of heritage,"[35] and on the Zimbabwean novel's histories of readership and circulation. The intertextual allusions to Yvonne Vera and Chenjerai Hove are both obvious and meaningful to the reader who "reads the referent." In addition, the novel is striking for the many surfaces on which writing appears, which often function as a commentary on the conduit of contradictions. In the first few pages alone, the reader finds individuals wearing shirts with a range of slogans and inscriptions, the decontextualized nature of the slogans referencing of course the practices of recycling northern rubbish into objects for which the global south is meant to express gratitude. But there is also a lighter, more hilarious, effect in the dissonance between the messages and the wearers of the garments. We see individuals wearing shirts that proclaim "Save Darfur," "Cornell," and a claimed allegiance to the Barcelona football team. These references unsettle the reader, and act as textual markers of the process of reading—they are coded instances of the conduit of contradictions.

The children's games are similarly disruptive of the opposition so often construed between local and transnational. They play a range of invented games that reference, amongst others, the raid on Abottabad, the television show *ER*, and the celebrity Paris Hilton. Karin Barber's definition of what a text is, as well as her discussion of the practices of entextualization, are particularly useful here. Barber defines a "text" as "the idea of weaving or fabricating—connectedness, the quality of having been put together, of having been made by human ingenuity."[36] A text is coherent because it is the result of a human's efforts to organize signs in such a way that they will become interpretable. What makes something a text is that it has been marked out for special attention,[37] and it is the fact of being detachable from their original context that sets texts in motion.[38] The games played by the children in the novel, like the clothes they wear, can be interpreted as recycled goods from elsewhere, rendering the children second hand, and their games and pursuits a poor copy of the shiny and new original. But there is a much more radical interpretation, available to the reader attuned to the conduit of contradictions in their games and re-enactments.[39]

This means the children's game is not derivative, a copy of the real thing. It is not a recycled and thus meaningless (or "rubbish") utterance. Entextualization is more than quotation; for the reader who sees the novel as an instance of the entextualization of "CNN" discourse, there is a very different effect than for the reader who understands the entextualizing agency which is locally inflected and accented. Read this way, the first half of the novel is not simply a world that is lost to the narrator, Darling, but instead the two halves of the novel are instances of mutual entextualization, with entextualization's agency and pleasure distributed diversely along the translational conduit. The references and texts are unmoored from their original contexts, and their meanings are determined precisely by this fluidity and restlessness. My argument is that the pleasure of a certain kind of entextualization relies on knowing that others, elsewhere along the pipeline, are precisely not able to make the same connections, nor to hear the many restless currents.

The significance of the novel's title, *We Need New Names*, is not immediately clear. The words appear in the novel during a discussion about the reassignment of roles and names in the children's performance of a scene from the NBC hospital drama series *ER*.[40] NoViolet Bulawayo's own writer's name (NoViolet means "with Violet," a reference to her mother Violet who died giving birth to her; the chosen surname Bulawayo locates both her origin and her connection to the place where she was born) is a richly affective acknowledgement of the author's as well as the novel's entextualization. When asked about the unusual names (to some western ears), the author replied:

> I come from a place of colourful names so I wanted to capture that in my work, after all my novel is many things including a celebration of my culture. Beyond that, they form a script of their own; they help illuminate character and tell stories.[41]

A number of readers in the transnational scene have remarked on the names of characters in the book, but as many know, Zimbabwean naming traditions in fact do include names such as "Bornfree" and "Godknows," given to characters in the novel.[42] Read from this point of view, the names in the novel are not there to add texture to the "CNN" version, but are instead simply references to the names of the people one knows, who are members of Zimbabwean families. A reader unfamiliar with this fact notices the names (notices them in an awkward way), but at the same time "reads over" them (or over-reads them as allegorical), and is not included in the conspiratorial set of references.

This sense of kinship was highlighted at the launch of the novel in Bulawayo, to which NoViolet Bulawayo returned after 13 years away.

In an article written for *Her Zimbabwe* (an online publication that publishes material related to women in Zimbabwe), Fungai Machirori described the event:

> Zimbabwean author NoViolet Bulawayo launched her novel, *We Need New Names*, long-listed for the prestigious Man Booker Prize and the Guardian First Book Award to a gathering of about 100 people in her home country ahead of a busy schedule that sees her attending a host of high level literary festivals in the coming weeks. In front of an audience made up of old high school friends and close family members—including sisters, cousins, nephews, and nieces, Bulawayo paid special tribute to her 74-year-old father (who has subsequently passed away), Noel Tshele, who she praised as a "master storyteller" with an engaged relationship to language which has influenced her own foray into the world of telling stories. "When I look in the mirror of my writer identity, I not only see myself, but I also see his shadow hovering there somewhere," she said before asking him to stand up to applause from the audience.[43]

In the description of those present, kinship connections are stressed, and in her own speech, NoViolet Bulawayo thanked the town that helped her to "raise" her novel—like one raises a child, and like the town raised the child she was. This framing of the novel serves to emphasize for whom the novel was written, as she writes in the acknowledgements: "And of course to Zim, beloved homeland, country of my people."[44] The thanks expressed are coded in isiNdebele: "Ngiyabonga mina!" in a declaration that embraces her (language) kin and performs for the transnational reader her exclusion (that is, if she even notices). On her blog, and used as a signature on emails, NoViolet Bulawayo includes the quotation from Chinua Achebe with which I introduced this chapter: "Let no one be fooled by the fact that we may write in English, for we intend to do unheard of things with it."[45]

Read alongside the expression of love and thanks, a certain kind of reader is placed here as secondary, at best eavesdropping, at worst simply irrelevant. The Bulawayo launch is the launch where the book (and author) are at home, and embedded in literary and familial networks. It is the celebration launch, and the local circulation is coded through an English which is aware of other languages and aware of other varieties of English/english. Awareness (conspiratorial awareness, even) of the anxious cosmopolitan circulation of the novel is part of the pleasure of this local reception.

The pleasure of this hometown audience is enhanced because they know that much of this private, conspiratorial reception remains "unheard" by others, in a communicative act similar to the ways James Scott theorized as the "hidden transcript," the communicative strategies through which the dominant order can be resisted.[46] The most sustained piece of African language text in the novel is the song sung by the troubled young man called Prince, a song which Bulawayo includes without gloss or footnotes: "*Sobashiy' abafowethu/ Savuka sawela kwamany' amazwe/ Laph' okungazi khon' ubaba lomama/ S'landel' inkululeko.*"[47] We do not hear the tune, of course, but printed on the page are the lyrics to a song which has deep histories as part of liberation struggles in Southern Africa, and was sung in camps where cadres of the ANC's armed wing, uMkhonto we Sizwe, trained.[48] A certain kind of reader, as Gikandi theorizes it, "reads over it," while for a different reader the deep meanings of the song are clear and resonant and call up a community for whom this is a shared memory.

The song is inserted here as a hidden transcript, which draws an intimate circle around those who understand (the language, the referent, the histories) and performs them to the exclusion of those who do not. The reader who does not know the referent may simply read over it, is unaware that she has missed anything; or she may experience the anxiety of exclusion—and both responses are, of course, the point of a hidden transcript. The pleasure, which includes the memory of the painful and resistant contexts of the song, draws together those who do know, and do understand. When the song then narrates the loss of family and place, it is crucial that this is done through the African language script, the memory is not *for* the uninformed reader. She is not included in the memory; and the other readers who do and can remember are— that is precisely the point. But nor are we to understand this particular 'diaspora' novel as one that narrates the character's movement into the space and time of monolingual English. Those who read the novel as an 'American' novel, or a novel written for the pleasure of the imagined 'American' reader, miss this crucial point. Darling's comment is pertinent here: "And then the problem with those who speak only English is this: they don't know how to listen; they are busy looking at you falling instead of paying attention to what you are saying."[49]

A 'heritage' song like this, written in or translated into English, might just be readable as a song about the movement from the past towards an English-language speaking future. Its translation into English might seem to promise a certain universality, reassuring the anxious reader in the scene of transnational reading, and confirming that leaving this broken place was a good decision. Written in isiNdebele like this, however, it retains the memory as untranslated, something which is not recorded for the pleasure or interest of the reader who does not "hear" it. It is a song about leaving hometowns and families, and finding oneself again, having crossed over into a foreign place. But let no one be mistaken to think that this new place can be self-satisfied that it is a good place. As Bookworm describes it in his piece "Diaspora Influence on Zim Literature," the experience of the migrant is too often to find that "the trees everywhere are as dry" as in Zimbabwe, and that "the arrival experience breaks them to the point of no recovery as the host lands become hostile sanctuaries."[50] The histories of the song also bring together various liberation struggles in Southern Africa, making the point clearly that Zimbabwe's troubles started long before people became disappointed in Mugabe, and underlining a transnational pan-African identity.

In response to the question whether she considers herself an "African writer," Bulawayo's answer is: "For me, I always insist that I am an African writer because it's true; I am an African... I feel that even if I deny that label, my work will scream otherwise". On her writer's website, NoViolet Bulawayo included for a while this striking image, as a visual equivalent of the answer (Figure 7.1).[51] In it, we see the author looking through a telescope, her hands cupped around the viewfinder and obscuring her face. What we see (looking as if through a cross section of a pipeline) is *her* looking; she is uninterested in whether we are looking at her or not. Right in the middle of the photograph is a small map of Africa, an earring drawing attention to the ear that hears the voices of 'home.' This picture, so unlike the typical authors' portrait, leaves us curious about what it is she sees. It is an awkward image, meant to unsettle—but also to please.

This chapter has attempted to theorize the reader who reads within, against, and through multilingual currents, who can read the references and take pleasure in the knowledge that other readers are at times excluded from this restless position of reading. Important is that this reader knows that the reader who speaks and reads only the one English

Figure 7.1 A portrait of the author: NoViolet Bulawayo.

has a more limited understanding of the nature of the transnationalism performed in the book. There are many englishes, as there are many homes. In the novel the definition of home is complex. "When somebody talks about home," thinks Darling, "you have to listen carefully to know exactly which one the person is referring to," or as I have theorized it here—where they are positioned along the conduit of contradictions.

In interviews, NoViolet Bulawayo repeatedly places her novel 'at home.' "My journey starts with hearing stories told mostly by my grandmother and father throughout my childhood," she says. And:

> I wanted a name that spoke and meant something to me so I chose one that allowed me to celebrate my late mother as well as my hometown—both are very dear to me, and I consider it more than a pen name.[52]

The international circulation of the novel, however, is not uncomplicatedly accepted. The transnational reader's buying power and the sponsorship of writing programmes and residencies support the writing; but the celebrated author has to be vigilant about the direction of flow in the "conduit," to prevent these extractive economies of knowledge.

We need New Names is a novel that has enlivened and reinvigorated the literary tradition 'at home,' and is a novel that is only partly interested in its transnational reception. Bosch Santana points out that the children in the novel

> smile for the cameras, but it's clear that smiling is not always what it seems, especially when it is described elsewhere in the novel as the "baring of teeth"—without looking closely we may not be able to tell the difference.[53]

And Mushakavanhu/Bookworm, writing about the night that Dambudzo Marechera was awarded the Guardian First Novel award, reminds his readers that Marechera used the occasion of the award ceremony to protest "against the hypocrisy of the [international] literary establishment." He concludes this piece, called "Caine Prize stifling African literature," by writing: "Take advantage of those whose mission is to take advantage of you and when it's time to run, don't hesitate."[54]

Acknowledgements

With thanks to Shepherd Mpofu, Sarah Chiumbu, and Lindelwa Dalamba for their insights and guidance, as well as their time. Thanks also to NoViolet Bulawayo for generously giving permission to use her photograph, and to Tinashe Mushakavanhu for his engagement. Thank you also to the two anonymous readers, and to the editors for their skilful and stimulating editing.

Notes

1 Chinua Achebe, *Morning Yet on Creation Day: Essays* (New York: Anchor Press, 1975), 9.
2 NoViolet Bulawayo, *We Need New Names* (London: Chatto & Windus, 2013).
3 Bulawayo, *We Need New Names*, 159.
4 Ato Quayson, *Oxford Street, Accra: City Life and the Itineraries of Transnationalism* (Durham: Duke University Press, 2014).
5 Quayson, *Oxford Street, Accra*, 31.
6 Ibid., 31.
7 Ashleigh Harris, "Awkward Form and Writing the African Present," *Johannesburg Workshop in Theory and Criticism* 7 (2014): 3, http://jwtc.org.za/test/ashleigh_harris.htm.
8 Eileen Julien, "The Extroverted African Novel," in *The Novel, Volume 1: History, Geography, Culture*, ed. Franco Moretti (Princeton, NJ: Princeton University Press, 2007), 684.
9 Harris, "Awkward Form," 3–8.
10 NoViolet Bulawayo, *We Need New Names* (Harare: Weaver Press, 2013).
11 Harris, "Awkward Form," 5.
12 Ibid., 6.
13 Ibid., 5.
14 Helon Habila, "*We Need New Names* by NoViolet Bulawayo—A Review," *The Guardian*, 20 June 2013, www.theguardian.com/books/2013/jun/20/need-new-names-bulawayo-review.
15 Philip Hensher, "Well, That's the End of the Booker Prize, Then," *The Guardian*, 18 September 2013, www.theguardian.com/books/booksblog/2013/sep/18/booker-prize-us-writers-end.
16 Ibid.
17 Ibid.
18 Binyavanga Wainaina, "Kenyan Author Attacks Insularity of British Fiction," *The Guardian*, 18 November 2011, www.theguardian.com/books/2011/nov/18/kenyan-author-insularity-british-fiction.
19 Ngũgĩ wa Thiong'o, *Decolonising the Mind: The Politics of Language in African Literature* (Oxford: James Currey, 1981).
20 Binyavanga Wainaina, "How to Write About Africa," *Granta* 92 (2005): 91–7.
21 NoViolet Bulawayo, "Codes Don't Exclude Readers from British Literature," *The Guardian*, 24 November 2011. www.theguardian.com/books/2011/nov/24/codes-exclude-readers-british-literature.
22 Stephanie Bosch Santana, "From the 'African Booker' to 'The Booker': NoViolet Bulawayo's *We Need New Names*," *Africa in Words*, 12 August 2013. http://africainwords.com/2013/08/12/from-the-african-booker-to-the-booker-noviolet-bulawayos-we-need-new-names/.
23 Bosch Santana, "'African Booker' to 'The Booker.'"
24 Bulawayo, *New Names*, 194–8.
25 Simon Gikandi, "Reading the Referent: Postcolonialism and the Writing of Modernity," in *Reading the "New" Literatures in a Postcolonial Era*, ed. Susheila Nasta (Cambridge: D S Brewer, 2000), 87–104.
26 Gikandi, "Reading the Referent," 90.
27 Ibid., 92.
28 Ibid., 92.
29 Ibid., 101.

30 For a fuller development of this concept of "accent," see Carli Coetzee, *Accented Futures: Language Activism and the Ending of Apartheid* (Johannesburg: Wits University Press, 2013).

31 Tinashe Mushakavanhu, "Review of *We Need New Names*," *The Standard*, 5 May 2013, www.weaverpresszimbabwe.com/index.php/reviews/101-we-need-new-names/556-review-of-we-need-new-names-the-standard.

32 Tinashe Mushakavanhu (writing as "Bookworm"), "Treason against Literature," *The Standard*, 9 February 2014, www.thestandard.co.zw/2014/02/09/treason-literature/.

33 Tinashe Mushakavanhu (writing as "Bookworm"), "Diaspora Influence on Zim Literature," *The Standard*, 2 March, 2014, www.thestandard.co.zw/2014/03/02/diaspora-influence-zim-literature/.

34 Mushakavanhu, "Diaspora Influence."

35 NoViolet Bulawayo, "Writer NoViolet Bulawayo Reflects on Zimbabwe," *Newsweek*, 25 September 2011, http://europe.newsweek.com/writer-noviolet-bulawayo-reflects-zimbabwe-67467.

36 Karin Barber, *The Anthropology of Texts, Persons and Publics: Oral and Written Culture in Africa and Beyond* (Cambridge: Cambridge University Press, 2007), 21.

37 Barber, *Anthropology of Texts*, 22.

38 Ibid., 22–3.

39 See, for example, Polo Moji, "New Names, Translational Subjectivities: (Dis)location and (Re)naming in NoViolet Bulawayo's *We Need New Names*," *Journal of African Cultural Studies* 27, no. 2 (2015): 181–90; Shirin Edwin, "(Un)solving Global Challenges: African Short Stories, Literary Awards and the Question of Audience," *Journal of African Cultural Studies* 28 no. 3 (2016): 359–71.

40 Bulawayo, *New Names*, 82.

41 David Smith, "NoViolet Bulawayo tells of heartbreak of homecoming in Mugabe's Zimbabwe," *The Guardian*, 4 September 2013, www.theguardian.com/world/2013/sep/04/noviolet-bulawayo-homecoming-mugabe-zimbabwe.

42 Busi Makoni, Sinfree Makoni and Pedzisai Mashiri, "Naming Practices and Language Planning in Zimbabwe," *Current Issues in Language Planning* 8 no. 3 (2007): 437–67.

43 Fungai Machirori, "NoViolet Bulawayo Pays Tribute to Father at Zimbabwe Book Launch," *Her Zimbabwe*, *The Guardian Africa Network*, 30 August2013,www.theguardian.com/world/2013/aug/30/zimbabwe-noviolet-bulawayo-book-launch.

44 Bulawayo, *New Names*, 294.

45 Achebe, *Morning Yet On Creation Day*, 9.

46 James C. Scott, *Domination and the Arts of Resistance: Hidden Transcripts* (New Haven: Yale University Press, 1990).

47 Bulawayo, *New Names*, 159.

48 Shirli Gilbert, "Singing Against Apartheid: ANC Cultural Groups and the International Anti-Apartheid Struggle," in *Composing Apartheid: Music For and Against Apartheid*, ed. Grant Olwage (Johannesburg: Wits University Press, 2008), 155–84.

49 Bulawayo, *New Names*, 194.

50 Mushakavanhu, "Diaspora Influence."

51 NoViolet Bulawayo's official author web site, http://novioletbulawayo.com/writing/.

52 Interview with NoViolet Bulawayo, "The Penname and *We Need New Names*," 11 August 2014 in *New Zimbabwe*, www.newzimbabwe.com/

showbiz-17260-NoViolet+The+alias+and+We+Need+New+Names/showbiz.
aspx.
53 Bosch Santana, "'African Booker' to 'The Booker.'"
54 Mushakavanhu (writing as "Bookworm"), "Caine Prize Stifling African Literature?" 30 March 2014 in *The Standard*, www.thestandard.co.zw/2014/03/
30/caine-prize-stifling-african-literature/.

Bibliography

Achebe, Chinua. *Morning Yet on Creation Day: Essays*. New York: Anchor
Press, 1975.
Barber, Karin. *The Anthropology of Texts, Persons and Publics: Oral and Writ-
ten Culture in Africa and Beyond*. Cambridge: Cambridge University Press,
2007.
Bosch Santana, Stephanie. "From the 'African Booker' to 'The Booker': NoViolet
Bulawayo's *We Need New Names*." *Africa in Words*, 12 August, 2013. http://
africainwords.com/2013/08/12/from-the-african-booker-to-the-booker-
noviolet-bulawayos-we-need-new-names/.
Bulawayo, NoViolet. Author Web Site. http://novioletbulawayo.com/writing/.
———. "Codes Don't Exclude Readers from British Literature." *The Guardian*, 24
November 2011. www.theguardian.com/books/2011/nov/24/codes-exclude-
readers-british-literature.
———. "NoViolet: The Penname and *We Need New Names*." *New Zimbabwe*,
11 August 2014. www.newzimbabwe.com/showbiz-17260-NoViolet+The+ali
as+and+We+Need+New+Names/showbiz.aspx.
———. *We Need New Names*. Harare: Weaver Press, 2013; London: Chatto &
Windus, 2013.
———. "Writer NoViolet Bulawayo Reflects on Zimbabwe." *Newsweek*, 25
September, 2011. http://europe.newsweek.com/writer-noviolet-bulawayo-
reflects-zimbabwe-67467.
Coetzee, Carli. *Accented Futures: Language Activism and the Ending of Apart-
heid*. Johannesburg: Wits University Press, 2013.
Edwin, Shirin. "Singing Against Apartheid: ANC Cultural Groups and the In-
ternational Anti-Apartheid Struggle." In *Composing Apartheid: Music for
and Against Apartheid*, edited by Grant Olwage, 155–84. Johannesburg:
Wits University Press, 2008.
———. "(Un)solving Global Challenges: African Short Stories, Literary Awards
and the Question of Audience." *Journal of African Cultural Studies* 28 no. 3
(2016): 359–71.
Gikandi, Simon. "Reading the Referent: Postcolonialism and the Writing of
Modernity." In *Reading the 'New' Literatures in a Postcolonial Era*, edited
by Susheila Nasta, 87–104. Cambridge: D S Brewer, 2000.
Habila, Helon. "*We Need New Names* by NoViolet Bulawayo—A Review."
The Guardian, 20 June 2013. www.theguardian.com/books/2013/jun/20/
need-new-names-bulawayo-review.
Harris, Ashleigh. "Awkward Form and Writing the African Present."
Johannesburg Workshop in Theory and Criticism 7 (2014): 3–8. http://jwtc.
org.za/test/ashleigh_harris.htm.

Hensher, Philip. "Well, That's the End of the Booker Prize, Then." *The Guardian*, 18 September 2013. www.theguardian.com/books/booksblog/2013/sep/18/booker-prize-us-writers-end.

Julien, Eileen. "The Extroverted African Novel." In *The Novel, Volume 1: History, Geography, Culture*, edited by Franco Moretti, 667–700. Princeton, NJ: Princeton University Press, 2007.

Machirori, Fungai. "NoViolet Bulawayo Pays Tribute to Father at Zimbabwe Book Launch." *Her Zimbabwe, The Guardian Africa Network*, 30 August 2013. www.theguardian.com/world/2013/aug/30/zimbabwe-noviolet-bulawayo-book-launch.

Moji, Polo. "New Names, Translational Subjectivities: (Dis)location and (Re)naming in NoViolet Bulawayo's *We Need New Names*." *Journal of African Cultural Studies* 27 no. 2 (2015): 181–90.

Mushakavanhu, Tinashe. "Review of *We Need New Names*." *The Standard*, 5 May 2013. www.weaverpresszimbabwe.com/index.php/reviews/101-we-need-new-names/556-review-of-we-need-new-names-the-standard.

———, (Writing as "Bookworm"). "Diaspora Influence on Zim Literature." *The Standard*, 2 March 2014. www.thestandard.co.zw/2014/03/02/diaspora-influence-zim-literature/.

———, (Writing as "Bookworm"). "Treason against Literature." *The Standard*, 9 February 2014. www.thestandard.co.zw/2014/02/09/treason-literature/.

Ngũgĩ wa Thiong'o. *Decolonising the Mind: The Politics of Language in African Literature*. Oxford: James Currey, 1981.

Quayson, Ato. *Oxford Street, Accra: City Life and the Itineraries of Transnationalism*. Durham, NC: Duke University Press, 2014.

Scott, James C. *Domination and the Arts of Resistance: Hidden Transcripts*. New Haven, CT: Yale University Press, 1990.

Smith, David. "NoViolet Bulawayo tells of heartbreak of homecoming in Mugabe's Zimbabwe." *The Guardian*, 4 September, 2013.

Wainaina, Binyavanga. "How to Write About Africa." *Granta* 92 (2005): 91–7.

———. "Kenyan Author Attacks Insularity of British Fiction." *The Guardian*, 18 November 2011. www.theguardian.com/books/2011/nov/18/kenyan-author-insularity-british-fiction.

8 Translation as a Motor of Critique and Invention in Contemporary Literature

The Case of Xiaolu Guo

Fiona Doloughan

This chapter will position translation as a particular mode of reading and of writing that draws not only on critical engagement with 'source' texts but also on the creative potentials of interaction between languages and cultures in the production of a 'target' text. Writers for whom English is not the sole means of communication or of expression, and whose circumstances or history are such that they have crossed cultures, tend to have increased awareness of cultural relativity and linguistic difference. This may be explicitly expressed or communicated in terms, for example, of a focus on a particular thematic or in relation to linguistic or generic choices. Indeed, for many such writers, the notion of translation itself, and what it might mean in the context of writing and meaning-making more generally, becomes a locus of interest. With access to more than one writing system and set of linguistic and cultural conventions comes the potential for enhanced creativity, and the kind of double vision or critical perspective that depends on or emerges from such a dual consciousness—as is the case for bilingual writers, for example.[1] Translation itself has become a hot topic, given continued debate about the contexts (literary, social, cultural, political, commercial) in which it can be seen to operate and the scope and extent of its influence.

That issues relating to translation are prevalent in our lives today is borne out by Sherry Simon's recent review in *Target*, a leading translation studies journal, of Susan Bassnett's 2011 *Reflections on Translation*: "What Bassnett shows so powerfully," Simon writes, "is how translation, more than one might have realized, is at the heart of our existence as readers, as theatre-goers, as citizens."[2] For more than a decade now, there has been increasing interest in, and discussion of, the meanings and import of translation, not just in relation to notions of linguistic and cultural exchange, but in broader social, political, and critical terms. Indeed, in the context of a recent international conference (July 2015) on the theme of "Innovation Paths in Translation and Intercultural Studies," organized by the International Association of Translation and Intercultural Studies, many of the talks by specialists in the field reflected awareness of translation's shifting social and cultural roles at a time of rapid technological change and political and economic challenges. It is timely, therefore, to reconsider the implications not only for production but also for the reception of work created by writers who engage critically and creatively with the "richness of diversity" that translation and translational practices, in a broad sense, open up.[3]

This chapter will argue that increasingly translation, in multiple senses, is integral to contemporary literary production and reception. In focusing on the work of Xiaolu Guo, a Chinese-born writer, now resident in the UK, it will illustrate the extent to which translation is implicated in shaping the construction of her narratives. It will do so against the backdrop of some recent theoretical and critical work in translation studies, comparative and world literature, and postcolonial and cultural studies, broadly speaking. In so doing, it will seek to build on a body of research that highlights the centrality of translation and translational practices in the production and circulation of contemporary writing, while addressing the consequences for readers of interaction with 'original' works that are already the product of more than one language and culture.[4]

The choice of Guo is motivated rather than contingent in the sense that her life history, as well as the concerns articulated in her fiction and in her films, reflect, and are a product of, processes of translation both literal and metaphoric. As a graduate of the Beijing Film Academy, as well as the recipient of a scholarship to the National Film and Television School, Beaconsfield, who has produced a number of award-winning films, and as a writer of fiction in both Chinese and English, whose inclusion in *Granta Best of Young British Novelists* 2013 stands as testimony to her literary status, Guo's trajectory is not untypical of that of many writers today who cross national and cultural borders. Indeed, a closer look at Guo's cinematographic and novelistic oeuvre would suggest that she has long been concerned with issues of translation in multiple senses. As I have shown in another context, as a film-maker Guo often treats similar themes to those realized in her novels (migration, alienation, loss) and imports into her fiction images and visual elements that support and extend the verbal, while her films often rely on poetry and metaphor in exploring their characters' worlds and feelings.[5] In other words, what can be seen to characterize Guo's work is a focus on extending the possibilities of one mode or medium by drawing on those of another. Thus her fiction is spatialized, while her films are, to an extent, novelized, or formally framed and edited, so as to import some of the devices of fiction into cinema. These can be considered translational narrative practices.

A Concise Chinese–English Dictionary for Lovers (2007), for example, employs a range of resources (intertextual, visual, linguistic, and cross-cultural) in addition to the imposition of a primarily conceptual mode of organization on what is otherwise a straightforwardly linear narrative detailing the life of a young Chinese woman residing in London, falling in love, and learning English over the course of a year. These resources function to disrupt linearity and encourage a reading and interpretation which sees a thickening of time and an opening up of intercultural spaces, as the here-and-now is filtered through the consciousness of a young woman who has come from elsewhere and who therefore, inevitably, has a comparative perspective. Her grounding in a different language, culture, and set of values serves as a critical lens to interrogate the presentation of what might otherwise appear as naturalized or normative customs and conventions in her new place of residence. Likewise, *She, A Chinese*, Guo's 2009 film in Chinese and English, seeks, in the director's words, to challenge "the traditional Chinese cinema style, to cross over cultural borders, with a fresh artistic language and a personal voice."[6] This artistic language and personal voice derive at least in part from a desire to produce a film that responds to Jean-Luc Godard's *La Chinoise* by reversing the direction of travel (from China to Europe) and by highlighting, perhaps somewhat ironically, the youthful rebellion and coming of age of a young Chinese woman in London. In any case, what is common in both instances is Guo's reliance on representational and expressive modalities that cut across languages and cultures, whether these relate to the language of literature or film, to Chinese or English, or to the cultures of the West or of the East.

What is of note is the fact that Guo's training as a film-maker is in documentaries, which at one level seek to show aspects of reality and to deal with social and cultural issues, broadly speaking. In *Late at Night: Voices of Ordinary Madness* (2013), shown at the British Film Festival, the viewer gets a sense of the extent to which Guo is driven by ideas rather than narrative. Yet this film, which might in a sense be described as a critique of capitalism or as the study of an underclass, in that it presents mostly marginalized figures living in the East End of London, is a highly wrought, formally structured film, which employs a series of cinematographic devices and fictional frames which, in effect, impose or create a reading path through the otherwise episodic and fragmented voices. There are stylized images and quotations on screen from a range of writers and philosophers, such as Beckett and Huxley, which have the effect of superimposing on the moving images and the talking heads a frame for reading. In short, the treatment of topics in Guo's films, whereby meaning is made at the level of form and in relation to the viewer's engagement with structure, including repetition and juxtaposition, demands an ability to read one mode in terms of another and to harness a translational logic. In her films, as in her fiction, Guo relies on sometimes explicit, sometimes implicit points of comparison and critique between East and West, communist and capitalist systems in their differential production of citizens, ideas of freedom and control, of inclusion and exclusion, of the creation of a sense of belonging or alienation. Of particular concern is the question of how particular societies produce certain types of people or ways of viewing the world, and what it means to feel at home in a culture or to experience dislocation. For those who move across cultures, whether voluntarily or out of necessity, notions of mobility and displacement, of being subjects in translation, are part of the texture of their lives as well as aspects of the spaces of imagination.

New Modes of Reading and Writing

Before turning in more detail to analysis of Guo's work, it would be useful to refer to societal, critical, and political contexts that inform current interest in translation in an extended sense, and that frame my reading of translation as a mode of literary production and reception as well as an interpretive space at the confluence of languages and cultures. What I want to highlight is the coexistence of a number of arguably interrelated, if apparently contradictory, phenomena, and their connection with extended concepts of translation. These relate to: changing and increasingly unstable relationships between language and nation; increased mobility and border crossing on the part of many contemporary writers, even if the effects of this mobility and border crossing are not evenly distributed or entirely predictable; and the rise of English as a lingua franca.

At a time when monolingualism can no longer be assumed to be the default position in many parts of the world, and when many writers writing in English have access to other languages and cultures and refer to them or employ them either covertly or overtly in their work, it is more difficult to maintain what for many is, in reality, a fiction.[7] The idea that languages and cultures are bounded and distinct, rather than mutually informing or complementary, has begun to be revisited, as have notions of translatability and equivalence more generally. The "default rule of monolingual speech" can no longer be maintained, as those who can, often do speak or write in more than one language, sometimes switching languages depending on the particular context, their sense of audience and of purpose, as well as the affective and intellectual values invested in one language or another.[8] Economic forces and political power also play their part in decision-making about which language or languages to use in a given situation: witness the rise of English and the imbalance in terms of what gets translated into and out of English across the globe.

Certainly, within a postcolonial and cultural studies paradigm there has long been recognition of the politics of language and the relevance of conceptions of, and approaches to, translation and translational writing to literary production. What has changed, in my view, is the fact that such issues can no longer be contained within bounded disciplinary or sub-disciplinary areas but constitute a challenge to literary studies more generally. Writing in English, indeed conceptions of English literature, its inclusions and exclusions, are subject to contradictory pressures: the simultaneous policing of, and movement across, borders (for example Apter's notion of 'checkpointization').[9] What it means to write in English, while accessing or employing other languages and cultures, is not necessarily the same today as 40 or 50 years ago, nor are readers necessarily schooled in similar ways of reading. The kind of work produced by Guo, for example, is alert to the creative and critical possibilities of linguistic and cultural border crossing as well as to the role of English in extending readership beyond those familiar with Chinese literature and culture. At the same time, her incorporation of extended notions of translation within her work, not just at the level of theme but also in terms of structural mechanisms and modes of organization, is evidence of an artistic and literary practice informed by the politics of style as well as by a bilingual aesthetics, in Sommer's terms.[10] As Ch'ien indicates in relation to what she calls the weirding of English, the "problem of interpretation and translation has become a subject for writers" from immigrant backgrounds or for those who have crossed linguistic and cultural, as well as geographic, borders.[11] Many of them, she asserts, "sustain a practice of linguistic polyculturality" and "challenge the existence of a normative standard for English" by drawing on the systemic properties or affordances of another language in the design and material realization of their narrative.[12] This can be seen in Guo's literary and narrative practice insofar as she constructs layered textual worlds with a comparative dimension where the materiality and cultural politics of language is always in play even as it serves as a critical lens and resource for creativity.

In both *A Concise Chinese–English Dictionary for Lovers* (2007) and *I Am China* (2014) the co-presence of Chinese and English is in evidence in a visible and material sense. The former explicitly treats the process of language acquisition, and in so doing is written in a kind of broken English which gets progressively more complex and sophisticated, both lexically and grammatically, as the young protagonist Z becomes more proficient. Comparison of the Prologue and Epilogue of the novel bears this out. Z's reflections as she leaves Beijing for London at the beginning of the narrative, for example, are couched in language that is syntactically and lexically simple, marked by the language of a learner.

> Now.
> Beijing time 12 clock midnight.
> London time 5 clock afternoon.
> But I at neither time zone. I on airplane. Sitting on 25,000 km
> above to earth and trying remember all English I learning in school.
> I not met you yet. You in future.[13]

As the narrative continues, what becomes clear is that despite some of the syntactic and lexical 'errors' made by Z, her thoughts and reflections are anything but simple. Already the kind of questions she poses in her broken English—"When a body floating in air, which country she belonging to?"—echoing her concern with time zones, travel and positionality, are indicative of a mind at work.[14] What becomes apparent is Z's philosophical disposition, as she subjects her experience in a new language and of a new culture to scrutiny.

By the end of the novel, the language has become more complex and visibly more 'correct.'

> It's a big aeroplane, with so many seats, so many passengers. Air China, with the phoenix tail drawn on the side. This time it takes me east. Which direction is the wind blowing now, I wonder? Coming to England was not easy but going back is much harder.[15]

While the narrator's philosophical disposition continues to be in evidence—she is still posing questions about the relationship between location and sense of self—what has changed, apart from the complexity and grammaticality of her language, is the 'thickness' of her experience. Time has passed in a new culture, the direction of travel has changed, and Z is a year older. With the passage of time she understands from the inside what it means to have been translated across time and space, and to be subject to translation by, as well as of, oneself. Returning to Beijing constitutes a kind of culture shock in reverse as she notes the changes that have taken place in her absence.

> The whole city is dusty and messy. Unfinished skeletons of skyscrapers and naked construction sites fill the horizon. The taxi drivers spit loudly on to the road through their open windows. Torn plastic bags are stuck on trees like strange fruits. Pollution, pollution, great pollution in my great country.[16]

This image of Beijing is evocative and the language used to project it is striking. The "skeletons of skyscrapers," the "naked construction sites," and the plastic bags "like strange fruit" are poetic and metaphoric. The qualifying of "construction site" by the adjective "naked" is unusual but meaningful, both complementing the image of rapid development in Beijing, with building projects in progress, and suggesting a kind of soulless cityscape. The kind of control and manipulation of language demonstrated here is that of a competent and linguistically playful narrator—witness the two meanings of "great" in evidence here. Reference to the natural world (trees, fresh air) and its despoiling and destruction (plastic bags, pollution) plays a narrative role here, but is also indicative of Guo's ongoing concern as a writer with the environment and its manmade destruction. It is difficult not to hear an echo of Billie Holiday's voice in the expression "strange fruit" to describe the torn plastic bags caught in the branches of the trees.

While in *A Concise Chinese–English Dictionary for Lovers*, use of English is marked and inflected with Chinese 'accents,' and notions of translation feature large in relation to movement and communication across cultures, in the case of *I Am China*, the presence of English-in-translation manifests itself in a less obviously mimetic way. Realization of the book's premise—the translation into English of assorted documents and letters by a translator at the invitation of a publisher—does not involve learner language, but that of a trained translator from Chinese into English, who is seen to grapple with the complexities of the translation process. Scottish-born translator Iona muses at intervals on the challenges of her task as well as on her own limitations as a translator. These challenges range from the organizational and lower level (for example, the bundle of documents she receives needs to be sorted), to higher-order skills and knowledges such as an understanding of colloquial as well as formal Chinese, and familiarity with Chinese history, literature, and culture. *I Am China* is a novel that reflects on processes of translation even as it demonstrates them by, for example, comparing different versions of a translation to test the possible meanings being made. In the context of a narrative where the question of whether an event has already taken place or is about to happen, differences between Chinese and English in their rendering of temporality become a crucial, not just an incidental, issue. Iona struggles with the translation of protagonist Jian's final two scribbled lines about the blueness and purity of the sea, as she tries to uncover what has happened to him and where he is:

> Then she changes the tense. Since Chinese has no tense indication with verbs it can be hard to determine the meaning.[17]

In rendering the lines in the future tense—"There, that sea, the bluest and purest sea. It will be the last blue I shall ever see," Iona is alerted to the possible undertones: that Jian is going there to die.[18] It is Jian's written correspondence with his girlfriend Mu which forms the substance of a major strand of the narrative. The novel's Prelude, which presents in italics the English translation of a letter dated 29 December 2011, is followed by a series of early chapters, told in the third person, which present to the reader the figure of Scottish-born translator Iona as she sets about her translation brief. These initial chapters set in April 2013 present to the reader a description of London, of Iona's flat, of her recent sexual encounter, and chart her engagement with the process of translating the documents before her, as she tries to piece together the story she uncovers. Translation is shown as a multifaceted practice, integral to the novel's design, narrative progression, and plotting. It serves both as narrative matter and as critical lens through which to explore what it means to live in translation or to be translated.

Brief commentary on the letter of 29 December 2011 from Jian to Mu illustrates some of the issues that translation can raise in terms of movement across languages and cultures. Take, for example, the opening sentence after the address to "Dearest Mu": "The sun is piercing, old bastard sky."[19] Already the inclusion of the phrase "old bastard sky" suggests a degree of foreignization, alerting the reader to the fact that s/he is reading in translation. In addition, mention of events and participants from a recognizably Chinese context (Tiananmen Square, Chairman Hu Yaobang) help remove the reader from his/her here-and-now to another time and place. While this process of entering another space and constructing a world on the basis of graphic and verbal triggers is true more generally of a process of reading and meaning-making, Guo's novel emphasizes the embeddedness of translational practices in the production and reception or interpretation of the narrative.

In effect, what is already happening is the emergence of new circuits of reading and writing, as Bassnett has called them, which are increasingly intercultural, or at the very least require sensitivity to the fact that English always operates in the presence of other languages and literatures.[20] Alastair Pennycook points to the ways in which English can always be reappropriated by those for whom it is one resource, amongst others, in their extended linguistic and expressive repertoires.[21] Utterances in English produced by speakers and writers for whom English is but one of a number of languages are not deficient by default, nor necessarily lacking in the idiomaticity assumed to be the prerogative of so-called native speakers. English that is described as 'broken' or 'accented' or that is perceived as a kind of 'translatorese' or 'translatese' may originate from a variety of speakers and writers and have multiple forms and functions.

Translational Spaces and the Construction of Narrative

As I have argued elsewhere in relation to the narratives produced by writers having access to English in addition to other languages and cultures, a situation that can no longer be presumed to be exceptional, the co-presence of these other languages and cultures, even where, on the surface, they do not seem to operate, creates a kind of translational space.[22] Whereas for Eva Hoffman, for example, acquisition and 'mastery' of English initially meant suppression and loss of her native Polish in order to acculturate to Canadian and American 'norms,' the work of writers such as Xiaolu Guo constructs and embodies a counternarrative by showing the extent to which English Only, rather than English Plus, is potentially limiting for both readers and writers at a time when, arguably, translation has become a primary modus operandi. The question of "[w]ho is addressed, and how, in the course of translation," and of the ways in which these questions relate to processes of migration, is, to an extent, entangled in the politics of space and of movement, as well as of language.[23] In other words, context, as well as co-text, is important in helping to decipher the meaning of what one is reading. In *I Am China*, for example, the treatment and status of those who are forced to leave their countries of origin, and the ways in which their claims are handled and 'translated' across jurisdictions, is one of the concerns of the novel. Kublai Jian, one of the central protagonists, is expelled from China on political grounds and lands in England, where he finds himself first in a psychiatric unit in Lincolnshire, having been declared by a doctor to suffer from "'borderline personality,'" then in an Immigration Removal Centre in Dover.[24] From here he is eventually transferred to an Asylum Centre in Switzerland, "one of a few refugees granted a transfer to a Third Country, owing to uncommon political status."[25]

What is of particular interest here is the way in which the novel narrativizes and embeds within itself aspects of a particular social and political reality. Jian's detention in the Lincolnshire psychiatric unit and his medicalization is shown to be the consequence of his inability to articulate his situation—he is after all a Chinese man from Beijing—in language that the authorities understand. (The question of whether or not an interpreter was present is not directly addressed, but what is made clear is Jian's frustration, incomprehension, and initial sense of powerlessness in the face of forces that feel alien to him). From a human point of view, his weariness, anger at his treatment, and sense of humiliation are understandable: "The words wouldn't come. He felt totally inert and unable to argue back or explain what was really wrong."[26] Jian's experience appears to be distorted and misrepresented by the language of power. However, he does take matters somewhat humorously into his own hands by writing to the Queen, a letter to which he receives a rather officious reply, informing him of the correct process for corresponding with her Majesty. The humour is in some ways a relief from the underlying bleakness of the book, notwithstanding the resilience and integrity of some of the characters. In distributing a manifesto at a music event in China, post-Tiananmen, Jian has taken a stand for freedom of expression and human rights, and has paid the price. His treatment in parts of Western Europe such as the UK, Switzerland, and France and his experience outside of China, illuminate the plight of those who find themselves caught up in systems they do not understand and over which they have little or no control. The human story revealed in diary entries and letters to his girlfriend Mu undercuts and disturbs the bureaucratic and hegemonic practices of states and territories.

The translation of Jian's narrative takes place at many different and overlapping levels: within the fictional frame, it is literally translated from Chinese into English by a freelance translator educated at the School of Oriental and African Languages (SOAS) in London—indeed there are representations of his handwriting in Chinese script within the novel followed by translator Iona's renderings in English; Jian is also 'translated' across cultures. He is removed from China and from his relational and familial ties, his cultural knowledge and his place within a particular society at a particular moment, and variously relocated. His location is shaped first by his status as 'a non-person,' someone who belongs to no country, since his visa has run out and he has been expelled from China, then as a refugee, as a temporary legal resident of one country (Switzerland), and as someone travelling and working under an assumed identity in another (France). His mobility is not of the transnational, cosmopolitan variety. In his travels and travails he encounters others like himself, those living on the fringes of society, surviving and making do, busking, working in restaurants, working on ships. Ultimately, however, the price for all of this 'freedom' is too high.

As I have begun to indicate, Guo's work also interrogates conceptualizations of translation in relation to border crossing, both linguistic and cultural, as well as in relation to narratives of migration. These narratives of translation can be read in the context of the social and political worlds which they index, as well as in relation to current theories of and discourses surrounding translation. In terms of language politics, modes of representation, and conceptualizations of translation at a time when English as a lingua franca may be seen as "[t]ranslation's defining moment," it is as well to look more carefully at the ways in which translation is narrated and represented.[27] Equally, it is important to examine the extent to which translation can be both a critical modus operandi and a driver of new modes of writing.

The following section will turn to Guo's work in relation to translation as motor of critique and invention. It presupposes, following Bakhtin, that the novel draws on heterogeneous discourses in its construction of narrative, even as it recognizes that the links between language and life, or between narrative shaping and the representation of particular types of social and political worlds through discourse, are heavily mediated and multilayered. It is important to bear in mind, however, that in her inclusion of visual images (samples of handwriting, record covers, photos, drawings, and other realia) as well as in her explicit representation of different sign systems and in her overt treatment of translation, Guo is explicitly marking her work as multimodal and multilingual. Even if, on the surface, her narratives are predominantly in English, it is English visibly in the presence of other languages and other sign systems. In her thematic as well as in her formal concerns, Guo points to the location of English today as a lingua franca: as a language of power, certainly, but also as a material resource on which to draw in her construction of narratives of translation that explicitly thematize stories of movement across languages and cultures, foregrounding issues of loss and/or gain in the process of encountering difference and translating self and other. My contention is that in relation both to individual works and across her corpus to date, Guo's work presents a critique of aspects of a translational culture, even as it depends on a reader's ability to recognize and engage with the double consciousness and bilingual aesthetics of the narrative voice.

Translation as Critique and Invention

A Concise Chinese–English Dictionary for Lovers is the dictionary-novel that brought Guo to the attention of an Anglophone public and was shortlisted for the Orange Prize for Fiction in 2007. The fact that it has been translated into a number of languages, including Italian, French, and Dutch, is indicative of its international reach and relevance beyond a purely Anglophone world. The challenges, both perceptible and imagined, of translating a work written in ostensibly 'broken' English into French would constitute the subject of another essay; but those who are interested in reading the 2008 translation into French by Karine Laléchère entitled *Petit dictionnaire chinois-anglais pour amants* will find one set of instructive solutions to the 'problem' of translating Chinese-inflected English used by an increasingly astute and proficient learner of English in London into 'broken' but progressively more complex French. Of course, in many ways this linguistic tour de force—the mimetic re-presentation of the language-learning process by a Chinese learner of English over the course of a year in London as she acquires grammatical structures, vocabulary items, and cultural knowledge while she experiences and gives voice to the frustrations and limits of cross-cultural understanding—is just one aspect of a work that foregrounds cultural translation and demonstrates what it means to be required to adjust to new cultural norms. The struggle for recognition and for self-definition is enacted at many levels: linguistic, cultural, and existential. But this is also a book that touches on resistant translation and resistance to translation, calling attention to the power differential between English and Chinese, even as it adopts strategies to subvert assumed hierarchies by demonstrating the advantages of English Plus. For while this is a novel directed towards an English-speaking audience, and one which by and large assumes little knowledge of China or Chinese other than stereotypical representations on the part of the reader, the narrator's refusal at a moment of frustration to continue writing in English and her switch to Chinese—a move requiring the ostensible intervention of an editor's translation into English—draws attention to the fact that it is the monolingual, rather than the bilingual or multilingual individual, who is disadvantaged or at a loss in today's world where an ability to speak or write more than one language is the norm.[28] In addition, in drawing on a pluricultural generic repertoire in the construction of her narrative, Guo is able to combine the linear and spatial potentialities of narrative to produce a new narrative form—the dictionary-novel.

Indeed Guo has spoken in interview at the Open University in 2013 about her search for method in writing her novel that originated as hundreds of messy pages typed up from the diaries she kept about her own observations and experiences as a young Chinese woman in England. In looking for a narrative thread, and seeking to turn a series of anecdotes and observations into a structured narrative, she drew on Barthes' *A Lover's Discourse* as a resource in terms of a search for form (an A–Z of quotations and observations about love) and a method that would allow her to combine narrative drive—what happens in the course of one year in the life of a Chinese woman in London—with topical and thematic control. To put it differently, the dictionary form, drawing as it does on thematic and definitional categories ('Home,' 'Privacy,' for example), allows for cultural and linguistic comparison in a story about accommodation and acclimatization, about translation of self and other, as well as about love. In terms of layout, too, the dictionary form permits a design that separates off abstractions or general definitional statements from the ensuing narratives, that test their legitimacy or their limits by relating episodes from experience that dramatize or personalize understanding and integration of new linguistic and cultural knowledge. In other words, formal arrangements of words, different scripts, and images on a page are seen to be motivated carriers of meaning in Guo's fiction, just as in her films style and length of shot, pacing, movement, gesture, inclusion of voice over, use of dialogue and text in more than one language, alongside music and colour, are all semiotic markers that carry meaning potential. As a film-maker as well as a novelist, short story writer, and poet, Guo's repertoire includes a range of resources to be deployed either singly or in combination to reinforce or disrupt a reader's or viewer's encounter with narrative. In terms of genre, Guo also demonstrates an ability to subvert expectations by creating generic blends such as her dictionary-novel, or using case notes and interviews to tell a story as she does in *UFO in Her Eyes*. It is as if she is constantly experimenting with forms of storytelling, using the affordances of the modes and media at her disposal while testing their limits. In this sense, access to more than one language and culture constitutes a set of resources to be marshalled and exploited in the creation of meaning. To write, then, is to engage in a set of translational practices aimed at creating for the reader through material features of language and design a story or cultural script about self in relation to other.

I Am China takes the preoccupation with translation as subject and dynamic, as critical lens and potential motor of creativity further. As well as being a structural principle mediating and constituting the novel, its embedding and realization at different levels in the narrative—at the level of story and of theme, at the level of plot and of motivating force to drive forward the action, as a device both literal and metaphoric—ensure that it is integral to the fabric of the work. Each of the nine chapters begins with an extract from an ancient Chinese text or with a Chinese proverb that is first represented in Chinese characters, then reproduced in a Romanized pinyin version, followed by a translation into English. Moreover, within sections of the text fragments of handwritten as well as printed Chinese characters are embedded, alongside English translations, ostensibly proffered by protagonist Iona Kirkpatrick, a professional translator from Chinese into English. In some sections, there are even notes inserted by the translator where, for example, she has had difficulty deciphering the handwriting, or where the expression used is one she is unfamiliar with because it is extremely colloquial.[29] There is also reference to real works of literature in translation (for example the Chinese and the English translation of a Russian novel by Vasily Grossman) and their resonances in the lives of the novel's protagonists, and there are fragments of other languages (such as French and German) woven into the fabric of the novel where the setting and/or narrative demands it. So, for example, when Jian has a French lesson at the Asylum Centre in Switzerland, there are some short phrases in French that both enact the subject of the lesson—saying where you are from—and provide an air of authenticity to the setting, while reinforcing the theme of 'self-translation.'

A good example of the way in which translation is both subject and object within the narrative—or to put it another way, both theme and commentary—reveals itself in a section of Chapter 2 of the novel entitled, with some irony, "Welcome to Dover." In this section, translator Iona is struggling to render the idiomaticity of one of Jian's letters to Mu, in which he refers to being exiled in England. Stuck in a camp in Dover, he feels himself to be nothing but a registration number. He relates his dreams and memories of China and of Mu, indicating the extent to which he misses them. On the page a section of that letter is reproduced complete with crossed out Chinese characters where in his haste to commit himself to paper, he has made a mistake. As well as commentary on the difficulties of the text, fragments of which are reproduced in the "original" with translated passages set off in italics, there is also, within a section of italicized translation, set off in square brackets, a translator's note: "not sure what this means. It's a new colloquial expression I've not heard before."[30] So in addition to the literal level at which translation operates (from Chinese into English) there is also within this 'literal' level an enactment of a meta-level of translational knowledge where the translator's presence is explicitly marked and her choices discussed. It is paratextual insofar as it is set off from the main text, not as a footnote, but simply in parenthesis within the narrative text. It draws attention to the role of the translator in interpreting meaning by selecting (or failing to select) particular 'equivalents.' In disrupting the illusion of a self-contained (fictional) work in translation, it highlights the operations required in the process of translation at the level of lexis and grammar. Yet there is a further level at which this reference to the task of the translator takes place, and that is within the third-person narrative where the narrator, rather than the fictional protagonist, comments on the difficulties of translation. So, for example, there is a passage in Section 11 of Chapter 2 ('Welcome to Dover') that articulates the role of translation as a kind of bridge-building between cultures and individual worlds.

> And it's like Iona is building this bridge again, through her reading, her translation. Building a bridge of meaning from their letters, and she has to choose the right words to keep the structure standing. And it is so hard. The Roman letters of English and the oriental characters of Chinese are not natural bedfellows. [...] How can she find the right translation for these swear words in English? If she had spent more time in Beijing's streets and markets and noodle stores on her year in China at university perhaps she would now grasp much more. One day, she thinks, she will master the language and understand the culture perfectly.[31]

The presence of a narrator is marked in this passage by use of the third person and by the tag—"she thinks"—that attributes knowledge of Iona's thoughts to someone with access to those thoughts. At the same time the reader is conscious of following Iona as she works through her translation and contemplates relations between the subjects of her translated portions of text. In the interrogative: "How can she find the right translation for these swear words in English?" there would seem to be an alignment between the perspectives of narrator and character, as the reader slips into Iona's head and appears to have unmediated access to her thoughts. This direct access is of course an illusion enabled by the choice of modality ('can') and use of the demonstrative pronoun 'these' (rather than those) which bring us closer to Iona's perspective. The reader thereby gains insight into the workings of translation and the difficult choices it demands of the translator.

In addition, translation—as an activity that involves first making sense of what one reads, and then rendering it into a form that enables another reader to decipher it and construct or co-construct meaning—is brought into close alignment with the production of text more generally. Indeed, there are explicit comparisons between the task of the translator and that of the writer of fiction: "Perhaps translating is another kind of story-telling: finding the writer's voice, unravelling the narrator."[32] As in any text, there is the question of who speaks and/or who narrates; and who sees or witnesses the unfolding action. The hand of the translator may not always be visible to those who read in translation but the translator will have ordered and organized the text in translation according to her understanding of events, their interrelationship, the behaviour and motivation of protagonists, and so on. It is made clear that with a language such as Chinese there is much to consider when rendering it into English. Apart from the thorny issue of tense and temporality, there is the question of tenor or tone, and of colloquial or street language mixed in with more formal registers. Then there is the relationship between text and context (as well as with co-text). What is particularly well demonstrated here is the extent to which translation is a dialogic process, not just in terms of a dialogue between writer and translator, but also between the words on the page and the context that informs those words and helps give them particular resonance. The translator must, in effect, resurrect or reinstate a context such that her eventual choice of wording can be read within and against the cultural norms operating in the source culture at the time, while paying attention to the norms of the target culture. Of course, it is not always possible to know what these norms might be with any degree of certainty, and this, I think, is the point. Words, in whatever language, relate both to one another within a text and also signal relationships beyond the world of the text. They are in dialogue with the world of the reader, as well as with the world of the writer. These worlds do not map directly on to one another but must be inferred and co-constructed. Just as a narrative text is the co-creation of a writer and reader, and a blend of the discourse of characters and a narrator or narrators, orchestrated by the hand of the author, so a translated text owes its particular configuration to a blend of voices, including that of the translator.

Moreover, in *I Am China* translation works to defer the construction of a narrative insofar as Iona's translations are effected randomly and in no particular order, given the fact that not all the documents are dated, nor are they all written by the same hand. Creating a narrative, therefore, becomes an activity assured by the translator as she researches the 'real' lives of the individuals whose stories she is representing through a selection of documents that have by chance come into her orbit. The reader is party to this effort at trying to detect a narrative thread; s/he becomes a kind of co-investigator in the biographical, cultural, and linguistic research conducted by Iona. But, as we have seen, Iona herself is implicated in the narrative, not only by virtue of her professional training as a translator but as an actor in the drama played out before the reader's eyes. Iona has a dual role as cultural and linguistic interpreter and as a participant in the production of the novel we are reading. In addition, in translating the lives of Jian and Mu, she is also translating herself. The uncovering of their story, which speaks of a critical period in modern Chinese life, pre-and post-Tiananmen Square, is also a stimulus to the creation of a life story for Iona herself. The process of delivering a book, based on her translations from the Chinese, of the lives and loves of Jian and Mu, a book whose publication is an act of defiance, forces Iona to reassess her own life and to create an alternative, more meaningful existence. What she reads and writes forces her out of her professional and personal corner and enables the construction of a different future, one where it looks like Jonathan of Applegate Books, who commissioned the translation in the first place, will play a personal, and not just a professional, role.

Conclusion

What this chapter has illustrated is the extent to which translation in an extended sense is part and parcel of the literary and critical landscape today. Literary production is visibly affected by the fact that English, increasingly, is being used by writers with access to other languages and cultures, many of whom focus on and thematize issues of translation. English clearly does not operate in a cultural and linguistic vacuum but always in the presence of other languages and literatures. While language politics remains an issue, there is a sense in which writers with English Plus are helping to change the terms of literary production, insofar as they are developing new literary forms and a new literary aesthetics based on translational modes of writing. In terms of reception, there are a number of attendant issues revolving around notions of readability, and the ability of monolingual readers to evaluate literature that depends on a bilingual or multilingual aesthetics. I have focused here on the work of Xiaolu Guo to illustrate the many senses in which translation features in her writing and to place this focus on translation both as a critical modus operandi and as a spur to enhanced creativity. A work such as *A Concise Chinese-English Dictionary for Lovers* has a mimetic relationship to translation insofar as it is constructed around the premise of language learning and indicates the extent to which languages and cultures appear to be constitutive of one another. Armed with a dictionary and a willingness to learn vocabulary and structures, Z translates her experience and her thoughts into increasingly complex English. Yet she remains a Chinese woman in London, and despite greater familiarity with English customs remains at a certain distance to the society and its values. In *I Am China* translation becomes even more central to the narrative even if it is staged in a different way. Through the figure of the translator, the accent is placed on translation as a dynamic and multidimensional process requiring knowledge and skill as well as perceptiveness and persistence. In this instance, translation is presented as an act of defiance as well as a labour of love. It drives the plot and serves to uncover the mystery at the heart of the lives of the protagonists. Translation becomes a vital (in both senses) mode of storytelling that alerts the reader to the ways in which biography—the story of a life—and history are textured according to linguistic, social, and cultural location. Not only is writing a form of translation, so too is reading.

Notes

1 Doris Sommer, *Bilingual Aesthetics: A New Sentimental Education* (Durham, NC: Duke University Press, 2004).
2 Sherry Simon, "Review of *Reflections on Translation*, by Susan Bassnett," *Target* 27 no. 1 (2015): 94.

3 Simon, "Review", 96.
4 See for example Steven Kellman, *The Translingual Imagination* (Lincoln: University of Nebraska Press, 2000); Sommer, *Bilingual Aesthetics*; Emily Apter, *The Translation Zone: A New Comparative Literature* (Princeton, NJ: Princeton University Press, 2006); Susan Bassnett, "Reflections on Comparative Literature in the Twenty-First Century," *Comparative Critical Studies* 3 no. 1–2 (2006): 3–11; Yasemin Yildiz, *Beyond the Mother Tongue: The Postmonolingual Condition* (New York: Fordham University Press, 2012); Tamar Steinitz, *Translingual Identities: Language and the Self in Stefan Heym and Jakov Lind* (Rochester, NY: Camden House, 2013); Maria Lauret, *Wanderwords: Language Migration in American Literature* (New York: Bloomsbury, 2014); Rebecca Walkowitz, *Born Translated: The Contemporary Novel in an Age of World Literature* (New York: Columbia University Press, 2015); Fiona Doloughan, *English as a Literature in Translation* (New York: Bloomsbury, 2016).
5 See Fiona Doloughan, "The Construction of Space in Contemporary Narrative: A Case Study," *Journal of Narrative Theory* 45 no.1 (2015): 1–17.
6 Xiaolu Guo, "She a Chinese: Director's Statement," *Xiaolu Guo*, http://www.guoxiaolu.com/FIL_SAC_director_statement.htm.
7 Yildiz, *Postmonolingual Condition*; Doloughan, *English as a Literature in Translation*.
8 Jan Blommaert, "Commentary: Superdiversity Old and New," *Language and Communication* 44 (2015): 83.
9 Emily Apter, "Translation at the Checkpoint." *Journal of Postcolonial Writing* 50 no. 1 (2014): 57, 68, 69, 72.
10 Sommer, *Bilingual Aesthetics*.
11 Evelyn Ch'ien, *Weird English* (Cambridge, MA: Harvard University Press, 2004), 28.
12 Ch'ien, *Weird English*, 21, 14.
13 Xiaolu Guo, *A Concise Chinese-English Dictionary for Lovers* (London: Chatto and Windus, 2007), 3.
14 Ibid., 3.
15 Ibid., 349.
16 Ibid., 350.
17 Xiaolu Guo, *I Am China* (London: Chatto and Windus, 2014), 313.
18 Guo, *I am China*, 313.
19 Ibid., 3.
20 Susan Bassnett, "Translation Studies at a Cross-Roads," *Target* 24 no. 1 (2012): 15–25.
21 Alastair Pennycook, "English as a Language Always in Translation," *European Journal of English Studies* 12 no. 1 (2008): 33–47.
22 Doloughan, *English as a Literature in Translation*.
23 Michaela Wolf, "'The Language of Europe Is Translation': EST amid New Europes and Changing Ideas on Translation," *Target* 26 no. 2 (2014): 233.
24 Guo, *I Am China*, 15.
25 Ibid., 106.
26 Ibid., 15.
27 Lance Hewson, "Is English as a *Lingua Franca* Translation's Defining Moment?," *The Interpreter and Translator Trainer* 7 no. 2 (2013): 257–77.
28 Guo, *Dictionary*, 179–80.
29 Guo, *I Am China*, 77, 72.
30 Ibid., 70–72.
31 Ibid., 78.
32 Ibid., 65.

Bibliography

Apter, Emily. *The Translation Zone: A New Comparative Literature*. Princeton, NJ: Princeton University Press, 2006.

———, "Translation at the Checkpoint." *Journal of Postcolonial Writing* 50 no. 1 (2014): 56–74.

Bakhtin, Mikhail. *Speech Genres and Other Late Essays*, eleventh edition. Translated by V. McGee and edited by C. Emerson and M. Holquist. Austin: University of Texas Press, 2007.

Bassnett, Susan. "Reflections on Comparative Literature in the Twenty-First Century." *Comparative Critical Studies* 3 no. 1–2 (2006): 3–11.

———. "Translation Studies at a Cross-Roads." *Target*, 24 no. 1 (2012): 15–25.

Blommaert, Jan, "Commentary: Superdiversity Old and New." *Language and Communication* 44 (September, 2015): 82–8.

Ch'ien, Evelyn. *Weird English*. Cambridge, MA: Harvard University Press, 2004.

Doloughan, Fiona. "The Construction of Space in Contemporary Narrative: A Case Study." *Journal of Narrative Theory* 45 no. 1 (2015): 1–17.

———. *English as a Literature in Translation*. New York: Bloomsbury, 2016.

Guo, Xiaolu. *A Concise Chinese-English Dictionary for Lovers*. London: Chatto and Windus, 2007.

———. *Petit dictionnaire chinois-anglais pour amants*, translated by Karine Laléchère. Paris: Buchet/Chastel, 2008.

———. *UFO In Her Eyes*. London: Chatto and Windus, 2009.

———. *She, A Chinese*. UK: DVD Optimum Releasing Ltd., [2009]/2010.

———. *I Am China*. London: Chatto and Windus, 2014.

———. "She, A Chinese: Director's Statement." *Xiaolu Guo*. www.guoxiaolu. com/FIL_SAC_director_statement.htm.

Hewson, Lance. "Is English as a *Lingua Franca* Translation's Defining Moment?" *The Interpreter and Translator Trainer* 7 no. 2 (2013): 257–77.

Kellman, Steven G. *The Translingual Imagination*. Lincoln: University of Nebraska Press, 2000.

Lauret, Maria. *Wanderwords: Language Migration in American Literature*. New York: Bloomsbury, 2014.

Pennycook, Alastair. "English as a Language Always in Translation." *European Journal of English Studies* 12 no. 1 (2008): 33–47.

Simon, Sherry. "Review of *Reflections on Translation*, by Susan Bassnett." *Target* 27 no. 1 (2015): 94–7.

Sommer, Doris. *Bilingual Aesthetics: A New Sentimental Education*. Durham, NC: Duke University Press, 2004.

Steinitz, Tamar. *Translingual Identities: Language and the Self in Stefan Heym and Jakov Lind*. Rochester, NY: Camden House, 2013.

Walkowitz, Rebecca. *Born Translated: The Contemporary Novel in an Age of World Literature*. New York: Columbia University Press, 2015.

Wolf, Michaela. "'The Language of Europe is Translation': EST amid New Europes and Changing Ideas on Translation." *Target* 26 no. 2 (2014): 224–38.

Yildiz, Yasemin. *Beyond the Mother Tongue: The Postmonolingual Condition*. New York: Fordham University Press, 2012.

9 Literary Adventures in Francophone Afropea

Léonora Miano and Music as a Language of Afro-Diasporic Subjectivity

Polo Belina Moji

Afropean (Afro-European) is a relatively new term that has been presented as a potentially important discursive category in the literary representation of Africans in Europe.[1] It is perhaps a reaction to the current identitarian crisis within the European Union about what constitutes a European identity, seen in the rise of nationalist sentiment through the success of right-wing parties such as the Dutch Party for Freedom (PVV), the French Front National (FN), and the United Kingdom Independence Party (UKIP). In France, the differentiation between '*français de souche*' [native French] and '*français d'origine*' [French by birth] foregrounds the questions of cultural purity and hybridity that influence diasporic subjectivity. Francophone Afropean literature can therefore be read through an ethnographic approach that focuses on the specificities of the African diaspora and blackness as a visual marker of difference for '*français d'origine*' of African descent.

The neologism 'Afropea' first appeared on the album *Adventures in Afropea I* (1993) by the Belgian-Zairian group, Zap Mama. The group's *a cappella* sound, promoted as "a myriad of vocal traditions from all over the world, but mostly the funky African Diaspora mixed with Euro-American traditions,"[2] is described as polyphonic, polyrhythmic, and poly-global by the album's producer David Byrne. This notion of a hybrid and polyphonic voice has been transformed into a literary aesthetic by Léonora Miano (born 1973), a Cameroonian writer who has been living in Paris since 1991. Miano is credited with introducing the term 'Afropean' into Francophone literature through a collection of short stories entitled *Afropean Soul et autres nouvelles* and the novel *Blues pour Elise—séquences afropéenes saison 1*.[3] The two texts are part of Miano's Afropean series, which also includes the novels *Tels les astres éteints* and *Ces âmes chagrines*.[4] Miano was awarded the Goncourt des Lycéens literary prize for her novels *Contours du jour qui vient* and *Les Aubes écarlates* which, with *L'Intérieur de la nuit*, form her Africa trilogy.[5] The difference between these two literary series is that Léonora Miano gives a philosophical base to her Afropean literary series through two philosophical collections of essays, *Habiter la frontière* and *Écrits pour la parole*.[6]

Écrits pour la parole includes the essay "Afropea," in which Miano frames Afropean subjectivity, "*Je suis*," as an "own speech" or a new space that bridges the dichotomy of a French colonial centre and formerly colonized periphery.[7] Miano therefore conceives of Afropean hybridity through the compresence or "assembling" of multiple affiliations, rather than the limited notions of purity and impurity that inform the differentiation between '*français de souche*' and '*français d'origine*.' This non-hierarchical, non-oppositional schema of subjectivity suggests a multiple rather than a double diasporic consciousness. Through an analysis of Miano's short story "Afropean Soul"[8] and the novel *Blues pour Elise—séquences afropéennes saison 1*, this chapter explores Francophone Afropea as a translingual affiliation to Afro-diasporic political and cultural subjectivity. I use Alexander Weheliye's *Phonographies: Grooves in Sonic Afro-Modernity*,[9] which proposes the production, circulation, and consumption of black music as a site for Afro-diasporic cultural affiliation, to read music as a 'language' of diasporic affiliations in Miano's literary works.

Music and the Diasporic Linguistic Abyss

In her definition of diaspora as a useful theoretical category, Kim Butler makes a convincing argument for diaspora studies to consider the specificities of "community formation" or networks of affiliation, rather privileging ethnographic descriptors.[10] Butler's approach is interesting in that it privileges relationality, focusing on five key dimensions which include "relationship with the homeland," "relationships with hostlands," and "interrelationships within communities of the diaspora."[11] Within this theoretical framework, black music can be seen as a mediator of interrelations within the communities of the Afro-diaspora across the globe. Indeed, Paul Gilroy's framing of blackness as a heterogeneous, 'open' signifier, which is characterized by polyphonic cultural expressions, can be read in this way.[12] Plurality and polyphonic artistic representation can therefore be interpreted as signifiers of a "globally mediated blackness,"[13] or Afro-diasporic networks of affiliation across Africa, the Americas, Europe, and the Caribbean. It must be noted that music, as a mediator of interrelations and an 'open' signifier of Afro-diasporic affiliation is influenced by the specific histories of African migration—from slavery, to present-day socio-economic and political reasons and conditions of diasporic dispersal.

Although studies such as *The Africa Diaspora: A Musical Perspective* interrogate music as the ultimate embodiment of blackness,[14] the link between music and Afro-diasporic subjectivity is more convincingly illustrated by studies of literature and music such as *Black Orpheus: Music in African American Fiction From the Harlem Renaissance to Toni Morrison.*[15] In his introduction to this edited volume, Simawe traces the figure of the black "orphic" self from Jean-Paul Sartre's foreword to the Francophone Négritude movement's *Anthologie de la nouvelle poésie nègre et malgache de langue française*[16] to its appropriation by African-American cultural movements in the 1950s in publications such as *Black Orpheus* magazine (1957). Having established the transatlantic Afro-diasporic affiliation, Simawe goes on to interrogate the notion that canonical African-American writing from the Harlem Renaissance on-wards uses music to circumvent the inherent (racial) ideologies embedded in language.[17] *Black Orpheus* explores the opposition between music as a site of black embodiment and language as a site of linguistically embedded racial constructs, suggesting that this dichotomy recreates the same racialized binaries that it seeks to subvert.[18] Although mindful of this critique, the usefulness of music as a mediator of Afro-diasporic interrelationships is illustrated by Paul Gilroy's personal history:

> black music provided me with a means to gain proximity to the sources of feeling from which our local conceptions of blackness were assembled. The Caribbean, Africa, Latin America, and above all America contributed to our lived sense of a racial self.[19]

Black musical production is shown to trace a genealogy and cartography of blackness as an embodied marker of racialized difference, which influences the collective subjectivity of Afro-diasporic communities in their respective hostlands.

The transatlantic slave trade constitutes a key moment in the diasporic dispersal of Africans or loss of Africa as a homeland. This moment is marked by the loss of African mother tongues—linguistic rupture—due to the loss of tribal affiliations. This linguistic void was filled by pidgin and creole languages bearing elements of African and European linguistic structures. This was driven by the need for a lingua franca through which slaves of differing tribal origins could communicate with each other, and the need of masters to communicate with slaves using elements of European languages.[20] Édouard Glissant's conception of rhizomic (relational) identities presents linguistic and cultural creolization as a signifier of hybridity or multiple sites of affiliation.[21] Creolization has since been proposed as a linguistic and literary aesthetic by fellow Caribbean scholars Jean Bernabé, Patrick Chamoiseau, and Raphaël Confiant in *Éloge de la Créolité*.[22] In framing his philosophy of multiple affiliations, Glissant starts with the metaphor of the abyss of the slave ship to imagine this loss of the homeland as a loss of linguistic expression: "feeling a language vanish, the word of the gods vanish, and the sealed image of even the most everyday object, even the most familiar animal vanish."[23] Based on the premise that language is a logical form that enables one to represent one's world,[24] this loss of language translates to the loss of power to represent one's world. The linguistic abyss of the slave ship can therefore be linked to Paul Gilroy's topos of diasporic "unsayability" based on the differentiated access to language created by slave histories and colonial hierarchies. The hegemony of colonial languages as logical forms of representing the world limits the expressive power of those who have limited access to them. Gilroy remarks that the rise of the significance of black music in the African diaspora is in inverse proportion to this "limited expressive power of language" to represent diasporic loss.[25] The notion of "unsayability" therefore transcends the realm of the linguistic to encompass the inability of language to express the lived experience.

Weheliye problematizes music, or "the singing voice," as a simple compensatory gesture for the loss of language, or loss of a literate, "signing voice." Through an analysis of Lionel Barret's dichotomy of the embodied "singing voice" of the black subject and the literate "signing voice"[26] of a disembodied (white) modern subject, Weheliye illustrates how framing music as a compensatory language risks recreating the racialized hierarchies of illiterate/literate or, pre-modern (singing)/ modern (signing). Weheliye therefore considers the ways in which the black "singing voice" is "(re) embodied" as both literate and modern through its literary representation as well as through the technologies of musical production, circulation, and consumption, in order to make an argument for music as a site for Afro-modernity.[27] He therefore delinks Afro-diasporic identity from a strictly racialized (political) identity, stating that it also relies on "cultural channels of membership because of the increased accessibility of African American cultural productions on the global marketplace."[28] I therefore read Léonora Miano's literary representation of both black musical production and the technologies of its circulation and consumption through this textual re-embodiment of black music as both a *literate* and a modern mediator of Afro-diasporic affiliation.[29]

Theorizing Francophone Afropean writing through the conflicting forces of "the embeddedness of place and language, and the untranslatability of the experience"[30] highlights the linguistic insufficiency of French when it comes to conveying the diasporic lived experience. In the case of Miano's writing, the relation to the hostland is mediated by the French language and its inability to fully capture the lived experience of the Afro-diasporic subject in France. Dominic Thomas notes the apparent impossibility of representing "black France" because the professed racial blindness of the French state prohibits the collection of racial statistics.[31] The "unsayability" of blackness as an experience in France is nuanced by William Franke's notion of conditional "unsayability"—namely, that some things are unsayable because of their circumstances (conditions) rather than being intrinsically so.[32] This conditional "unsayability" can therefore be read as the underlying dynamic that informs the use of music as a compensatory language in Miano's novelistic representation of Francophone Afropean subjectivity. Although re-conceptualized as literate, "music does not rely on meaning making in the same way as language [...]—it calls attention to its texture and confluence rather than striving for intelligibility."[33] Music communicates the texture of the lived experience of Miano's Francophone Afro-diasporic subjects, as well as their political and cultural affiliations to globally mediated blackness, in a way that compensates for the expressive lacunae of French and novelistic language.

I argue that both *Afropean Soul* and *Blues pour Elise* are characterized by heteroglossia or multiple speech types, not least as a result of the insertion of black music in the text. To do so, I stretch Mikhail Bakhtin's list of novelistic style-unities—which consist of narration, individualized speech, extra-authorial, semi-literary, and oratory elements[34]—to incorporate stylized sonic aspects of the literate "singing voice." This addition of music to the stylistic range of the novelistic form allows us to read it as a stylized form of language within the text. Miano's narrative can therefore be read as a site of linguistic contact between the text (the signing voice) and music (the re-embodied singing voice). This allows us to frame the interplay between the sonic and textual elements of Afropean narrative as a form of linguistic code-switching—the multiple forms through which speakers of multiple languages will alternate between and integrate languages in order to fill linguistic gaps, express an ethnic identity, or achieve particular discursive aims.[35] One could read this code-switching as both an 'unmarked' language choice, which is expected and familiar for certain readers, and a 'marked' choice, which the author employs as a socially meaningful speech act of subjectivation.

"Afropean Soul" and the Conditional Unsayability of French Blackness

> "J'écris dans l'écho des cultures qui m'habitent: africaine, européenne, africaine américaine, caribéenne [...]. Écrire *en français,* ce n'est pas écrire *français.*"[36]

> [I write in the echo of the cultures which inhabit me: African, European, African American, Caribbean [...]. To write *in French* is not to write *French.*]

The essay "Habiter la frontière"—the title of which echoes Homi Bhabha's notion of border locations as spaces of postcolonial subjectivation[37]—links Miano's conception of multiple consciousness to the Glissantian notion of relationality. She describes the border as inherently multiple, characterized by the continuous contact between worlds and the meeting of languages which creates a hybrid universe.[38] Miano's conceptualization of Afropean literature is influenced by Glissant's philosophy of rhizomic identities—the Deleuzian notion of a rhizome (network) root that develops multiple branches instead of having a single stem.[39] Drawing on this Glissantian conception of relational identity, she describes her writing as an aesthetic produced by projecting her interiority—"inhabiting" multiple cultures—onto the French language.[40]

The problematization of Francophonie is seen in the subtitle of *Afropean Soul et autres nouvelles*, *Petites histoires de pièces rapportées*. This subtitle plays on the double meaning of the expression *pièce-rapportée*, which can mean a family member who is not a blood relative (family by marriage) and has come to mean the addition of any new person to a pre-existing community. Miano's collection of *Petites histoires de pièces rapportées* depicts Francophone Afropean subjects through this schema of a somewhat problematic affiliation to the French linguistic and cultural 'family.' This problematization of Francophonie as a site of linguistic and cultural affiliation mirrors the concerns of Emily Apter's "Theorizing Francophonie," in which she interrogates differing definitions of the Francophone community. These include descriptors such as a "planetary cartography," a "postcolonial ontology," a "linguistic platform," or a "multiplicity of linguistic life-forms," which are deemed inadequate due to what Apter calls "disciplinary negation" that defines the Francophone identity.[41] According to this negation, Francophone affiliation is defined through *not* being a French subject yet being linguistically affiliated to French culture. The Afropean figure of the '*français d'origine*' would conform to this schema of an enlarged French family that is defined by the negation of *not* being a blood relation or a native '*français de souche.*'

Francophonie deterritorializes the French language beyond its national borders, delinking French as a linguistic community from French as a cultural site of affiliation.[42] As *The Cambridge Introduction to Francophone Literature* puts it, defining oneself as Francophone is not to conceive of oneself as French. "The word 'Francophone' alludes to identity without ever quite conferring it."[43] The implicit subordination of Francophonie to 'true' French is evident in Daniel Larangé's introduction to *De l'écriture africaine à la présence afropéenne*, in which he describes Afropean literature as a mere offshoot of a French literature that is "so rich and complex" that it is collapsing under the its own weight.[44] It also foregrounds the differentiated relation to France that makes it impossible for a Francophone Afropean subject who is a French citizen, or '*français d'origine*,' to fully inhabit France as their homeland.

The short stories in *Afropean Soul et autres nouvelles* adopt a dual insider–outsider perspective to interrogate the often racialized hierarchy implied between being '*français de souche*' [native French] and '*français d'origine*' [French by birth]. All five of the short stories in this volume construct Afropean subjectivation (or soul) through the trope of a para-doxically deterritorialized affiliation to France as a home/hostland. The pivotal story is "Afropean Soul," in which an unnamed young man living in Paris wonders whether being Afropean means that he is a "national" subject; "si l'identité des Afropéans était nationale."[45] The narrative is set against a backdrop of a French society that is grappling with an identitarian crisis. Assimilationist laws such as the prohibition of the veil (2004), the derogatory characterization of *banlieue* [ghetto] youth by the then Minister of the Interior, Nicolas Sarkozy (2005), as well as an upsurge in political support for the right-wing Front National party, have made the protagonist acutely aware of his blackness as a marker of exclusion despite the supposed inclusiveness of French citizenship. Yet despite his growing sense of alienation, the young man's experience lis-tening to community radio stations in his immigrant neighbourhood of Paris underlines his rejection of Africa as a homeland. He criticizes the Africanized French pronunciation and syntax of the radio presenters, and feels alienated by African music being played:

> La musique diffusée n'était qu'un brouhaha continu, dépourvu d'harmonie. Il ne se sentait pas particulièrement proche de ceux qui s'exprimaient, ne vivait pas comme un Africain exilé en France. Il était un *Afropéen*, un Européen d'ascendance africaine.[46]

> [The music being broadcast was nothing but an unending brouhaha, devoid of harmony. He did not feel particularly close to those who were talking, did not live like an African exiled in France. He was an *Afropean*, a European of African descent.]

The unspecified African music seems disharmonious or lacking in ex-pressive power to the young man because he does not feel affiliated to the cultural community that it represents. This "singing voice" from an African homeland that he has never known is in discord with his self-affiliation to an Afropean—"a European of African descent"—identity. This figure of the Afropean French citizen therefore subverts the migratory schema of Francophonie, which is based on the conception of France as a hostland for the Francophone African diaspora, and not a homeland. In line with Kim Butler's definition of diasporic community in terms of a relation with a homeland and hostland(s),[47] the disharmony of African music can be read as a signifier of the young man's conception of France as his homeland, in the same way that his hyper-awareness of French syntax and pronunciation denotes his linguistic affiliation to French. The "Afro" in Afropean therefore refers to blackness as an ethno-cultural site of diasporic affiliation[48] and as a visible marker of a minority status in the European context,[49] rather than a relation of loss to Africa as a homeland. As the introduction to *Francophone Afropean Literatures* puts it, "Afropeans do not identify themselves in terms of either/or in relation to the country of their ancestry and the European nation of their birth, but rather in relation to the transnational, diasporic space that is Black Europe."[50]

The young protagonist remains nameless, suggesting that he is a generalized representation of Afropean subjectivity. Although he does not identify with the loss of an African homeland, the young man faces the conditional 'unsayability' of being black in France against a backdrop of rising anti-immigrant sentiment. These conditions have destabilized the assumption that being Afropean gives him equal access to France as a homeland: "Le jeune homme se demandait si l'identité des Afropéens était nationale. Il avait toujours cru les identités multiples." [The young man asked himself if the identity of Afropeans was national. He has always believed in multiple identities.][51] This context reframes France as both a home and hostland in which he is internally exiled—a citizen who is rendered different by his racially marked body despite a state policy of racial blindness. The internal exile or 'unsayability' of black France as Afropean lies in this lived contradiction of socially visible blackness and political racial blindness. This unsayable interiority or 'soul' lies at the heart of Miano's "Afropean Soul."

Miano uses an oblique musical reference to link the 'unsayable' lived experience of Francophone Afropea to globally mediated Afro-diasporic blackness: "la couleur de sa peau n'était pas d'ici. Il était devenu soudain une bande ethnique à lui tout seul"[52] [the colour of his skin was not from here. He had suddenly become an ethnic group of his own]. Footnotes mark the intentional link between the expression "Une bande ethnique à lui tout seul" and a French track entitled "Je suis une bande à moi tout seul" by the underground rap group La Rumeur. The relationship between rap music as an Afro-diasporic musical genre and Afropean subjectivity can be understood through the manner in which rap deliberately breaks the linguistic conventions of dominant languages such as English or French through changes to the syntax, pronunciation, orthography, and so forth. As a musical form, it is globalized through 'street language' and the inflection of a 'singing' voice with speech patterns to convey a lived experience that is outside of the dominant culture. Although the insertion of La Rumeur in a footnote suggests an openness to readers who would not recognize the musical reference in the text, only those in the minority 'we-group' would recognize the subversive nature of the reference. Understanding this code requires insider knowledge that La Rumeur are an underground group who refuse to adapt the radical political message of their lyrics for French radio, relying on word of mouth (rumours) to attract audiences to their shows. I read this link to subversive, underground culture through Paul Gilroy's assertion that the power of black music as a site of Afro-diasporic affiliation lies in its ability to organize the consciousness of blackness as a (political) struggle.[53] The reference to the radical politics of La Rumeur obliquely foretells the awakening of the protagonist's black consciousness or affiliation to blackness as a political community.

It is significant that the young man works in the anonymous job of a telemarketer along with colleagues who are mainly of immigrant descent—"issus de minorités ethniques" [ethnic minorities]—but, like him, are fortunate enough to speak accent-less French.[54] Obliged to all adopt the "neutral" name of Dominique Dumas, the anonymity of the telephone masks the visibility of their skins as markers of their difference: "*Il effaçait la couleur*" [It erased colour].[55] The young man observes that by "becoming" Dominique Dumas in their professional interactions, he and his colleagues inscribe themselves in what is considered to be the norm of French national identity. Playing the role of Dominique Dumas can therefore be read as a metaphor for the role-playing through which Afropean subjects are obliged to negotiate their blackness in France. The 'unsayability' of blackness is therefore presented as a norm that is enforced by a "monochromatic" management or the dominance of whiteness.[56] The trope of awakening (political) consciousness traces the young man's journey from considering himself to be alone—"une bande ethnique à lui tout seul"—to a sense of collective struggle. After searching immigrant radio stations, interrogating definitions of "nation," and questioning the racialized structure of his workplace, he finds a sense of racial (political) community when he comes across the funeral procession of a fellow black immigrant who was killed by French police. Noticing the heterogeneity of the black skins—"from honey to ebony"—that surround him, the protagonist is struck by their collective plight as a visible minority.[57]

Inasmuch as Francophone Afropeanism has the potential to construct a relativism that abolishes the divides of inside/outside within Francophonie,[58] this is shown to be mediated by the 'unsayability' of French blackness as lived experience as opposed to a globally mediated blackness in French. "Afropean Soul" problematizes the conflation of an African homeland with blackness. It also considers what it means for an Afro-diasporic subject to consider Europe as one's homeland, or "one possible world of French speakers among many"[59] that can co-exist with others within the national space. "Afropean Soul" therefore represents the soul through Franke's notion of "self-unsaying," where the soul constitutes the self as an "inexpressible core of mystery."[60] The interiority of the Francophone Afropean "soul" and its political affiliation to the black Afro-diasporic struggle is presented as having the latent potential to destabilize the hierarchical ownership of France as a homeland that privileges autochthony.

Polyphony and the "Signing Voice" in *Blues pour Elise*

Somewhat erroneously compared to the television show *Sex and the City*,[61] *Blues pour Elise* focuses on the lives of cosmopolitan black women who employ English to describe themselves as the "Bigger than Life" crew. The novel deliberately steers away from the classic diasporic tropes of socio-economic precarity and longing for a lost homeland as sites of black struggle. It focuses on the identitarian struggles of seemingly assimilated middle-class Afropean subjects, French citizens who are relatively at ease in the cosmopolitan centre of Paris (*intramuros*), as opposed to marginalized immigrant neighbourhoods (*banlieues*) on the outskirts of the city. *Blues pour Elise* uses the story of a secondary character, Elise, a Cameroonian immigrant who has made France her homeland, and her daughter Shale, an Afropean French citizen who has never known Africa, to associate differentiated access to language with the diasporic experience. The linguistic abyss of the slave ship[62] is mirrored by the fact that Shale and her older half-sister Estelle are forever severed from the African language of their parents, for whom Douala becomes "le langage des secrets, celui d'émotions dont l'expression échappait au langage social" [the language of secrets, of emotions whose expression eluded social language].[63] Shale's loss of language is presented in contrast to Elise's recourse to diglossia. For Elise, French is the 'they-language' or social language of the hostland, and it cannot express or 'say' her Afro-diasporic interiority. She has the possibility of Douala as a 'we-language' that compensates the expressive lacuna of French and maintains a sense of relation with her homeland. She does not give this option to her daughters, who can only express themselves through the French language and have to find other compensatory strategies or sites of affiliation through which to express their Afro-diasporic subjectivity *in French*. I analyse how the lived experience of Francophone Afropea is embedded in Afro-diasporic political struggle through the author's depiction of blackness as a translinguistic site of affiliation.

Using Weheliye's problematization of the separation between a literate text and non-literate black music, I argue that by structuring her narrative (signing voice) according to black musical forms, Miano portrays the multiplicity of the lived experience according to differentiated access to language (literacy) of the novel's characters. Miano explicitly describes her writing as "L'écrit surgi du jazz" [writing that springs from jazz],[64] and this is evident in the morphology of *Blues pour Elise*. Jazz is a music that is multi-instrumental and polyrhythmic, characterized by distinctive solos, instrumental dialogues as well as improvisational segments. This is reflected in the novel's schema of polyphonic narration. The novel is structured as eight verses (chapters) and two improvisational segments (interludes). The polyphonic narrative is composed of Amahoro, Akasha, Malaïka, and Shale—four friends of differing Afro-diasporic descent living in Paris—as the principal voices, with interventions from a multitude of secondary voices—including that of Elise—which create an intimate mosaic of Francophone Afropean lived experiences.

The novel opens with Akasha, a woman of mixed Caribbean and Cameroonian descent, whose narrative voice is characterized by code-switching between French and Creole. Her French is inflected with

Creole expressions such as *"une femme poto mitan"* [a woman who is the central pillar of a home], *"pié bwa"* [a tree] and *"ladjé mwen"* [leave me], as well as creolized French syntax such as *"du temps long-temps,"* which is modelled on the Creole expression *"au tan lontan."*[65] Moreover, her Martinican heritage is highlighted through intertextual references to *Cahier d'un retour au pays natal* [Notebook of a Return to the Native Land] (1939), Aimé Césaire's seminal text of Négritude. These linguistic openings and instances of intertextuality are signalled through explanatory footnotes. Footnotes are also used to explain musical references such as *bèle*, traditional music from Martinique, or *tambouyés*, traditional Caribbean percussionists. This first chapter establishes Miano's use of paratextual devices, such as footnotes, to 'translate' the different ways in which the French language is inflected by the diverse linguistic and cultural affiliations that characterize the African diaspora. In a game of transparency and opacity, Miano also maintains the defamiliarization of the French language by peppering the entire novel with English expressions and Douala culinary references, which are not always translated in the footnotes. As didactic devices, footnotes draw attention to the referencing of key texts such as Eldridge Cleaver's seminal US Black Power prison memoir *Soul on Ice* (1968).[66] This self-conscious, heteroglossic intertextuality grounds the novel in black Afro-diasporic struggle.

The literacy of the 'signing voice' is also portrayed through a differentiated access to the histories of black political struggle. Asakha is depicted as being highly conscious of black identity politics, militantly maintaining her natural hairstyle and openly criticizing black women's efforts to subscribe to a white aesthetic by straightening their hair.[67] Her voice is contrasted with that of Amaharo, who is portrayed through a highly commoditized black musical production and colloquial Parisian French. Sporting a T-shirt with the slogan "Michael was Black"[68] and dancing to "Marley,"[69] this character affiliates herself to an Afro-chic black aesthetic rather than a deep consciousness of black struggle. Amaharo's preoccupation with her appearance and with her boyfriend does not make her immune to living with blackness as a marker of difference within French society. Frustrated when her boss inappropriately asks if she has ever had a white lover, she observes that divulging the race of her loved one implies adopting a political stance that she does not care to engage with. Despite her professed 'apolitical' stance regarding race, Amaharo's conclusion that "l'imaginaire occidental demeurait éminemment sensible à ce qui touchait la sexualité des Noirs" [the Western imaginary remained incredibly alert to anything related to black sexuality] shows her awareness of the everyday politics of living in a racially marked body.[70] As with the narratives of Malaïka and Shale, Amaharo's voice is less marked by the explanatory footnotes that highlight Akasha's embeddedness in the history and philosophy of Afro-diasporic black struggle.

Malaïka's internal monologue explores the social value of being able to speak 'good' French. She remarks that her fiancé Kwame—an English-speaking migrant of Sub-Saharan origin—speaks French about as well as Jane Birkin, English model-turned-actress and long-time companion of the iconic French singer, Serge Gainsbourg. Birkin, whose subsequent musical and cinematic career have earned her the French *Ordre National du Mérite*, observes: "In France I could say anything I wanted and make mistakes in French and people laughed,"[71] but this is certainly not the case for Kwame. Malaïka's reference to the French 'we-joke' about Jane Birkin therefore illustrates the racialized hierarchy within French society, into which Birkin has successfully integrated, whereas Kwame's grammatical errors mark him as a foreigner. Aware that the other members of the "Bigger than Life" crew do not think that Kwame is good enough for her, Malaïka is haunted by the prospect of a *marriage gris* [marrying to obtain the right to stay in France] because of Kwame's precarious migrant status, highlighting the dilemma of her privileged status as a French citizen.[72] The distinction between Malaïka and Kwame also illustrates a diasporic hierarchy, created by waves of migration, between Francophone subjects of African descent who consider France as their homeland and those who are in the more precarious position of considering it their hostland.

The novel's two interludes, meanwhile, can be read as improvisational segments in which Bijou, a secondary character who is unrelated to the main protagonists, gives a solo linguistic performance of *Camfranglais* (Cameroonian, French, and English). Titled *"Ton pied mon pied"* [your foot, my foot]—an expression which denotes friendship in *Camfranglais*—these interludes depict long-distance telephone conversations during which Bijou describes her life in France to a friend in Cameroon.[73] The intermingling of Douala words such as *"mboutoukou"* [bumpkin], untranslatable exclamatory sounds such as *"Tchiip"* and *"hein,"* French, English words, and colloquial Cameroonian expressions creates an improvisational aspect that one would associate with 'unmarked' or unconscious instances of code-switching. "Allô? Asso! C'est moi Bijou... Tu reconnais quand même ma voix, hein? C'est how?... Je knowais que Mbeng était strong, mais là... Je wanda sur le gars-là." [Hello? Asso! It's me Bijou... You at least recognize my voice, *hein*? How is it? ... I knew that Mbeng was hard but now I wonder about that guy].[74] Bijou's two linguistically opaque crescendos of code-switching are rendered partially transparent by the paratextual device of a glossary at the end of the novel, which translates some unfamiliar words and expressions into French. While this reflects the novel's representation of the stylized speech of individual characters, the colloquial orality amplifies the novel's heteroglossia through the interplay of linguistic transparency and opacity.

In the essay "Habiter la frontière," Miano describes the border as inherently multiple, characterized by the continuous contact between worlds and the meeting of languages which creates a hybrid universe.[75]

This hybridity opposes the "monolingual intent" of Western languages, which linguistically replicate the schema of a (neo)colonial centre and (ex)colonized periphery.[76] The influence of Édouard Glissant's philosophy of relational or rhizomic identities and the idea that rhizomic subjectivity arises from a network of affiliations rather than a single cultural root is evident in the polyphonic 'jazz' narration that in *Blues pour Elise* paints a complex tableau of a hybrid Afropean universe. There are generational shifts, as illustrated by Elise and her daughter Shale—notably the latter's loss of Doula as an African mother tongue. There are differences in legal status, as illustrated by Malaïka's concerns about marrying a non-French citizen. There are also differences in social class, when one compares the representation of Bijou to that of the four middle-class "Bigger than Life" women. The multilingualism of Francophone Afropea is also evident in the novel's heteroglossia. Akasha's use of Creole, Kwame's broken French, Bijou's pidgin Camfranglais, and the self-naming in English of the "Bigger than Life" crew, all highlight the linguistic porosity of French, or the differentiated access to it as a logical form through which to represent the world. Other than framing the racialized hierarchy of French society as a site of affiliation to an Afro-diasporic political struggle—the conditional 'unsayability' of blackness—the novel also raises questions about diasporic hierarchies based on waves of migration and social class. Whereas "Afropean Soul" presented the figure of the young man as a generalized representation of Francophone Afropea, *Blues pour Elise* problematizes the idea of a homogeneous Afropean identity.

Black Mix-Tape: The "Singing Voice" of Black France

The title of *Blues pour Elise* makes an obvious reference to African-American musical traditions and the genealogy of black writers who, from the Harlem Renaissance onwards, have employed textual representations of blues music in their writing.[77] Moreover, Nicki Hitchcott notes that the title makes reference to Beethoven's famous composition, *Für Elise*.[78] Significantly, this piece of European classical music has been rearranged by Erik Morales as the jazz standard, *Blues für Elise*. These intertextual references, as well as the interplay between the title and subtitle, foreground multiple sites of affiliation—African-American and European. As an Afro-diasporic musical genre, the roots of the blues can be traced to the work songs of African-American slaves and the linguistic abyss of slave histories, and are credited with influencing musical genres from jazz to rap.[79] In the essay "Écrire le blues" Miano attributes her African-American musical influences to growing up in Douala in Cameroon.[80] This musical genealogy traces a modern tri-continental network of affiliation through the purchase of her father's records in Paris, American musical production, and African music. It concurrently marks a generation shift, from the blues and jazz associated with her father, to the funk and hip hop of the author's own youth. *Blues pour Elise* is structured as though it was the author's personal music collection, in which every chapter (excluding the interludes) represents a different mix-tape of black experience. I return to Weheliye and the ways in which he reads black music as a "singing voice that is (re) embodied"[81] as both literate and modern through its literary representation in order to analyse Miano's presentation of the black mix-tape as a literate "singing voice."

Each chapter in *Blues pour Elise* is followed by an italicized "*Ambiance sonore*," or soundtrack. Though music often features (whether overtly or obliquely) in the narrative, there is rarely a direct relation between the music in the chapter and the '*ambiance sonore*' that follows it. Miano simply provides lists of artist names and tracks, which demand an intertextual reading based on prior knowledge of diverse and sometimes obscure musical references, for example: "***Ambiance sonore:** Ça t'fait du bien. Je n'ai pas confiance, **Valery Boston**. H.A.P.P.Y, **Sandra Nkaké**, Malaïka, **Miriam Makeba**.*"[82] Although Weheliye proposes an Afro-diasporic cultural membership that is mediated by the globalized accessibility of African-American cultural production,[83] I would argue that *Blues pour Elise* presents this 'we-group' membership as mediated by the transnational circulation and multilingual consumption of black music from all over the world. This mix-tape echoes Miano's notion of multiple cultural affiliations in "Habiter la frontière." Valery Boston is a Parisian-born singer of Caribbean descent, and Sandra Nkaké is a Cameroonian-born Parisian singer, while the South African anti-apartheid songstress Miriam Makeba was made an honorary French citizen in 1990. It also frames Afro-diasporic cultural membership according to multiple linguistic affiliations. Although Valery Boston sings in French, Sandra Nkaké's "H.A.P.P.Y" is in English, and Makeba's "Malaïka" is in the East African lingua franca, Swahili. While the soundtrack (mix-tape) varies the rhythm and adds a sonic texture to the text, the reader who is unfamiliar with some or all of the musical references can also feel 'tone deaf.' Therefore this 'we-code' can also be understood through the creation of differing levels of sonic opacity depending on the level of identification with the music being referred to.

Nevertheless, *Blues pour Elise* does establish a strong transatlantic affiliation through an early reference to the African-American gospel song "When the Saints Go Marching In," popularized by Louis Armstrong's 1938 jazz recording. Indeed, Akasha frames her decision to stop being depressed in opposition to the gospel song's suggestion of heavenly rewards for (black) suffering on earth: "When the saints go marching in [...] I don't want to be in their number. C'était sur terre qu'elle voulait être félicitée" [It was on this earth that she wanted to be rewarded].[84] Later in the narrative, Michel and Gaëtan listen to a radio interview in which a singer explains how she was inspired to name her album *Daughters of the Dust* after a movie by African-American film-maker

Julie Dash.[85] Considered a classic black feminist movie, *Daughters of the Dust* has the distinction of being the first feature film directed by an African-American woman to be shown in American cinemas. Set in 1902, the film depicts the story of a mother and two daughters—descendants of West African slaves who have retained a creolized African culture on an isolated slave plantation island in Georgia—on the eve of departure to the mainland.[86] The film's tension—retaining a unique cultural identity by staying, or opting for integration by leaving—becomes the context for a conversation in which Gaëtan (a Frenchman who grew up in an unnamed African country) complains that his new girlfriend Shale's attitude is not 'African' enough. The music inspired by *Daughters of the Dust* can therefore be read as a "singing voice" that intervenes as a third (critical) interlocutor in a conversation about an essentialized Africanness that resists integration with other cultures. Music mediates a certain amount of reflexivity in the text. Having sex to the rhythm of Ron Isley's "Between the Sheets" prompts Shale's half-sister Estelle to relate her own sexual experience to the globalized consumption of black sensuality through African-American soul music. Her sexual pleasure is heightened by connecting to the eroticism of soul tracks such as "Sexual Healing" and "Til the Cops Come Knockin" by Marvin Gaye,[87] a singer who was killed by his deeply religious father for the 'sin' of producing sexual music. Soul music is literally the "singing voice" that speaks to and about Estelle's sexuality, just as *Daughters of the Dust* comments on Gaëtan's essentialist conception of Shale's Africanness. In both cases the "singing voice" blends with the voices of the novel's characters, amplifying the novel's polyphony, allowing an array of artistic voices to mediate and comment on the interiority of the characters.

Blues pour Elise can therefore be read as an orchestrated text—requiring the reader's double engagement with seeing and hearing texts[88] or engagement with the "signing and singing voices." This orchestration is visibly marked by the *Ambiance sonore* (mix-tape) at the end of each chapter, as well as the musical references embedded in the text. These narrative devices highlight the diversity of black music production—blues, soul, Caribbean *bèle*, Swahili folk songs, hip hop, funk, rhythm, and jazz. Music or "singing voices" not only amplify the novel's polyphonic and polyrhythmic narration, they also frame Miano's literary interrogation of the (sometimes everyday) politics of blackness by intervening with critical or reflexive voices in the midst of the text. The sonic texture of the novel reinforces the notion of music as a site that expresses a communal experience or a 'we-group.' Miano plays with the transparency and opacity of her musical references, varying the ability of individual readers to 'hear' certain sonic aspects of the text. This creates a sonically complex schema of 'we-group' experiences of being able to hear and see the text (singing and signing voices) and 'they-group' experiences of being able to only see the text (the signing voice).

Conclusion

"Afropean Soul" and *Blues pour Elise* enact Léonora Miano's conception of Francophone Afropean subjectivity as multiple linguistic and cultural affiliations in different ways. The short story, written in 2008, introduces the term 'Afropean.' It establishes the problematic of the 'unsayability' of the black lived experience in France in the context of increased anti-immigrant sentiment, associating it with a globalized racial struggle or Afro-diasporic political community. Although music is subtly used to signal blackness as a political Afro-diasporic affiliation through an oblique reference to the subversive rap group *La Rumeur*, it is not used as an expressive throughout the text. *Blues pour Elise—séquences afropéenes saison 1* (2010) then engages with the question of differentiated access to language and the multiplicity of Francophone Afropea. Through the extensive use of black music as a "singing voice" that textures the lived experience of blackness, the novel frames music as an expressive language of Afro-diasporic cultural affiliation.

Weheliye delinks Afro-diasporic identity from a strictly racialized political affiliation by proposing the globalized accessibility (circulation and consumption) of African-American music as a site of cultural Afro-diasporic affiliation. However, my analysis of Miano's *Blues pour Elise* as a text that orchestrates the written (signing) voice and the sonic (singing) voice exposes the globalized diversity of Miano's black musical references. Although there is a clear African-American bias, the geographic spread of the musical references creates a schema of transcontinental affiliations—America to the Caribbean, Africa and Europe—and translingual affiliations—through English, French, Swahili, Creole, as well as slang. Furthermore, Miano links the histories of black musical production to the "singing voice." The play on intertextuality therefore casts the novel's "singing voices" as literate (signing) voices that intervene in, or commentate on, the narrative. This interplay of narrative and music constitutes a form of linguistic and cultural code-switching. It enables black music to act as a language that compensates the conditional 'unsayability' of Francophone Afropea, as part of a globalized Afro-diasporic lived experience, *in French*.

Notes

1 See Sabrina Brancato, "Afro-European Literature(s): A New Discursive Category?" *Research in African Literatures* 39 no. 3 (2008): 1–13; John Nimis, "Corps sans titre: 'Fleshiness' and Afropean Identity in Besora's 53cm," in *Francophone Afropean Literatures*, ed. Nicki Hitchcott and Dominic Thomas (Liverpool: Liverpool University Press, 2014), 48–63; Daniel S. Larangé, *De l'écriture africaine à la présence afropéenne: Pour une exploration de nouvelles terres littéraires* (Paris: Editions L'Harmattan, 2014).

2 Zap Mama, *Adventures in Afropea 1*, Luaka Bop, 1993, compact disc. Wording on the CD sleeve of the 1993 release of the album. *Adventures in Afropea 1* went on to top *the American Billboard* world music charts in 1993.

3 Léonora Miano, *Afropean soul, et autres nouvelles* (Paris: Flammarion, 2008); *Blues pour Elise: séquences afropéennes: saison 1* (Paris: Plon, 2010).

4 Léonora Miano, *Tel les astres éteints* (Paris: Plon, 2008); *Ces âmes chagrines* (Paris: Plon, 2011).

5 Léonora Miano, *Contours du jour qui vient* (Paris: Plon, 2011); *Les Aubes écarlates* (Paris: Plon, 2009); *L'Intérieur de la nuit* (Paris: Plon, 2005).

6 Léonora Miano, *Habiter la frontière* (Paris: L'Arche Editeur, 2012); *Écrits pour la parole* (Paris: L'Arche Editeur, 2012).

7 Miano, "Afropea," in *Écrits pour la parole*, 28, 28.

8 Miano, "Afropean Soul," in *Afropean Soul*, 53–68.

9 Alexander G Weheliye, *Phonographies: Grooves in Sonic Afro-modernity* (Durham, NC: Duke University Press, 2005).

10 Kim D. Butler, "Defining Diaspora, Refining a Discourse," *Diaspora: A Journal of Transnational Studies* 10, no. 2 (2001): 194.

11 Butler, "Defining Diaspora," 195.

12 Paul Gilroy, "'Jewels Brought from Bondage': Black Music and the Politics of Authenticity," in *The Black Atlantic: Modernity and Double Consciousness* (Cambridge, MA: Harvard University Press, 1993), 72–110.

13 Dominic Thomas, *Black France: Colonialism, Immigration, and Transnationalism* (Bloomington, IN: Indiana University Press, 2007), 82.

14 Ingrid Monson, ed., *The African Diaspora: A Musical Perspective* (New York, NY: Routledge, 2004).

15 Saadi A. Simawe, ed., *Black Orpheus: Music in African American Fiction from the Harlem Renaissance to Toni Morrison* (New York, NY: Garland Publishing, 2000).

16 Jean-Paul Sartre, "Orphée noir," foreword to *Anthologie de la nouvelle poésie nègre et malgache de langue française*, by Léopold Sédar Senghor (1948; repr. Paris: Presses Universitaires de France, 1969).

17 Saaid A. Simawe, "Introduction: The Agency of Sound in African American Fiction," in *Black Orpheus*, xxii.

18 Jacquelyn A. Fox-Good, "Singing the Unsayable," in *Black Orpheus*, 5.

19 Gilroy, *Black Atlantic*, 193.

20 Randall M. Miller and John David Smith, *Dictionary of Afro-American Slavery* (Westport, CT: Greenwood Publishing Group, 1997), 28.

21 Edouard Glissant, *Poétique de la relation: Poétique III*, vol. 3 (Paris: Gallimard, 1990).

22 Jean Bernabé, Patrick Chamoiseau and Raphaël Confiant. *Éloge de la créolité* (Paris: Gallimard, 1993).

23 Edouard Glissant, *Poetics of Relation*, trans. Betsy Wing (Ann Arbor: University of Michigan Press, 1997), 7.

24 William Franke, "Varieties and Valences of Unsayability," *Philosophy and Literature* 29, no. 2 (2005): 496.

25 Gilroy, *Black Atlantic*, 74.

26 Lindon Barrett, *Blackness and Value: Seeing Double* (New York, NY: Cambridge University Press, 1999), 114.

27 Weheliye, *Phonographies*, 36–40.

28 Ibid., 148.

29 Ibid., 6.

30 Brancato, "Afro-European Literature," 6.

31 Thomas, *Black France*, 17.

32 Franke, "Varieties," 496.

33 Weheliye, *Phonographies*, 69.

34 Mikhail Bakhtin, "Discourse in the Novel," in *The Dialogic Imagination: Four Essays by MM Bakhtin*, trans. Michael Holquist and Caryl Emerson (Austin, TX: University of Texas Press, 1981), 262.

35 Barbara E. Bullock and Almeida Jacqueline Toribio, "Themes in the Study of Code-switching," in *The Cambridge Handbook of Linguistic Code-switching*, ed. Barbara E. Bullock and Almeida Jacqueline Toribio (Cambridge: Cambridge University Press, 2012), 3.
36 Miano, "Habiter la frontière," in *Habiter la frontière*, 25–32, 29 (emphasis in the original).
37 Homi K. Bhabha, *The Location of Culture* (New York: Psychology Press, 1994).
38 Miano, "Habiter," 25.
39 Glissant, *Poétique de la relation*, 11.
40 Miano, "Habiter," 25.
41 Emily S. Apter, "Theorizing Francophonie," *Comparative Literature Studies* 42 no. 4 (2005): 297.
42 Apter, "Theorizing Francophonie," 298; Patrick Corcoran, *The Cambridge Introduction to Francophone Literature* (Cambridge: Cambridge University Press, 2007), 8.
43 Corcoran, *Cambridge Introduction*, 10.
44 Larangé, *De l'écriture*, 7.
45 Miano, "Afropean Soul," in *Afropean Soul*, 53–68, 53.
46 Ibid., 53 (emphasis in the original).
47 Butler, "Defining Diaspora," 195.
48 Brancato, "Afro-European Literatures," 2–3.
49 Fatima El-Tayeb, *European Others: Queering Ethnicity in Postnational Europe* (Minneapolis: University of Minnesota Press, 2011), xxi.
50 Nicki Hitchcott and Dominic Thomas, eds., *Francophone Afropean Literatures* (Liverpool: Liverpool University Press, 2014), 4.
51 Miano, "Afropean Soul," 53.
52 Ibid., 54.
53 Gilroy, *Black Atlantic*, 36.
54 Miano, "Afropean Soul," 57.
55 Ibid.,57.
56 Ibid., 57.
57 Ibid., 60–64.
58 Apter, "Theorizing Francophonie," 302–303.
59 Ibid.
60 Franke, "Varieties," 491.
61 Hitchcott, "Sex and the Afropean City"; Larangé, *De l'écriture africaine*.
62 Gilroy, *Black Atlantic*; Glissant, *Poétique de la relation*.
63 Miano, *Blues*, 123.
64 Miano, *Habiter*, 16.
65 Miano, *Blues*, 23, 13–31.
66 Ibid., 27–8.
67 Ibid., 32–40.
68 Italicized in the original text.
69 Miano, *Blues*, 42.
70 Ibid., 46.
71 Barney Hoskyns, "Jane Birkin: 'No, Serge, I won't lick my lips and pout." *The Guardian*, 1 April 2015, www.theguardian.com/music/2015/apr/01/jane-birkin-no-serge-i-wont-lick-my-lips-and-pout.
72 Miano, *Blues*, 65–71.
73 Ibid., 58–9; 104–105.
74 Ibid., 58–9.
75 Miano, "Habiter," 25.
76 Glissant, *Poetics*, 19.
77 See Simawe, *Black Orpheus*; Weheliye, *Phonographies*.

78 Hitchcott, "Sex and the Afropean City," 131.
79 Elijah Wald, *The Blues: A Very Short Introduction* (New York, NY: Oxford University Press, 2010).
80 Miano, "Écrire le blues," in *Écrits pour la parole,* 9.
81 Weheliye, *Phonographies,* 37–8.
82 Miano, *Blues,* 76.
83 Weheliye, *Phonographies,* 148.
84 Miano, *Blues,* 14.
85 Ibid., 50–51.
86 Julie Dash, *Daughters of the Dust: The Making of an African American Woman's Film* (New York, NY: New Press, 1992).
87 Miano, *Blues,* 90.
88 Julie Ann Huntington, *Sounding Off* (Philadelphia, PA: Temple University Press, 2009), 123.

Bibliography

Apter, Emily. "Theorizing Francophonie." *Comparative Literature Studies* 42 no. 4 (2005): 297–311.

Barrett, Lindon. *Blackness and Value: Seeing Double.* New York: Cambridge University Press, 1999.

Bernabé, Jean, Patrick Chamoiseau, and Raphaël Confiant. *Éloge de la créolité.* Paris: Gallimard, 1993.

Bhabha, Homi K. *The Location of Culture*: New York: Psychology Press, 1999.

Bhaktin, Mikhail. "Discourse in the Novel." In *The Dialogic Imagination: Four Essays by MM Bakhtin.* Translated by Michael Holquist and Caryl Emerson, 259–422. Austin: University of Texas Press, 1981.

Brancato, Sabrina. "Afro-European Literature(s): A New Discursive Category?" *Research in African Literatures* 39 no. 3 (2008): 1–13.

Bullock, Barbara E. and Almeida Jacqueline Toribio. "Themes in the Study of Code-switching." In *The Cambridge Handbook of Linguistic Code-Switching,* edited by Barbara E. Bullock and Almeida Jacqueline Toribio, 1–18. Cambridge: Cambridge University Press, 2012.

Butler, Kim D. "Defining Diaspora, Refining a Discourse." *Diaspora: A Journal of Transnational Studies* 10, no. 2 (2001): 189–219.

Corcoran, Patrick. *The Cambridge Introduction to Francophone Literature.* Cambridge: Cambridge University Press, 2007.

Dash, Julie. *Daughters of the Dust: The Making of an African American Woman's Film.* New York: New Press, 1992.

El-Tayeb, Fatima. *European Others: Queering Ethnicity in Postnational Europe.* Minneapolis: University of Minnesota Press, 2011.

Fox-Good, Jacquelyn A. "Singing the Unsayable." In *Black Orpheus: Music in African American Fiction from the Harlem Renaissance to Toni Morrison,* edited by Saadi A. Simawe, 1–40. New York: Garland Publishing, 2000.

Franke, William. "Varieties and Valences of Unsayability." *Philosophy and Literature* 29 no. 2 (2005): 489–97.

Gilroy, Paul. *The Black Atlantic: Modernity and Double Consciousness.* Cambridge, MA: Harvard University Press, 1993.

Glissant, Edouard. *Poétique de la relation: Poétique III.* Vol. 3. Paris: Gallimard, 1990.

————. *Poetics of Relation.* Translated by Betsy Wing. Ann Arbor: University of Michigan Press, 1997.

Hitchcott, Nicki. "Sex and the Afropean City: Leonora Miano's *Blues pour Elise.*" In *Francophone Afropean Literatures*, edited by Nicki Hitchcott and Dominic Richard David Thomas, 124–37. Liverpool: Liverpool University Press, 2014.

Hitchcott, Nicki, and Dominic Richard David Thomas, eds. *Francophone Afropean Literatures.* Liverpool: Liverpool University Press, 2014.

Hoskyns, Barney. "Jane Birkin: 'No, Serge, I won't lick my lips and pout.'" *The Guardian*, 1 April 2015 www.theguardian.com/music/2015/apr/01/jane-birkin-no-serge-i-wont-lick-my-lips-and-pout.

Huntington, Julie Ann. *Sounding Off.* Philadelphia, PA: Temple University Press, 2009.

Larangé, Daniel S. *De l'écriture africaine à la présence afropéenne: Pour une exploration de nouvelles terres littéraires.* Paris: Editions L'Harmattan. 2014.

Miano, Léonora. *L'Intérieur de la nuit.* 2005.

————. *Contours du jour qui vient.* Paris: Plon, 2006.

————. *Afropean soul, et autres nouvelles.* Paris: Flammarion, 2008.

————. *Tel les astres éteints.* 2008.

————. *Les Aubes écarlates.* Paris: Plon, 2009.

————. *Blues pour Elise: séquences afropéennes: saison 1.* Paris: Plon, 2010.

————. *Ces âmes chagrines.* Paris: Plon, 2011.

————. *Écrits pour la parole.* Paris: l'Arche Editeur, 2012.

————. *Habiter la frontière, Tête-à-tête.* Paris: L'Arche Editeur, 2012.

Miller, Randall M, and John David Smith. *Dictionary of Afro-American Slavery.* Westport, CT: Greenwood Publishing Group, 1997.

Monson, Ingrid. *The African Diaspora: A Musical Perspective.* New York and London: Routledge, 2004.

Nimis, John. "Corps sans titre: 'Fleshiness' and Afropean Identity in Besora's *53 cm.*" In *Francophone Afropean Literatures*, edited by Nicki Hitchcott and Dominic Richard David Thomas, 48–63. Liverpool: Liverpool University Press, 2014.

Sartre, Jean-Paul, "Orphée noir." Foreword to Léopold Sédar Senghor, *Anthologie de la nouvelle poésie nègre et malgache de langue française*, ix–xliv. 1948. Reprint, Paris: Presses Universitaires de France, 1969.

Simawe, Saadi A., ed. *Black Orpheus: Music in African American Fiction from the Harlem Renaissance to Toni Morrison.* New York: Garland Publishing, 2000.

————. "Introduction: The Agency of Sound in African American Fiction." In *Black Orpheus: Music in African American Fiction From the Harlem Renaissance to Toni Morrison*, xix–xxv.

Thomas, Dominic Richard David. *Black France: Colonialism, Immigration, and Transnationalism.* Bloomington: Indiana University Press, 2007.

Wald, Elijah. *The Blues: A Very Short Introduction.* New York: Oxford University Press, 2010.

Weheliye, Alexander G. *Phonographies: Grooves in Sonic Afro-modernity.* Durham, NC: Duke University Press, 2005.

Zap Mama. *Adventures in Afropea 1*, Luaka Bop, 1993, compact disc.

10 Translation and the Multilingual Film Text
Defining a Public

Moradewun Adejunmobi

The debate about language and literary expression in Africa has often focused on the role of vernaculars or mother tongues in creative writing by Africans. But given widespread multilingualism, especially in African cities, shouldn't this in fact be a debate about multilingual literary expression? That is the question I wish to address in this chapter by examining multilingualism in Nigerian popular film. An established convention amongst many African writers involves using a single language to represent the different languages spoken by the many characters in the literary text.[1] In principle, African film-makers should not face the same conundrum and could simply reproduce, as is, the diverse languages spoken by characters of different social class and ethnic backgrounds. In practice, however, many popular films in West Africa are monolingual,[2] while the majority of multilingual films are subtitled into a single language, thus effacing the multilingualism represented in the film. In order to make sense of what I describe as a pervasive monolingual address, even in African multilingual films, I explore in this chapter how the multilingual film narrative defines its publics.

There are several reasons for turning to film, and in this case Nigerian films, in a review of questions pertaining to multilingualism and literature. First, a discussion of popular film offers an opportunity to highlight differences between the written text and the filmed text when it comes to multilingual practice. The similarities and differences are especially significant for an understanding of how imaginative texts travel around the world and convene their diverse publics. Secondly, the films in question here have been made for initial distribution in a country where multilingualism is the norm for urban residents. The ways in which language addressivity is handled in film texts initially made available to multilingual publics within the space of the nation-state will likely provide insight into the relationship between multilingualism and the circulation of imaginative narratives on a more geographically dispersed scale.

Much of what has been written about multilingualism in film is dedicated to European cinema. To take an example, Christopher Wahl describes polyglot cinema as a European film genre.[3] By comparison, multilingual film from the countries of the global south has received scant scholarly attention, though citizens in many middle- and low-income countries are polyglot, and the state itself often acknowledges more than one language as an official language. Thus, the case studies in Verena Berger and Miya Komori's edited book, *Polyglot Cinema*, refer only to multilingual cinema from Western Europe.[4] In his work, Lukas Bleichenbacher focuses on multilingualism in Hollywood, while Carol O'Sullivan presents a comparative study of multilingualism in both Hollywood and European cinema.[5] Wahl, and others who have adopted his proposed taxonomies, interprets the multilingual film in Europe as a sign of the growing salience of immigrant groups and other minority language speakers in European countries. By contrast, multilingualism in African film appears to derive from a different set of considerations.

I make a number of arguments in this chapter. To start with, I propose that the languages used in a film text, and the decision to translate or not translate parts of the dialogue, are means by which texts 'define' a public. In matters of language, defining a public often entails choosing between what I describe as a monolingual address and a multilingual address. A monolingual address is usually associated with a more expansive and less restricted public, while a multilingual address often correlates with a more enclosed public. Second, and for the most part, multilingual films are made available to dispersed publics around the world by adopting a strategy of monolingual address. Similarly, though, and in highly multilingual communities, domestic circulation of multilingual films likewise rests on monolingual address and selective translation.

How might this apply to multilingualism in literature? Rebecca Walkowitz describes World Literature as referring to "works of literature produced any place in the world, or all works that begin in one place and then move out to other places."[6] Extrapolating from the positions to be developed in this chapter, I might expand significantly on that definition. Thus, I describe as World Literature literary texts that can be inserted into a corpus associated with authors of disparate affiliations, and that can be made available to geographically dispersed publics by adopting a monolingual address usually in the more or less accredited registers of a global language. Here, the term 'global language' refers to a language that has acquired a large number of geographically dispersed second-language speakers. In this respect, it is worth recalling Casanova who states that "the political centrality of a language—or, as I wish to say, its linguistic capital—can be determined by the number of multilingual speakers it has..."[7] Whether the imaginative work characterized as World Literature is monolingual or multilingual in composition, translation ensuring monolingual address into and from the accredited registers of global languages is usually required for defining its geographically dispersed publics.

To illustrate these arguments, I look to the Nigerian film industry, popularly known as Nollywood. It is Africa's largest film industry in terms of its output. The emergence of Nollywood in the final decades of the twentieth century marks an expansion of the cinema and film land-scape in Africa, bringing commercially oriented and popular film into prominence alongside the more politically oriented and aesthetically ex-perimental films that predominated in African film-making for most of the twentieth century. In this chapter, I will consider a selection of films belonging to the 'New Nollywood' trend in Nigerian film-making. *Onye Ozi* and *Àbèní* (2006) will serve as examples of monolingualism, while *Phone Swap* (2012) and *Confusion Na Wa* (2013) will serve as examples of multilingualism in popular Nigerian film-making.[8]

The Public and Addressivity

I speak of public here in the same sense as does Michael Warner, that is, an as entity that comes into existence "in relation to texts and their circulation," as a "space of discourse organized by nothing but the discourse itself."[9] Warner further clarifies that publics involve "discursive circulation among strangers."[10] For this reason amongst others, several scholars distinguish between the notion of public and audience. Karin Barber states, for example, that the public is "an audience whose members are not known to the speaker/composer of the text, and not necessarily present, but still addressed simultaneously and imagined as a collectivity."[11] Media and communication technologies are often the enabling elements for the circulation of discourse amongst strangers who are unknown to the author/composer and maybe even to themselves.

While the text's interpellation of presumed strangers and often anonymous interlocutors makes for the publicness of a public, Barber warns against assuming that all texts are designed for a maximum level of accessibility to a given public.[12] As she notes in her work on the anthropology of texts, there were and are certain kinds of oral texts in Africa that were designed to be relatively obscure.[13] In effect, and since all texts do not offer the same degree of accessibility to potential readers/viewers/consumers, so also do publics not enjoy the same levels of publicness, or offer similar types of engagement with the text in matters pertaining to language comprehension.

With respect to degrees of publicness and types of engagement, we might also consider another crucial dimension of the interaction between text and public, namely the addressivity of the text. Mikhail Bakhtin, in speaking about discourse, states that "an essential (constitutive) marker of the utterance is its quality of being directed to someone, its *addressivity*."[14] Applying similar notions to the public, Warner observes that the public exists "only by virtue of being addressed."[15] Of special interest here is the addressivity of film texts towards particular publics. In this respect, I understand a mode of address as a way of designat-ing the perspective that governs the orientation of a particular kind of media content or text towards particular types of potential spectators, viewers, or readers at a given point in time. Modes of address result from a combination of factors including the features of a text, its format, and genres, distribution mechanisms, languages of composition and translation, and diverse interventions affecting circulation of the text. The deployment of selected languages within the dialogue of a film and the translation of the dialogue used in a film into other languages are both addressive interventions that contribute towards demarcating potential publics for a film. A text that defines its prospective publics using a single language exhibits monolingual address, while a text that defines its prospective publics using multiple languages at the same time exhibits multilingual address.

Though the exact composition of a public is rarely predictable prior to the distribution of a text, and is not fully knowable even afterwards, authors, directors, translators, and sundry distributors of texts frequently deploy diverse modes of address with the goal of defining a prospective public for the texts under their purview. Some modes of address grant access into powerful fields of interactions or networks of publishing and distribution while other modes of address constrain admission into such fields of interactions.[16] In this respect, and as Walkowitz notes in one of her essays on World Literature, some literary texts appear to be designed for travel to far-flung publics, while others are not.[17] Modes of address are frequently the means by which texts can be, and are, specifically prepared for travel.

Modes of address are often intentional on the part of cultural brokers with a stake in the aesthetic and/or financial values associated with a given text.[18] Accordingly, these cultural brokers might deploy particular modes of address within and around the text, but are not always successful in reaching the public prospectively demarcated. Indeed, unanticipated publics regularly emerge around texts,[19] while defined publics decline to take up a text. In this respect, one might usefully distinguish between intentional, inadvertent, and achieved addressivity. The diverse modes of address adopted for a text indicate how critical figures associated with the text are envisioning or defining a public for the text. It is often easier to identify a text's mode of address than it is to provide a full accounting of the public generated by a text.

Nigerian Multilingual and Monolingual Films

Very few films in Nigeria's vast annual output of films can be described as multilingual. Indeed, and to the contrary, the dominant trend in Nigerian films is the practice of vernacular monolingualism, or "monolingualism in the indigenous language of a postcolony."[20] Vernacular monolingual films invent a fictional universe where one language suffices for most communication, and code-switching is rare or completely absent. The predominant languages in Nigerian monolingual films are English, Yoruba, Hausa, Igbo, but also Edo, Efik, and other languages. Kunle Afolayan and Kenneth Gyang, directors of *Phone Swap* and *Confusion Na Wa* respectively, belong with a group of film-makers trying to chart new directions for the Nigerian film industry and often described as New Nollywood film-makers. One of many innovations pioneered by Afolayan, and also adopted by Gyang, is the making of multilingual films.[21]

The film *Phone Swap* is a romantic comedy. Akin, who works in the finance industry, and Mary, a seamstress, are the principal figures in the film. Both reside in Lagos, the commercial capital of Nigeria. When they bump into each other at the domestic airport in Lagos, both take a fall which sends their phones scattering across the airport floor. Passersby help Mary and Akin back to their feet, and help retrieve their phones. Unfortunately, and because Mary and Akin have identical Blackberry phones, they end up with each other's handsets. Following text messages received on Mary's phone, Akin gets on the wrong flight, as does Mary, who is new to flying. By the time the mix-up is discovered, it is too late. Mary and Akin end up in unexpected locations, and have to persuade each other to try and intervene in the domestic and professional problems that compelled each one to undertake a journey away from Lagos in the first place. The film ends with a second more promising encounter at the airport, when Mary and Akin exchange phones on their return to Lagos.

The succession of misunderstandings that unfold in *Confusion Na Wa* also starts with a misplaced phone, though this film offers a much darker take on the travails that follow in the wake of its loss. Emeka, who lives a respectable middle-class life in an unnamed Nigerian city, inadvertently drops his phone during a melee in a crowded street. Small-time gangsters Chichi and Charles recover the phone, and when Emeka makes contact, try to blackmail him into buying it back. Emeka is understandably eager to recover his phone, and with all the more reason as it holds incriminating evidence about the fact that he is having an affair. Emeka's phone—which Chichi and Charles make liberal use of while it is in their possession—is the element that links the stories of several other characters facing challenges either in their private or professional lives. Those challenges are intensified by the calls made on Emeka's phone and lead to a series of crossed signals, as well as Chichi's murder towards the end of the film when he is mistaken for his friend, Charles.

The plot for both stories starts out in a Nigerian city, or is substantially set in an urban environment. Although Yoruba-English bilingualism is commonplace amongst the host and Yoruba-speaking community of Lagos,[22] the setting for most of *Phone Swap*, Afolayan deliberately creates a story involving characters who practice alternative forms of bilingualism and multilingualism. Akin in *Phone Swap* is Yoruba-speaking, but as an educated professional, conducts most of his conversations in English, except when he is speaking to his mother. Mary, Akin's love interest in the film, is Igbo, and this is the language she speaks in phone conversations with her father, who is located in a different region of Nigeria. With her peers at work and neighbours in Lagos, she speaks Pidgin. And with her social superiors, she speaks English. Mary's soon to be ex-boyfriend, Tony, is also an Igbo man living in Lagos who speaks Igbo, Pidgin, or English, depending on whom he is addressing. Akin's soon to be ex-girlfriend, Gina, is a citizen of another West African country, Ghana. Typically, she speaks English with Akin and his associates, but in moments of anger reverts back to Ghana's de facto if unofficial lingua franca, Twi.

Similarly, in *Confusion Na Wa*, characters in an unnamed Nigerian city speak a variety of languages. Most frequently, Chichi and Charles converse in Pidgin when they speak to each other, and continue speaking in Pidgin when making calls on Emeka's phone to people they do not know or have never met. The title of the film itself is in Pidgin and could be loosely translated as: 'confusion is trouble.' Emeka speaks English with his girlfriend/mistress, Isabella, but he is Igbo, and there are scenes where he speaks Igbo to his wife. Isabella, the woman that Emeka is having an affair with, is married to Bello, who speaks both Hausa and English in the film. In the course of the story, we see Bello speaking Hausa to a police officer and a bus conductor. With dialogue in four or five languages, both *Phone Swap* and *Confusion Na Wa* would seem to qualify as multilingual films, although a significant proportion of the dialogue is in Standard Nigerian English. Frequently and at various points, the protagonists of both films engage in brief or extended conversations in a language other than English. Some, like Mary in *Phone Swap*, speak in three languages during the film. And even where some characters do not show their polyglottism, they do speak entirely or mostly in a language other than English.

Both films engage in what Carol O'Sullivan calls "vehicular matching," that is, depiction of languages as they are actually spoken.[23] Indeed, one might describe the primary motivation for multilingualism in both films as the desire to present the postcolonial nation as a reflexively multilingual space. Afolayan and Gyang aim for sociocultural authenticity in their representation of linguistic practice. Gang members, especially in southern Nigeria, do conduct their conversation in Pidgin when they are from different ethnic groups, and in this respect *Confusion Na Wa* is socially authentic. Likewise, and as in *Phone Swap*, it is entirely plausible that an Igbo resident of Lagos would speak Pidgin to her peers and neighbours, English to her employer and other social superiors, and Igbo to members of her own family. When Akin ends up by mistake in the south-eastern part of the country where Igbo is spoken, several characters alternate between Pidgin and Igbo, or speak entirely in Igbo. Akin uses his proficiency in English to distance himself from associates and family in a way that is consistent with social practice in Nigeria. His mother, seeking to re-establish close ties with him, insists on speaking Yoruba to him. And as a foreigner in Nigeria, Gina's exasperation with her ex-boyfriend Akin, and outbursts in Twi, fit into expected speech patterns and are performed to comedic effect in the film. In the multilingual postcolony, as depicted by Afolayan, and Gyang, multiple languages thrive side by side. And yet, misunderstandings due to language and translation appear to be rare. Transitions from one language to another occur seamlessly and without drama in these Nigerian multilingual films, unlike in European polyglot films, which foreground moments of interruption in communication due to an alternation of languages. Multilingualism as represented in Nigerian multilingual films is often unmarked and unremarked upon.

If Nigeria's multilingual films seek to represent the ethnic and especially social complexity of the nation in its fullness, Nigeria's monolingual films, by contrast, transform the nation, and indeed the world, into the preserve of a single ethno-linguistic group. The lengths to which Nigeria's monolingual films go to make its postcolonial subjects monolingual are perhaps most striking in the films in indigenous languages. The story in the film *Àbèní*, for example, unfolds across two countries, one in which an official language is English (Nigeria), and the second where the official language is French (Bénin). While it is true that there are substantial Yoruba-speaking populations in both countries, the characters in *Àbèní* are able to conduct their personal and professional lives almost entirely in Yoruba even as they circulate between work spaces in Bénin and work spaces in Nigeria.[24] In this film, when characters from Nigeria are confronted with characters speaking French in Bénin, or when characters from Bénin are confronted with characters speaking English in Nigeria, incomprehension ensues and communication comes to a halt. To all intents and purposes, effective dialogue is possible in only one language: Yoruba. Even more remarkable is Obi Emelonye's film *Onye Ozi*. The plot follows the travails and eventual triumph of Metumaribe, an Igbo-speaking Nigerian in the United Kingdom. Metumaribe's adventures in London bring him in contact with a succession of Igbo-speaking individuals. What is more, the only white Britons that he ever encounters in trying to resolve his challenges all speak Igbo! This does not amount to the artifice of representing what is supposedly spoken English using Igbo. That would illustrate what O'Sullivan calls "homogenization," or the representation of multiple languages using a single language.[25] Instead, viewers are called upon to imagine the existence of an entirely Igbo-speaking universe at the centre of the United Kingdom's most cosmopolitan city.

Monolingual films in English account for a prominent proportion of Nigeria's total film output. These films are shown and sold in Nigeria without subtitles in indigenous languages. Monolingual films in some indigenous languages, notably Yoruba and Igbo, are fairly consistently subtitled into English for viewing within Nigeria.[26] As indicated earlier, multilingual films are relatively rare, and everything suggests that the protocols for making these films available within and outside Nigeria are still very much in flux. In *Phone Swap*, for example, subtitling into English is consistent. Every time a character speaks a language other than English (Pidgin, Igbo, Yoruba, Twi), it is subtitled in English. By contrast, subtitling is inconsistent in *Confusion Na Wa*, leading to complaints amongst some Nigerian viewers.[27] It is also worth noting that fewer alternations between languages occur in *Confusion Na Wa*. A lot of the dialogue in Pidgin is subtitled into English, especially at the beginning of the film, but there are also conversations in Igbo that are not subtitled. Furthermore, there are moments when the two gangsters, Charles and Chichi, inexplicably shift from Pidgin to Standard Nigerian English.

Shared Idioms and the Public

Relevant to the discussion here is Kwesi Kwaa Prah's characterization of Africans as "one of the most multilingual groups of people in the world."[28] With respect to the West African region where Nigeria is located, Evershed Amuzu and John Victor Singler observe that it is "a region where polyglottism is the norm."[29] Given pervasive multilingualism and polyglottism in West Africa, a number of questions come to mind. If we can make sense of the fact that both publicly backed and commercially oriented media naturally default to a monolingual address in nations with a long history of state-imposed monolingualism, and where many citizens are monolingual, how do we explain the apparent predominance of monolingual addressivity in mediated texts produced for publics in countries where multilingualism is the norm, and where most citizens are polyglots?

To start with and in responding, we should take note of the ways in which polyglots in multilingual communities communicate with other polyglots. In the highly multilingual settings around the world, what prevails is a situation that Norman Denison has characterized as one of "functional plurilingualism."[30] Where functional plurilingualism is the norm, the typical adult speaks several languages, and uses different languages for communication in different contexts. While code-switching is well established across Africa, and has been documented in many different settings, communication in highly multilingual contexts across Africa more commonly involves the use of a shared language,[31] or what I have described here as a monolingual address. In effect, community members either learn each other's languages, or deploy a local language of wider communication as a shared language. While monolingual address in mediated texts undoubtedly perpetuates local language hierarchies, imposing what Vicente Rafael calls "an imperializing monolingualism,"[32] monolingual address is actually the norm in Africa's highly multilingual communities. In other words, African polyglots typically use a single language of their language repertoire with specific interlocutors in specific contexts, and do not necessarily deploy multiple languages from their language repertoire in every speech event involving the same interlocutors. It is this practice of using whatever languages are shared in common with different interlocutors that Denison calls functional plurilingualism and others describe as functional multilingualism.

The functional multilingualism of many African cities, which allows residents to use different languages for different purposes, is itself a shared experience. But it is a shared experience that most commonly manifests itself in a single idiom.[33] Code-switching too can be thought of as a shared idiom, though it is often a shared idiom amongst speakers who seek to distinguish themselves from other kinds of polyglots, in effect establishing sub-cultural communication. In contemporary Africa, mixed languages and code-switching have been most frequently associated with the elaboration of urban identities,[34] or peer communication, especially amongst urban youth.[35] While mixed languages can become a more widely used form of speech in African urban settings, or rise in status,[36] even in the highly multilingual communities of African cities, the mixing of languages often functions as a specialized code that allows speakers to separate themselves from other polyglots around them.[37]

Because a shared idiom, and especially a monolingual address, is presumed to heighten rather than to depress degrees of publicness, or communication amongst strangers, the shared idiom of a public's discourse almost always defaults to monolingual address, even where public discourse involves commentary on a multilingual text in a multilingual community. Similarly, and in film texts, mixed languages restrict rather than expand the public defined for a text, even within the nation where the mixed languages are commonplace.[38] I do not imply here that publics emerge around a text only when they have proficiency in the languages of the text. Instead, I suggest that publics as discursive formations often adopt a monolingual address, and that a monolingual address generally correlates with an expanded rather than a restricted degree of publicness. To the extent that all forms of mediation constitute systems for making public, or 'publishing,' it comes as little surprise that those author/composers and sundry distributors of mediated texts seeking maximum publicness tend to impose a monolingual address on the text, even in the instance where it is ostensibly multilingual in formation.

Translation and Circulation of Texts

Where reader/viewers do not have proficiency in the language of the text, translation becomes necessary as a way of making the text accessible to an additional set of readers/viewers beyond those who share the languages of the text. Translation, then, operates as a mode of address for extending degrees of publicness emerging around a text. With translation, too, there is a choice of adopting a monolingual or a multilingual address, that is, translating the source text using a single or multiple languages.

In some source texts, we observe a monolingual address towards a primary language public, or a public that shares the same language as that used in the text. The films *Àbèní* and *Onye Ozi*, like most Nigerian films in indigenous languages, are examples of monolingual address towards primary language publics in Yoruba and Igbo respectively. When films with a monolingual address are translated through subtitling or dubbing, they then present a monolingual address to a public that does not have proficiency in the language of the source text. We see this with many monolingual Nigerian films in indigenous languages, which are comprehensively subtitled into a single language of wider communication for domestic viewing. Thus, the version of *Àbèní* sold in Nigeria was subtitled into English, while the version sold to spectators in Bénin was subtitled into French. The existence of monolingual address in several different languages in Nigerian film-making further confirms the extent to which the logic of the shared idiom dominates the definition of publics for films made available to multilingual communities and polyglot spectators within Nigeria. However, and if the monolingual address of Nigeria's indigenous language films does violence to a multilingual reality (as also happens with English-language films), widespread subtitling for domestic publics recovers the trace of multilingualism, confirming the coexistence of multiple languages within the publics of the African postcolony. The widespread exclusion of English-language films from subtitling or dubbing would seem to indicate designation of English as a shared idiom for speakers of many other languages.

In the case of a multilingual film like *Phone Swap*, the fact that subtitling occurs in a single language would suggest that the film actually offers a monolingual address towards a public that is probably multilingual. If the film-makers anticipated a primary language public for this film within Nigeria, there would be no need then for subtitling, since the viewers could be expected to follow all the dialogue in the different languages used. Instead of defining a primary language public, the language politics and practices of this film are to be associated with a monolingual address to a multilingual public by way of 'selective' translation.[39] When translation for a highly multilingual narrative is selective rather than comprehensive, it is an indication of incomplete congruence between languages used in the film and the language repertoires of an anticipated multilingual public.

The inconsistent subtitling of *Confusion Na Wa* is indicative of oscillation between different definitions of a potential public. Subtitling of exchanges in Pidgin between the gangster protagonists of the film, Charles and Chichi, would suggest that the prospective public is envisioned as unfamiliar with Pidgin but conversant with English, which also has a substantial presence in the film.[40] The absence of subtitling in English for conversations in Igbo between Emeka and his wife seems to point towards defining for the film a public that is Igbo-speaking (and as such Nigerian), but also familiar with Standard Nigerian English which is never subtitled in the film.

There are additional implications to note when monolingual address based on translation is adopted for a multilingual film.[41] If, as I have noted elsewhere,[42] translation is superfluous in a multilingual community where everyone shares the same language repertoires, it is also superfluous for a multilingual text when readers/viewers have proficiency in all the languages used in the text. The subtitling of versions of *Phone Swap* shown and sold within Nigeria into a single language is a way of anticipating divergence in the language repertoires of its presumably local multilingual public. A refusal to translate the multilingual text is certainly possible, but equates with reduced publicness even in a largely multilingual context. A further option would be multilingual address in translation, or a translation practice that aims for consistent multilingualism in the target text. As it turns out, multilingual address in translation is rare both for the domestic and foreign publics of Nigeria's multilingual films. When, for example, *Phone Swap* was shown at the Nollywood Film Festival in Paris in 2013, all the languages in the film were subtitled into different registers of a single language: French.

When scholars of literature speak of the "multilingual circulation" of literature in the contemporary age,[43] it is important to note that this expression primarily references for them texts composed in single languages which exhibit monolingual address prior to, and after, translation. If texts of this sort "circulate in several literary systems at once,"[44] it is because they are very quickly translated into additional languages, and not because the texts are initially composed in more than language. In such instances, the text may be subject to supplementary editorial interventions designed to enhance circulation in other literary systems.[45] Furthermore, the literary systems in which these kinds of texts circulate tend to be associated more with powerful languages than with the mother tongues of the authors, except when those mother tongues are also global languages. To the extent that World Literature texts can be described as "born translated,"[46] it is often by virtue of being "compositional translations" usually written in global languages. As I have indicated elsewhere, "compositional translations" are texts that appear to be translations or are passed off as translations, but for which no source texts exist.[47]

In the case of African literature, a number of bilingual works have been published, especially in poetry, but comprehensively multilingual texts are rare.[48] Multilingualism in African literary texts more often involves occasional code-switching between a European and an indigenous language, frequently juxtaposed with a direct or indirect translation of indigenous language expressions into a European language.[49] This kind of 'multilingualism' more often functions as a gesture signalling the deployment of an indigenous language in reported speech than as a commitment to consistent representation of a multilingual world. By contrast, the dialogue in films like *Phone Swap* and *Confusion Na Wa* exhibits multilingual address and involves regular rather than occasional alternation between several languages. Likewise, and despite their deployment of multiple languages, neither *Phone Swap* nor *Confusion Na Wa* would fit Walkowitz's notion of comparison literature, a term which she uses to characterize texts where "global comparison is a formal as well as thematic preoccupation."[50] Indeed, and as intimated earlier, the rationale behind the use of multiple languages in these Nigerian films is less comparison than it is commitment to the authentic portrayal of a particular nation's sociocultural reality.

In contrast, *Timbuktu*,[51] the award-winning film by the Mauritanian-Malian film director, Abderrahmane Sissako, would seem a better fit for the cinematic equivalent of comparison literature, as a multilingual film with translation, interpretation, and comparison of a global order as thematic concerns.[52] Unlike *Phone Swap* and *Confusion Na Wa*, where transitions between languages never interrupt communication, *Timbuktu* foregrounds instances when a breakdown in communication occurs between characters speaking different languages. This film, about the clash between the values of a transnational militant Islamic movement and those associated with a locally rooted Muslim community, uses lack of proficiency in the languages spoken by different characters as a metaphor for the disregard for local culture exhibited by the transnational militant group. In one example, an English-speaking member of the militant group insists on marrying an underage girl against the wishes of her parents, though he cannot speak directly to her mother and must use two interpreters to make his wishes known. In another example, a Tuareg nomad imprisoned by the militant group enquires in growing frustration whether anyone speaks his language, Tamasheq. *Timbuktu* repeatedly depicts the actual process of interpretation, and what is omitted as the militant fighters issue orders and judgements, which are then fully or only partly interpreted into the diverse languages spoken locally.

While I have no confirmation regarding reception of the film in the home country of the film-maker, it is certainly possible that when viewed in some regions of Mali (and especially northern Mali),[53] *Timbuktu* might offer multilingual address without translation to a domestic public. However, there can be no doubt that this film's ability to travel within the nation-state, within Africa, and along the most prestigious circuits for global film distribution, rests in large part on subtitling and monolingual address in singular global languages. Unlike 'born translated'

literary works, then, whose ability to travel is enhanced by the fact of being already written in a global language, polyglot films from the global
south that aspire for visibility in world cinema circuits are preferably
composed in languages other than English, and may be multilingual.
However, they must then be subtitled, so as to exhibit monolingual address for the benefit of geographically dispersed publics. If it is to 'travel,'
the multilingual film from the global south has to adopt monolingual
address by way of translation.

African writers may better secure global attention for their work
by writing in the valued registers of a global language or by having
their work translated into such languages. The same is not true for
African film-makers, who improve their chances for global attention by
making a film in indigenous languages, whether it is monolingual or
multilingual, and subsequently using translation to adopt a monolingual
address for dispersed publics. The commitment to authentic portrayal
of social reality by Afolayan and Gyang has made their films natural
candidates for inclusion in film festivals and diverse film award events
within and outside Africa. However, recent experience suggests that a
film relying on multilingual dialogue based on an alternation between
English and other languages will be disqualified from consideration
in the Best Foreign Language Film category of Hollywood's Academy
awards because "English isn't a foreign language."[54] These films, as multilingual texts relying heavily on regional accents of global languages, do
not comfortably inhabit the foreign-language film category frequently
assigned to the films from the global south that secure the most prestigious critical attention at international film festivals or award events.

In conclusion, the multilingual narrative is not incompatible with
the very notion of publicness, but in the absence of translation, it often
signals a restricted rather than an expansive publicness. As discussed
here, the multilingual film is made legible, even for local, highly multilingual spectators, mainly through selective translation that enhances a
monolingual address in a shared idiom. The principle of monolingual
address, then, is not limited to monolingual texts. Whether the literary
or film text is monolingual or multilingual, monolingual address coupled with translation into a shared idiom remains the usual prerequisite
for expanded publicness, both within local multilingual communities as
well as with geographically dispersed audiences that may or may not be
monolingual.

Notes

1 For more on this, see Moradewun Adejunmobi, "Literary Translation and
  Language Diversity in Contemporary Africa," in *Intimate Enemies: Translation in Francophone Contexts*, ed. Kathryn Batchelor and Claire Bisdorff,
  (Liverpool: Liverpool University Press, 2013), 22–3.
2 Popular films are to be distinguished from African art house films which do
  often seek to represent contemporary forms of multilingualism.

3 Christopher Wahl, "Discovering a Genre: The Polyglot Film," *Cinemascope, Independent Film Journal* 1 (2005): 7.
4 Verena Berger and Miya Komori, *Polyglot Cinema: Migration and Transcultural Narration in France, Italy, Portugal and Spain* (Vienna: Lit Verlag, 2010).
5 See Lukas Bleichenbacher, *Multilingualism in the Movies: Hollywood Characters and Their Language Choices* (Tübingen: Narr Francke Attempto Verlag, 2008) and Carol O'Sullivan, "Multilingualism at the Multiplex: A New Audience for Screen Translation," *Linguistica Antverpiensia*, New Series, 6 (2007): 81–95.
6 Rebecca Walkowitz, "Close Reading in an Age of Global Writing," *Modern Language Quarterly* 7 no. 2 (2013): 171.
7 Pascale Casanova, *The World Republic of Letters*, trans. by M.B. DeBevoise (Cambridge, MA: Harvard University Press, 2004), 20.
8 *Onye Ozi*, dir. Obi Emelonye, The Nollywood Factory, 2013; *Àbèní*, dir. Tunde Kelani, Mainframe Film and TV Productions, 2006; *Phone Swap*, dir. Kunle Afolayan, Golden Effects, 2012; *Confusion Na Wa*, dir. Kenneth Gyang, Cinema Kpatakpata, 2013.
9 Michael Warner, "Publics and Counterpublics," *Public Culture* 14 no. 1 (2002): 50.
10 Warner, "Publics and Counterpublics," 87.
11 Karin Barber, *The Anthropology of Texts, Persons and Publics: Oral and Written Culture in Africa and Beyond* (Cambridge: Cambridge University Press, 2007), 139.
12 Ibid., 168.
13 Ibid., 79–86.
14 Mikhail Bakhtin, *Speech Genres and Other Late Essays*, trans. Vern W. McGee, ed. Caryl Emerson and Michael Holquist (Austin: University of Texas Press, 1986), 95.
15 Warner, "Publics and Counterpublics," 50.
16 See Moradewun Adejunmobi, *Vernacular Palaver: Imaginations of the Local and Non-Native Languages in West Africa* (Clevedon: Multilingual Matters Press, 2004), 65; Rebecca Walkowitz, "Location of Literature," *Contemporary Literature* 47 no. 4 (2006): 533.
17 Walkowitz, "Close Reading," 172.
18 Such cultural brokers include authors, directors, translators, publishers, and distributors amongst others.
19 See for example Barber, *Anthropology of Texts*, 356, for examples of unintended publics emerging around texts.
20 Adejunmobi, "Vernacular Monolingualism," 173.
21 Afolayan's first film, *Iràpàdà* (2007), was also a multilingual film.
22 On bilingualism in central Lagos, see Emmanuel Adedun and Mojisola Sodipe, "Yoruba-English Bilingualism in Central Lagos-Nigeria." *Journal of African Cultural Studies* 23 no. 2 (2011): 121–32.
23 O'Sullivan, "Multilingualism at the Multiplex," 82–3.
24 For a more detailed analysis of *Àbèní*, see Adejunmobi, "Vernacular Monolingualism."
25 O'Sullivan, "Multilingualism at the Multiplex," 82.
26 Systematic subtitling is not as commonplace in Hausa language films.
27 In one blog, for example, Kemi Filani, a self-identified Nigerian, complained about the failure to provide subtitles for the Igbo language conversations in the film. Kemi Filani, "Confusion Na Wa." www.kemifilani.com/2014/05/kfb-movie-confusion-na-wa-confused-mei.html.
28 Kwesi Kwaa Prah, "Multilingualism in Urban Africa: Blessings or Bane?" *Journal of Multicultural Discourses* 5 no. 2 (2010): 170.

29 Evershed Amuzu and John Victor Singler, "Codeswitching in West Africa," *International Journal of Bilingualism* 18 no. 4 (2014): 330.

30 Norman Denison, "On Plurilingualism and Translation," in *Theory and Practice of Translation*, ed. Lillebill Gräh, Gustav Korlén, and Bertil Malmberg (Bern: Peter Lang, 1978), 313.

31 Prah, "Multilingualism in Urban Africa," 171.

32 See Vicente L. Rafael, "Translation, American English, and the Insecurities of Empire," *Social Text* 27 no. 4 (2009): 3. Amuzu and Singler ("Codeswitching in West Africa," 330) likewise observe that West African polyglottism is increasingly hierarchically oriented rather than geographically oriented.

33 Thus, for example, and as noted by Mike Kuria, multilingual street performance in Nairobi, Kenya was often accompanied by what he called the preacher–interpreter method of translation, where dialogue in one language would be translated into another language, and mistranslation itself became a subject of comedy. Mike Kuria, "Transcending Boundaries: Comedy in the Streets of Nairobi," in *African Languages Literature in the Political Context of the 1990s*, ed. Charles Bodunde (Bayreuth: Bayreuth African Studies, 2001), 99.

34 See for example Eline Versluys, "Multilingualism and the City: The Construction of Urban Identities in Dakar (Senegal)," *City & Society* 20 no. 2 (2008): 282–300.

35 See Mungai Mutonya, "Redefining Nairobi's Streets: A Study of Slang, Marginalization and Identity," *Journal of Global Initiatives* 2 no. 2 (2007): 169–85.

36 See Peter Githinji, "Ambivalent Attitudes: Perception of Sheng and its Speakers," *Nordic Journal of African Studies* 17 no. 2 (2008): 113–36.

37 Complaints about Swahili-English mix known as Sheng in Kenya by those lacking proficiency in this mixed language have been documented. These are usually adults rather than youth, which is why it can function as a specialized code for peer communication amongst youth. See Chege Githiora, "Sheng: Peer Language, Swahili Dialect or Emerging Creole?" *Journal of African Cultural Studies* 15.2 (2002): 169–70. Jan Blommaert describes, for example, the exclusive identities associated with campus Swahili in Dar es Salaam, Tanzania. Jan Blommaert, "Codeswitching and the Exclusivity of Social Identities: Some Data from Campus Kiswahili," *Journal of Multilingual and Multicultural Development* 13 no. 1 (1992): 67–8.

38 When for example, Beur film-makers in France (second generation North African immigrants) began making films in which French dialogue was mixed with slang and neologisms, the majority French public was often unable to follow the dialogue. For more on this, see Alec Hargreaves and Leslie Kealhofer, "Back to the Future? Language Use in Films by Second-Generation North Africans in France," in *Polyglot Cinema*, ed. Verena Berger and Miya Komori (Vienna: Lit Verlag, 2010), 76.

39 Selective translation here is translation into a language widely used in the film dialogue. This is to be distinguished from the kind of subtitling that accompanies indigenous language films with a monolingual address, and which involves subtitling the film text into a language that is either completely absent from the film dialogue or has at best minimal presence in the film. In Yoruba and Igbo language films for example, where subtitling occurs, it is into a language that is for the most part absent from film dialogue.

40 Pidgin is very widely spoken in Nigerian cities. As such, it is difficult to imagine Nigerian spectators requiring subtitling of dialogue in Pidgin. Related varieties of Pidgin are widely spoken in Sierra Leone and Cameroon, and Pidgin has a growing presence in southern Ghanaian cities.

41 A similar kind of language politics has been reported for *Solino*, the bilingual German/Italian film by Fatih Akin, the Turkish-German film-maker, which was dubbed entirely into German when it was released in Germany. See David Gramling, "On the Other Side of Monolingualism: Fatih Akin's Linguistic Turns," *The German Quarterly* 83 no. 3 (2010): 364.

42 Adejunmobi, "Vernacular Monolingualism," 169.

43 See Walkowitz "Location of Literature," 530; Wen Jin, "Transnational Criticism and Asian Immigrant Literature in the U.S.: Reading Yan Geling's Fusang and Its English Translation," *Contemporary Literature* 47 no. 4 (2006): 572–3.

44 Walkowitz, "Location of Literature," 529.

45 See Wen Jin, "Transnational Criticism," 572, on how the translator excised passages from Mandarin language text for English language readers.

46 Rebecca Walkowitz, "Comparison Literature," *New Literary History* 40 (2009): 570.

47 Moradewun Adejunmobi, "Translation and Postcolonial Identity: African Writing and European Languages," *The Translator, Studies in Intercultural Communication* 4 no. 2 (1998): 166.

48 See, for example, Adejunmobi, "Translation and Postcolonial Identity," 174–8, and Peter Hawkins, "Translation and its Others: Postcolonial Linguistic Strategies of Writers from the Francophone Indian Ocean," in *Intimate Enemies: Translation in Francophone Contexts*, ed. Kathryn Batchelor and Claire Bisdorff (Liverpool: Liverpool University Press, 2013), 39–40, on bilingual poetry.

49 The most extensive discussion of this is to be found in Chantal J. Zabus, *The African Palimpsest: Indigenization of Language in the West African Europhone Novel* (Amsterdam: Rodopi, 1991).

50 Walkowitz, "Location of Literature," 536. See also Walkowitz, "Comparison Literature." It is worth pointing out that, in the latter, despite discussing an instance of multilingual writing as an example of comparison literature, Walkowitz remarks that most comparison literature tends to be written in English (571).

51 *Timbuktu*, dir. Abderrahmane Sissako, Arte France Cinéma, 2014.

52 The languages used in *Timbuktu* are Bambara, Tamasheq, French, Arabic, and English. For more on the film's multilingualism, see Fatin Abbas, "Abderrahmane Sissako's Oscar-Nominated 'Timbuktu' Transcends the Present,"http://africasacountry.com/abderrahmane-sissakos-oscar-nominated-timbuktu-transcends-the-present/.

53 While Bambara is widely spoken in Mali, Tamasheq is more of a regional language that is better represented in the north rather than the south though it has a presence in several other countries of the West African Sahel.

54 For more on disqualification of multilingual films using English from consideration as 'foreign language films' for the Oscars, see Felicia Chan, "When is a Foreign Language Film Not a Foreign Language Film? When It Has Too Much English in It: The Case of a Singapore Film and the Oscars," *Inter-Asia Cultural Studies* 9 no. 1 (2008): 97–105.

Bibliography

Abbas, Fatin. "Abderrahmane Sissako's Oscar-Nominated 'Timbuktu' Transcends the Present." http://africasacountry.com/abderrahmane-sissakos-oscar-nominated-timbuktu-transcends-the-present/.

Àbèní, Dir. Tunde Kelani, Mainframe Film and TV Productions, 2006.

Adedun, Emmanuel and Mojisola Sodipe. "Yoruba-English Bilingualism in Central Lagos-Nigeria." *Journal of African Cultural Studies* 23 no. 2 (2011): 121–32.

Adejunmobi, Moradewun. "Translation and Postcolonial Identity: African Writing and European Languages." *The Translator, Studies in Intercultural Communication* 4 no. 2 (1998): 163–81.

———. *Vernacular Palaver: Imaginations of the Local and Non-Native Languages in West Africa*. Clevedon: Multilingual Matters Press, 2004.

———. "Literary Translation and Language Diversity in Contemporary Africa." In *Intimate Enemies: Translation in Francophone Contexts*, edited by Kathryn Batchelor and Claire Bisdorff, 17–35. Liverpool: Liverpool University Press, 2013.

———. "Vernacular Monolingualism and Translation in West African Popular Film." In *Writing and Translating Francophone Discourse: Africa, The Caribbean, Diaspora*, edited by Paul Bandia, 167–87. Amsterdam: Rodopi, 2014.

Amuzu, Evershed and John Victor Singler. "Codeswitching in West Africa." *International Journal of Bilingualism* 18 no. 4 (2014): 329–45.

Bakhtin, Mikhail. *Speech Genres and Other Late Essays*. Translated by Vern W. McGee, edited by Caryl Emerson and Michael Holquist. Austin: University of Texas Press, 1986.

Barber, Karin. *The Anthropology of Texts, Persons and Publics: Oral and Written Culture in Africa and Beyond*. Cambridge: Cambridge University Press, 2007.

Berger, Verena and Miya Komori. *Polyglot Cinema: Migration and Transcultural Narration in France, Italy, Portugal and Spain*. Vienna: Lit Verlag, 2010.

Bleichenbacher, Lukas. *Multilingualism in the Movies: Hollywood Characters and Their Language Choices*. Tübingen: Narr Francke Attempto Verlag, 2008.

Blommaert, Jan. "Codeswitching and the Exclusivity of Social Identities: Some Data from Campus Kiswahili." *Journal of Multilingual and Multicultural Development* 13 no.1 (1992): 57–70.

Casanova, Pascale. *The World Republic of Letters*. Translated by M.B. DeBevoise. Cambridge, MA: Harvard University Press, 2004.

Chan, Felicia. "When is a Foreign Language Film Not a Foreign Language Film? When it Has Too Much English in It: The Case of a Singapore Film and the Oscars." *Inter-Asia Cultural Studies* 9 no. 1 (2008): 97–105.

Confusion Na Wa. Dir. Kenneth Gyang, Cinema Kpatakpata, 2013.

Denison, Norman. "On Plurilingualism and Translation." In *Theory and Practice of Translation*, edited by Lillebill Gräh, Gustav Korlén, and Bertil Malmberg, 313–25. Bern: Peter Lang, 1978.

Filani, Kemi. "Confusion Na Wa." www.kemifilani.com/2014/05/kfb-movie-confusion-na-wa-confused-mei.html.

Githinji, Peter. "Ambivalent Attitudes: Perception of Sheng and its Speakers." *Nordic Journal of African Studies* 17 no. 2 (2008): 113–36.

Githiora, Chege. "Sheng: Peer Language, Swahili Dialect or Emerging Creole?" *Journal of African Cultural Studies* 15 no. 2 (2002): 159–81.

Gramling, David. "On the Other Side of Monolingualism: Fatih Akin's Linguistic Turns." *The German Quarterly* 83 no. 3 (2010), 353–72.

Hargreaves, Alec and Leslie Kealhofer. "Back to the Future? Language Use in Films by Second-Generation North Africans in France." In *Polyglot Cinema*, edited by Verena Berger and Miya Komori, 75–87, Berlin: LIT Verlag, 2010.

Hawkins, Peter. "Translation and its Others: Postcolonial Linguistic Strategies of Writers from the Francophone Indian Ocean." In *Intimate Enemies: Translation in Francophone Contexts*, edited by Kathryn Batchelor and Claire Bisdorff, 36–48. Liverpool: Liverpool University Press, 2013.

Jin, Wen "Transnational Criticism and Asian Immigrant Literature in the U.S.: Reading Yan Geling's Fusang and Its English Translation." *Contemporary Literature* 47 no. 4 (2006): 570–600.

Kuria, Mike. "Transcending Boundaries: Comedy in the Streets of Nairobi." In *African Languages Literature in the Political Context of the 1990s*, edited by Charles Bodunde, 91–102. Bayreuth: Bayreuth African Studies, 2001.

Mutonya, Mungai. "Redefining Nairobi's Streets: A Study of Slang, Marginalization and Identity." *Journal of Global Initiatives* 2 no. 2 (2007): 169–85.

Onye Ozi. Dir. Obi Emelonye, The Nollywood Factory, 2013.

O'Sullivan, Carol. "Multilingualism at the Multiplex: A New Audience for Screen Translation." *Linguistica Antverpiensia*, New Series 6 (2007): 81–95.

Phone Swap. Dir. Kunle Afolayan, Golden Effects, 2012.

Prah, Kwesi Kwaa. "Multilingualism in Urban Africa: Blessings or Bane?" *Journal of Multicultural Discourses* 5 no. 2 (2010): 169–82.

Rafael, Vicente L. "Translation, American English, and the Insecurities of Empire." *Social Text* 27 no. 4 (2009): 1–23.

Versluys, Eline. "Multilingualism and the City: The Construction of Urban Identities in Dakar (Senegal)." *City & Society* 20 no. 2 (2008): 282–300.

Wahl, Christopher. "Discovering a Genre: The Polyglot Film." *Cinemascope, Independent Film Journal* 1 (2005): 1–8.

Walkowitz, Rebecca. "Location of Literature." *Contemporary Literature* 47 no. 4 (2006): 527–45.

———. "Comparison Literature." *New Literary History* 40 (2009): 567–82.

———. "Close Reading in an Age of Global Writing." *Modern Language Quarterly* 7 no. 2 (2013): 171–95.

Warner, Michael. "Publics and Counterpublics." *Public Culture* 14 no. 1 (2002): 49–90.

Zabus, Chantal J. *The African Palimpsest: Indigenization of Language in the West African Europhone Novel*. Amsterdam: Rodopi, 1991.

11 Afterword

Paul F. Bandia

The chapters in this book speak to the inescapable centrality of language diversity in its various manifestations and conceptualizations in literature and culture, as well as to the role or significance of translation, viewed pragmatically or metaphorically, in the characterization of multilingualism in the current context of globalization. It is now commonly acknowledged that multilingualism is the prevalent linguistic experience in contemporary societies worldwide, whether within nation-states, postcolonial societies, colonial métropoles, or pre-industrialized traditional societies. It is a common misconception to think of multilingualism as a literary theoretical construct mainly in terms of transnational encounters involving distant cultures, often between the global south and the global north, or as the result of the spread of empire and the consequent power differential or imbalance. This is a point that Rachael Gilmour and Tamar Steinitz touch upon in their introduction to this volume, but one which we might yet think through further. Crucially, there is a strong dynamic of multilingual experiences and practices within fairly homogeneous traditional societies operating predominantly as oral cultures. Homogeneity may not always imply monolingualism, especially in cultures of orality which seem more porous and more conducive to multilingual experiences, and where the border between languages is not always as rigid or clearly demarcated as is the case between written language cultures. Often, for societies steeped in orality, multilingualism is a way of life. There is a kind of fluidity of discourse between and amongst neighbouring languages and cultures buoyed by age-old or historical relations between peoples or ethnicities and the simple need to communicate with each other for a variety of social, economic, or political interests. It is therefore not unusual, in societies of orality, to find people of a certain generation who speak many neighbouring languages at will as a part of everyday experience. This insular multilingualism is at the heart of many traditional societies that have remained fairly consistent and intact in the face of modernity. In other words, multilingualism is often the result of internal rather than external forces, and is at the basis of a certain degree of societal cohesion.

Thus it is somewhat limiting to think of multilingualism mainly from the perspective of a transnational or migratory experience, as is often the case in the current context of globalization. If anything, it is more likely that the preponderance of multilingual practices triggered by colonization on a global scale simply built on existing multilingual experiences (or realities) in the colonies, and perhaps also on the multilingual histories of the colonizer nation-states themselves. What may differ is the enhanced awareness of power differentials and linguistic hierarchies that remained a determining factor for life under colonization, whether in regards to the potential for upward mobility or the desire to participate in civil society. This is not to say that all languages were equal in traditional societies before the advent of colonization. Rather, it is to affirm that with colonization, language became a major factor in the life experiences of the colonial subject due to the imposition of an alien imperial language that trumped local languages in matters of power and prestige. The colonial experience of multilingualism is manifest in the various discourses of colonial administration, religious missionaries, traders, as well as anthropologists and linguists who were active agents at the crossroads of the encounter between colonized and colonizer. Colonial governmentality ('gouvernementalité') imposed the language of the métropole for officialdom, but sought communication with colonial subjects through the native interpreter or translator. Religious missionaries engaged in large-scale translation activity into indigenous languages for proselytization, while anthropologists and linguists resorted to the services of native informants for cross-cultural communication purposes. Contact and interaction between the language of colonization and indigenous languages gave rise to hybrid vehicular languages such as pidgins and creoles, which became handy tools for traders and other mercantilists in the multilingual complexity of the colony. Some of these hybrid languages are lingua francas today and provide the basis or link that holds together various language experiences within the postcolony.

The native interpreter, translator, or linguist is the embodiment of colonial multilingualism, a figure that bridges the gap between an alien imperial presence and a historically multilingual and multi-ethnic society. As a gifted linguist and polyglot, the colonial native interpreter was an important figure in the colonial enterprise, derided by some as an enabler of colonization and held in awe by those who feared his power and influence within the colonial establishment. His skills closely mirror those of the *griots* in traditional societies, who were revered for their heritage as repositories of history and culture and for their multilingual abilities. However, unlike the *griot*, the colonial native interpreter was working not for their own immediate society but rather for an alien imperial power. Therefore, colonial multilingualism served as a necessity for the consolidation of colonization, as well as the means for ensuring communication in colonial societies between colonized people of various ethnicities and the agents of the colonial enterprise.

Postcoloniality is often expressed in literature and other art forms in terms of its characteristic multilingualism and pluralism. For postcolonial societies, multilingualism has become the norm, as various ethnicities are forced to cohabit within a nation-state mapped out without regard for traditional ethnic boundaries. As is well known, the creation of independent postcolonial nation-states came with the splitting up of major ethnic groups which now belonged to different nations, and the lumping of various, sometimes hostile, ethnic groups within the same emerging nation or country. This created the conditions for a forced multilingualism in which language hierarchy and issues of prestige and power are inescapable. The dominance of the imposed colonial language in official and public domains has left the various local languages vying for recognition and competing for influence, often with the result of ethnic strife or conflict. Multilingual practices in the postcolony are, in other words, deeply embedded in various conditions of diglossia between the colonial language of prestige and the indigenous languages. This diglossia, with its implied hierarchy of languages, has led in turn to the proliferation of new and shifting linguistic codes for communication across ethnicities and for the assertion of postcolonial identities. The linguistic layering characteristic of postcolonial societies calls for multilingual practices and translation as a way of life. This is often showcased in postcolonial literature and other art forms in terms of the use of multiple languages through discourse strategies such as code-switching, code-mixing, or the encoding or transcoding of various indigenous linguistic specificities within the matrix of the global colonial language.

Hybrid languages such as pidgins and creoles that have become lingua francas in many postcolonies are themselves the product of multilingualism, the encounter of various language communities and the blending of codes for wider communication. However, as identity markers of postcolonial societies, such hybrid varieties have yet to garner prestige as the means of literary expression for postcolonial societies. For all the hopes of some writers in the decolonizing Caribbean, for example, there are very few instances where these languages have been used in whole literary productions such as novels. They are often interspersed in novels written in the global colonial language, where they serve as signposts of an identitarian politics of postcoloniality. The interpolation of these hybrid varieties in colonial language literature thus offers, it must be said, only a partial challenge to the dominance of global languages. In some contexts, creoles have been widely used in education, religious activities, politics, and even in literature, yet often with an intra-national rather than a transnational reach. Take, for instance, Britta Schneider's account in this volume of multilingualism in Belize, where English is the language of officialdom and Belizean Kriol is the country's lingua franca and a marker of Belizean identity, in spite of the increasing demographic dominance of Spanish-speakers. The European and African heritage of

Kriol, and also its attachment to English as a global language of prestige, confers upon Kriol its own sense of prestige and resistance to the threat of Spanish. This is a clear indication that postcolonial multilingualism, while assertive of postcolonial identity, is quite heavily dependent on dominant colonial languages for its global relevance: rich and complex multilingual practice remains circumscribed within the matrix of the colonial language.

Multilingual currents run through transnational or global experiences ingrained in cultures of migration and diaspora. The migrant condition dictates a multilingual existence, even if and when migration takes place between geographical locations that share a common global language. Migration creates and depends on multilingualism. The already-polyglot migrant—most migrants hail from multilingual societies—living in a Western host society possesses a double consciousness (to borrow W.E.B. Du Bois' term[1]), which makes it possible to navigate the perils of metropolitan multilingualism by adopting an outsider–insider attitude. These increasingly common experiences of language produce in literature a kind of bilingual aesthetics, in Doris Sommer's terms:[2] through the double vision or dual consciousness of bilingual writers, translation as a stylistic and formal feature becomes, as Fiona Doloughan argues in this volume, integral to contemporary literary production. Such conditions of living and writing can also give rise to the sense of homelessness in two or more languages described here by Steven Kellman. Translingual writers engage in practices of "languaging" which, according to Walter Mignolo, are a form of "border thinking," engaging the space or "the border or line that divides and unites modernity/coloniality"[3] and offering, as Kellman notes, "a vantage point from which to launch a successful foray against hegemonic thinking."

In spite of its multilingual fabric, we must recall that the linguistic scene of a Western metropolis is almost always dominated by a global language. Migrants therefore quickly learn to fashion language varieties for communication within their own communities, while adopting the dominant language for interaction with the host society. Thus Western cities become ever more multilingual, while these processes at the same time result in expanded varieties of European languages in a context of what can be referred to as minority cosmopolitanism. In her chapter, for example, Rachael Gilmour discusses the relationship between the linguistic local and global in contemporary Glasgow, where a multilayered literary Scottish–Asian Glaswegian-speak exposes at the level of language the power dynamics of class and race. Contemporary migrant literatures are replete with such variants to a global language, which is moulded or transformed to reflect the lived experiences of migrants. The replication of such experiences across the globe is the basis of the trace of multilingual practices running through migrant communities in the diaspora.

In many ways, the polyglot and translingual dimensions of migration can be explained in terms of translocation, in which the latter mirrors a translational experience both metaphorically and pragmatically. Translocation as migration involves the translation, or carrying across, of cultures and linguistic attitudes into the metropolitan or global medium of communication. The result is a form of globalism of language through a process of transfusion and translation of multiple experiences in a context of cultural and linguistic encounter. As Rita Wilson points out in her chapter on contemporary Italian urban writing by translingual authors, migrants are indeed "fragmented beings," having experienced a "triple disruption" ("loss of place; entering into an alien language; surrounded by people, cultures, of different social behaviours and codes"). Translation becomes a means to establish links and hold the fragments together by renegotiating new hybrid identities within the dialectic between the local and the global. The language of globalism evokes a form of 'global speak' in its various incarnations across the globe, for example resulting in what has been referred to as 'global English,' which is the subject of several chapters in this book. The formation of 'global English' can therefore be viewed as a centripetal translating practice that pulls varied cultural and linguistic experiences towards a centre that remains hegemonic even as it becomes more pluralistic. In the context of globalization, the manufactured pluralism of the metropolitan centre overshadows the multiple and rich multilingual experiences in the peripheries, while ultimately negating the need for translation at all.

This situation raises various questions. The domain of World Literature has come under scrutiny for its alleged homogenizing tendency, which has led to the rise of the so-called global English by relying heavily on Western, Anglophone systems of production and circulation. Critics have pointed to the overwhelming presence or influence of Anglo-American English in World Literature, promoting a type of diversity-in-monolingualism, as it were. Global English takes on multiple influences and subsumes or synthesizes them into a matrix that purports to represent a variety of experiences—or even, the full range of experience—through a global language that remains determined by the imperial centre. How does this globalism of language square with issues of (un)translatability (as raised recently by Emily Apter, and discussed in several chapters in this volume)?[4] Is global English a language of translation? If so, does it render translation obsolete? How fluent or transparent are literatures or discourses in global English for communities across the globe? Are peripheral cultures and linguistic experiences being short-changed in the globalism of imperial languages such as English? Or do some benefits accrue for peripheral productions in the unrelenting march towards globalization? In her chapter, Fiona Doloughan highlights the indispensable role of translation in a context whereby a global language such as English is increasingly being used by polyglot writers with access to other languages and cultures. These writers adopt translation as a mode of writing, developing new literary forms and aesthetics as they bring their multilingual experiences to bear on a global language. The multilingual aesthetics of such writing, and the reading processes they demand, recall translational modes that can be referred to as writing-as-translation and reading-as-translation respectively. Multilingual writing therefore challenges the normative standard for English, and its recourse to translational modes of resistance draws attention to the power differential or inequality between English and the other peripheral languages. Citing Chinua Achebe's well-known position regarding diversity within the English language,[5] Carli Coetzee discusses NoViolet Bulawayo's novel as an example of "a novel that can be diverse (or translated) *within* itself; circulating as it does among diverse audiences and in multiple discursive spaces." In Bulawayo's novel "the local and the transnational are complexly interwoven rather than oppositional," and readers who can read locally challenge the transnational narrative emphasized by its cosmopolitan reception. The novelistic blending of the local and the global, the national and the transnational or the diasporic in postcolonial and World Literature is necessarily grounded in multilingualism and transculturality. Yet it is also important to note that some inherently multilingual societies may show a preference for monolingualism in artistic productions for a variety of reasons, including the mere desire to reach a wider audience. In discussing multilingualism in Nigerian popular film production, Moradewun Adejunmobi here raises the issue of language addressivity, whereby "multilingual films are made available to dispersed publics around the world by adopting a strategy of monolingual address." In the complex situation Adejunmobi discusses, monolingual address is more expansive and less restrictive while multilingual address is aimed at a more enclosed public, though it should be pointed out that multilingual films reach their various audiences by monolingual address through selective translation. Multilingualism in Nigerian popular film seeks to represent the postcolony as a socially complex, multilingual, and multi-ethnic space. Yet, according to Adejunmobi, vernacular *monolingualism*—addressivity in a particular indigenous language—seems to be the dominant trend in Nigerian film production. Translation plays a role in adopting another kind of monolingual address, as indigenous languages are often subtitled into a lingua franca or a global language such as English. It is just one of the ironies highlighted in this volume, that films produced in the global south, where multilingualism is often the norm, must have recourse to translation to effect monolingual address for the benefit of a wider audience both locally and globally. This speaks to the power of global English and to its ability to function as the matrix through which other language cultures and varieties of English can be subsumed and conveyed in the current context of globalization.

It is interesting to note that while the Anglo-American paradigm of 'World Literature' seems to rely on an imposed global English for its imperial reach, the Francophone concept of 'Littérature-monde' is rather a negation of the imperial extension of Hexagonal French, seeking or creating alternatives that reflect the linguistic and cultural realities within a greater Francophonie. The expression of this greater Francophonie obviously includes the French resulting from subversive linguistic practices within the métropole itself, often by people of migrant origins who seek to assert their identity in the face of hegemonic and nationalistic tendencies. As Polo Moji indicates in her chapter, "the embeddedness of place and language, and the untranslatability of the experience" highlights the insufficiency of French when it comes to conveying diasporic lived experience. This diasporic experience is defined beyond the dichotomous homeland–hostland paradigm to include multiple and varied experiences of diaspora living in the hostland. Moji points out that in Léonora Miano's writing, "the relation to the hostland is mediated by the French language and its inability to fully capture the lived experience of the Afro-diasporic subject in France." Citing Paul Gilroy, Moji points in fact to the "limited expressive power of language" to represent diasporic loss.[6] This is compounded by the "conditional 'unsayability' (Gilroy) of being black in France against a backdrop of rising anti-immigrant sentiment." It becomes therefore necessary to resort to other forms of artistic expression such as music to communicate "the texture of lived experience of Miano's Francophone Afro-diasporic subjects, as well as their political and cultural affiliations to globally mediated blackness, in a way that compensates for the expressive lacunae of French and novelistic language." The use of multiple forms of language in the Afropean narrative, including code-switching strategies both between languages and between sonic and textual elements, are indicative of a desire to find ways around the imposed silences.

In a context where distinctions are made not only between immigrants and hosts, but also in terms of blood or ancestral relations to the indigenous populations, terms of exclusion such as "*français d'origine*" and "*français de souche*" emerge. The former, "*français d'origine*" (French by birth), is meant to emphasize the fact that even those born in France but whose ancestral roots are elsewhere are considered different from the "*français de souche*" (native French), whose ancestry is rooted in the French territory. By contrast, in other Francophone societies built on immigration, such as Québec, to be "*d'origine*" is taken as a synonym of to be "*de souche*," simply implying a natural born citizen. This indeed explains why it becomes crucial for the Afropean French to develop various strategies for identity formation and assertion by resorting to multilingualism and resistance to the hegemonic monolingualism of French. Within Francophonie, Québec seems to present a somewhat unique case of multilingualism, as suggested in Christopher

Larkosh's chapter in this volume. A fairly multilingual and multicultural society immersed within the official bilingualism of Canada, the province seems to prefer a model of interculturalism between the host population and the non-native communities, and holds onto a rigid official monolingualism in French. Québec's growing awareness of its own "globalized late modernity" viewed against the background of conflicting cultural and identity politics—faced with the overwhelming presence of Anglo-American culture and an ever-increasing need for immigrants—has thwarted attempts at promoting a multilingual and multicultural existence in favour of maintaining and strengthening a centralized form of monolingualism. Québec's apparent limited presence in the discourse of World Literature may have to do with its own preference for an inward-looking, self-preserving literary practice, rather than the result of some 'Paris-centrique' or Anglo-American definition and domination of the field. Larkosh's chapter, pulling against this tendency, postulates an alternative Québec imagined through the crossing of borders both linguistic and physical.

In a noteworthy spin on centre/periphery questions, we have seen a spate of canonization of periphery-inspired literatures through prestigious literary prizes such as the Man Booker Prize or the Prix Goncourt. The language used in various nominated works dealing with the periphery often deviates from the mainstream metropolitan variety, grounded in a kind of hybrid or transnational expression—a 'world speak' that exploits multilingualism and multiculturalism through a process of translation, and transcends geographical and cultural borders. Take, for example, Patrick Chamoiseau's *Texaco*, which won the 1992 Prix Goncourt. It is a novel written in French, but a French moulded to capture or reflect the Antillean world view, couched in a language that expresses the creoleness ('*créolité*') of the French Antilles. To ensure its global reach, this linguistic experimentation with creoleness is grounded securely in what can be described as a global French, understandable across the Francophone universe, but posing a serious challenge to the hegemony of metropolitan French. The reading of the novel is itself a translation process that requires a back and forth movement between languages and worlds, between the creole imaginary and the French world view. In fact, it is quite likely that one could find more people capable of navigating the reading process for this novel at depth within the wider Francophonie than one would in mainland France. Yet the novel was highly acclaimed by critics, and won one of France's most prestigious and exclusive literary prizes. There are still more examples in the Man Booker Prize competition, from Salman Rushdie's *Midnight's Children* (named the "Booker of Bookers") all the way to Marlon James's *A Brief History of Seven Killings*, but the point is that although language globalism might be stifling multilingual experiences in peripheral societies, literatures that draw on such multilingual realities arc able to enhance their appeal worldwide and influence the global language and global tastes significantly. They are literatures of translation by translocated beings, written within the matrix of a global language, that resonate with polyglot and diverse linguistic communities across the world. Given the contemporary experiences of globalization and migration, the world is increasingly interconnected, highlighting the need for a developed understanding of multilingual and multicultural currents and relations. This is a fact that flies in the face of dismissive, mocking, and reactionary comments such as those recently uttered by the current British Prime Minister, Theresa May, who in the context of Brexit has criticized the expression "citizens of the world," claiming it means "citizens of nowhere"—when indeed, a significant proportion of the world's population identifies as such. The chapters in this volume reveal the anachronism of such views, being propagated currently by the extreme-right and nationalist wave sweeping across the West, and can be read as a challenge to ideologies of linguistic and cultural purism.

Notes

1 W.E.B Du Bois, *The Souls of Black Folk*, ed. Brent Hayes Edwards (Oxford: Oxford University Press, 2008).
2 Doris Sommer, *Bilingual Aesthetics: A New Sentimental Education* (Durham, NC: Duke University Press, 2004).
3 Walter D. Mignolo, *Local Histories/Global Designs: Coloniality, Subaltern Knowledges, and Border Thinking*, rev. ed. (Princeton, NJ: Princeton University Press, 2012), xvi, xxii, 226.
4 Emily Apter, *Against World Literature: On the Politics of Untranslatability* (London: Verso, 2013).
5 Chinua Achebe, "The African Writer and the English Language," in *Morning Yet On Creation Day* (London: Heinemann, 1975), 55–62.
6 Paul Gilroy, *The Black Atlantic: Modernity and Double Consciousness* (Cambridge, MA: Harvard University Press, 1993).

Bibliography

Achebe, Chinua. "The African Writer and the English Language." In *Morning Yet On Creation Day*, 55–62. London: Heinemann, 1975.
Apter, Emily. *Against World Literature: On the Politics of Untranslatability*. London: Verso, 2013.
Du Bois, W.E.B. *The Souls of Black Folk*. Edited by Brent Hayes Edwards. Oxford: Oxford University Press, 2008.
Gilroy, Paul. *The Black Atlantic: Modernity and Double Consciousness*. Cambridge, MA: Harvard University Press, 1993.
Mignolo, Walter D. *Local Histories/Global Designs: Coloniality, Subaltern Knowledges, and Border Thinking*, rev. edition. Princeton, NJ: Princeton University Press, 2012.
Sommer, Doris. *Bilingual Aesthetics: A Sentimental Education*. Durham, NC: Duke University Press, 2004.

List of Contributors

Moradewun Adejunmobi is Professor in African Studies at the University of California, Davis. She is the author of *Vernacular Palaver: Imaginations of the Local and Non-Native Languages in West Africa* (2004), as well as several articles on translation, multilingualism, and intercultural communication in West African literature and popular culture.

Paul F. Bandia is Professor of French and Translation Studies at Concordia University, Montreal, and an Associate Fellow at the W.E.B. Du Bois Institute for African and African American Research at Harvard University. With interests in translation theory, he has published widely in the fields of translation studies and postcolonial literatures and cultures. He is the author of *Translation as Reparation: Writing and Translation in Postcolonial Africa* (2008), editor of *Writing and Translating Francophone Discourse: Africa, the Caribbean, Diaspora* (2014), and co-editor of *Charting the Future of Translation History* (2006) and *Agents of Translation* (2009), as well as the first issue of *TTR* vol. 23 Rencontres Est-Ouest/East-West Encounters (2010).

Carli Coetzee is the editor of the *Journal of African Cultural Studies*, an Honorary Research Fellow in the School of Literature, Language and Media at Wits University, and a Research Associate in the African Languages and Cultures department at SOAS, University of London.

Fiona Doloughan is Senior Lecturer in English (Literature and Creative Writing) at the Open University, Milton Keynes, England. She works principally in the area of contemporary narrative fiction with a focus on creativity and translation. She is author of two monographs, *Contemporary Narrative: Textual Production, Multimodality and Multiliteracies* (Continuum, 2011) and *English as a Literature in Translation* (Bloomsbury, 2016).

Rachael Gilmour is Reader in Postcolonial and World Literatures in the Department of English at Queen Mary University of London. Her research has explored the politics of language, language-learning, multilingualism, and translation, in South African and British literature and culture. She is co-editor of *The Journal of Commonwealth*

Literature, and her publications include *Grammars of Colonialism: Representing Languages in Colonial South Africa* (2006), and *End of Empire and the English Novel since 1945* (2011), edited with Bill Schwarz, as well as the forthcoming *Bad English: Literature and Language Diversity in Contemporary Britain.*

Steven G. Kellman is the author of *The Translingual Imagination* (University of Nebraska Press, 2000) and editor of *Switching Languages: Translingual Writers Reflect on Their Craft* (Nebraska, 2003). His other books include *Redemption: The Life of Henry Roth* (Norton, 2005), *The Plague: Fiction and Resistance* (Twayne, 1993), *Loving Reading: Erotics of the Text* (Archon, 1985), and *The Self-Begetting Novel* (Columbia University Press, 1980). He served four terms on the board of directors of the National Book Critics Circle, and was the 2006 recipient of the NBCC's Nona Balakian Citation for Excellence in Reviewing. Kellman is Professor of Comparative Literature at the University of Texas at San Antonio.

Christopher Larkosh is Associate Professor of Portuguese at UMass Dartmouth. His research in comparative literary and cultural studies transits not only spaces commonly associated with the Portuguese-speaking world, but also Québec, Argentina, Central Europe, the Middle East, South Asia, and the Far East. His research has appeared in *TTR* and *The Translator*, as well as *Translation Studies*, on which he also collaborated as Reviews Editor from 2012 to 2014. He has edited *Re-Engendering Translation: Transcultural Practice, Gender/Sexuality and the Politics of Alterity* (Routledge, 2011), and two co-edited volumes on interculturality: *Writing Spaces* (Kaohsiung: NSYSU Press, 2013) and *KulturConfusão: German-Brazilian Inter-culturalities* (Berlin: De Gruyter, 2015). He is also currently Director of Tagus Press at the University of Massachusetts Dartmouth and co-editor of its online journal *Portuguese Literary and Cultural Studies*.

Polo Belina Moji is Lecturer in French and Francophone Studies at the University of the Witwatersrand (South Africa). She completed a PhD in Comparative Literature at the Université de Sorbonne Nouvelle (France) in 2011. She was a postdoctoral fellow at the University of Pretoria (South Africa), where she co-convened Research at UP. She works principally in the areas of feminist and cultural studies, critical race theory and comparative (Anglophone/Francophone) African literature. Her current research focuses on Francophone Afro-European literary and cultural production.

Britta Schneider is Researcher in the Department of English Philology at Freie Universität Berlin, Germany. Her research interests include sociolinguistics of globalization, language ideology, language policy, epistemology of language and multilingualism, and superdiversity. Her publications include *Salsa, Language and Transnationalism* (Multilingual Matters, 2014), and she runs a research project on multilingualism in Belize, funded by the German Research Council (DFG).

Tamar Steinitz is Lecturer in the Department of English and Comparative Literature at Goldsmiths, University of London, and has worked as a literary translator between English and Hebrew. Her research explores modern and contemporary transnational literature, with a focus on translingualism and translation. She is the author of *Translingual Identities: Language and the Self in Stefan Heym and Jakov Lind* (Camden House 2013).

Rita Wilson is Professor of Translation Studies in the School of Languages, Literatures, Cultures and Linguistics at Monash University (Melbourne). She has published widely on contemporary Italian literature, women's writing, and on the relationship between migration, self-translation, and identity. She is currently the Academic Co-Director of the Monash-Warwick Migration, Identity, Translation Research Network.

Index